Poverty Reduction and Economic Growth: Current and Emerging Issues

Poverty Reduction and Economic Growth: Current and Emerging Issues

Kyle Greiner

NY Research Press
New York

Published by NY Research Press
118-35 Queens Blvd., Suite 400,
Forest Hills, NY 11375, USA
www.nyresearchpress.com

Poverty Reduction and Economic Growth: Current and Emerging Issues
Kyle Greiner

International Standard Book Number: 978-1-64725-418-6 (Hardback)

Cataloging-in-Publication Data

Poverty reduction and economic growth : current and emerging issues / Kyle Greiner.
p. cm.
Includes bibliographical references and index.
ISBN 978-1-64725-418-6
1. Poverty. 2. Poverty--Prevention. 3. Economic development. I. Greiner, Kyle.
HC79.P6 P68 2023
339.46--dc23

Contents

Preface

Every book is initially just a concept; it takes months of research and hard work to give it the final shape in which the readers receive it. In its early stages, this book also went through rigorous reviewing. The notable contributions made by experts from across the globe were first molded into patterned chapters and then arranged in a sensibly sequential manner to bring out the best results.

Poverty refers to a situation or state in which a person or community lacks the financial resources and necessities essential for maintaining a minimum standard of living. It usually has multiple economic, social, and political causes and effects. Poverty-ridden individuals and households are often unable to make ends meet and they seldom have access to proper housing, clean water, healthy food, and medical facilities. Poverty reduction is a set of economic and humanitarian measures or policies aimed at bringing the poverty-stricken individuals out of poverty. Economic growth is the most effective tool for eliminating poverty and improving the standard of living in developing nations. It has also resulted in better access to opportunities and basic services, creation of new jobs, improved incomes, and increased pace of poverty reduction. This book discusses the current and emerging issues in poverty reduction and economic growth. Coherent flow of topics, student-friendly language, and extensive use of examples make it an invaluable source of knowledge.

It has been my immense pleasure to be a part of this project and to contribute my years of learning in such a meaningful form. I would like to take this opportunity to thank all the people who have been associated with the completion of this book at any step.

Kyle Greiner

Understanding Economic Growth and Poverty Reduction

Over the last two decades, research interest on the interaction between economic growth and poverty reduction has increased considerably, particularly after limited success of macroeconomic adjustment policies in the nineties as well as heterogeneous results of economic growth and poverty reduction across countries.

From the microeconomic perspective, three important questions were at the focus of attention. First, is economic growth always associated with poverty reduction? Second, does inequality hamper the scope of economic growth to reduce poverty? Third, does poverty and inequality limit subsequent growth? Similarly, in macroeconomics one of the most debated issues was if poor economies grow automatically faster than rich ones in such a way that over the long run disparities decrease. This topic has been extensively studied across countries but not that much within them, particularly in developing countries.

Answers to these questions are of extreme relevance for designing policy interventions. For instance, if policy makers assume that economic growth always trickles down to the poor, the central policy objective would be to achieve high and sustained growth, and abstain from implementing poverty alleviation programs. If inequality is not considered as an obstacle for economic growth, one would refrain of implementing redistributive policies, for example through the taxing system. Similarly, the assumption of automatic reduction of disparities among countries or regions over time would reduce the need of policies to foster growth in poor countries. Answers to these question affect not only the evolution of research in development economics, but also policy implementations that influence people's daily life.

Usually, microeconomic empirical research on the link between poverty and growth is not linked to the macroeconomic one. Many reasons explain this lack of connection, which is observable not only in Colombia but elsewhere. One is that the most common used growth models, the neoclassical and endogenous, do not explicitly account for an explanation of the growth-poverty relation as they depart from aggregate production functions with output explained as a function of aggregate capital and labor. One further reason is the source and relevance of data. While poverty analysis is based on data from household surveys, the aggregate growth analysis uses national accounts. As it is well known, estimates of household consumption obtained by these two sources have large discrepancies, and therefore attempts to combine them are risky. Furthermore household survey data is usually available for short periods of time, while growth models are conceived to explain growth in the long run.

More importantly, the focus of attention in each one of these fields goes in a different direction. Growth studies frequently concentrate on finding macroeconomic growth determinants or on testing the most important implication of the neoclassical model, namely the convergence hypothesis (Durlauf et al., 2005). Relevant policy implications in this field are those that foster growth. On the contrary, poverty analysis focuses on understanding the dynamics and determinants of poverty reduction, as well as on finding appropriate poverty measurement concepts and tools. In this literature, growth is relevant only if it is poverty reducing and economic policy implications are those that are poverty alleviating. Note that growth in this field of analysis refers to the percentage change of the mean income or mean expenditures of the households, while growth analysis at the macroeconomic level refers to aggregated growth in production of all sectors of the economy.

Even though the fields of growth theory and poverty analysis are difficult to link with each other empirically and theoretically, they have a common underlying question which goes frequently unnoticed. The poverty-growth-inequality analyisis is concerned with how economic growth leads to poverty reduction, depending on changes in the distribution among households or individuals. The growth convergence literature looks at whether disparities between poor countries or regions disappear over time. Implicitly both are concerned with a reduction in poverty although using different instruments and levels of aggregation. Recent efforts have been done to link these two fields through the convergence hypothesis derived from the neoclassical growth model. For instance, Ravallion (2009) finds that a high poverty rate in the initial period makes it harder to achieve subsequent growth, explaining why countries with a large incidence of poverty do not grow faster than the richer.

As a contribution to understanding the dynamics of poverty and economic growth on a country case basis, this dissertation explores empirically in how far growth has been beneficial for the poor in Colombia and if regional disparities have diminished over time. The dissertation is composed of four essays. The first two essays use a micro-data based approach and different dimensions of poverty measurement. The third and fourth essays use macroeconomic aggregates to test for convergence among Colombian departments. As will be observed, a central characteristic of this dissertation is that it studies poverty and growth convergence multidimensionally, given the limitations of income alone to capture all aspects of well being, be it at the household or at an aggregated level.

Addressing the growth-poverty-inequality relation and the convergence hypothesis questions is of vital importance for a country like Colombia. The country has been immersed for many years, and particularly in the last quarter of the twentieth century, in a cycle of low growth, elevated poverty rates and high inequality. There is a large contrast between living standards in densely populated industrialized areas and rural areas rich in diversity and natural resources, many of them dominated by violent groups involved in domestic conflict and illicit activities.

The domestic conflict, between the government, guerrillas and paramilitary groups, originated in the mid fifties in a context of political turbulence, but also high economic disparities. One possible way for reducing the burden of the ongoing domestic conflict, is to offer universal access to social services and human capital formation for expanding the capabilities of people and the freedom to chose among different alternatives of life beyond conflict and evolvement in illegal activities. For this purpose, it is necessary to understand how economic growth influences inequality and poverty, and if at least in the long run, disparities among regions are getting lower.

Chapter 1 offers an analysis of the evolution of income poverty and inequality at the household level and its sensitivity to short run economic fluctuations. It investigates if household income growth (per capita) contributed to poverty reduction between 1996 and 2005 and in how far its evolution was associated to the boom and bust cycle experienced by the country in that period. For this purpose this chapter uses annual Household Surveys for all years between 1996 and 2005 and applies for the first time in Colombia the methodology of "Pro-Poor Growth" suggested by Ravallion and Chen (2004). This methodology allows analyzing changes between two periods of time along the entire income distribution. It allows us to make judgements on changes in income for households ranked in percentiles below a selected poverty threshold, compared to those above it. Moreover, this essay presents standard 'Foster Greer and Thorbecke' poverty indicators (Foster et al., 1984) and several inequality indicators. It also reviews economic issues and policy reforms to contextualize reasons behind changes in poverty and how the distribution of household income was affected by the economic recession of 1999.

This study contributes to the discussion on the impact of economic crisis on the poor. Results show that poverty figures and household income in Colombia are highly sensitive to business cycle fluctuations and labor market conditions. It also confirms that variability is larger in low percentiles of the income distribution, particularly during economic recessions. While the speed of poverty reduction was very low in the years previous to the economic recession, the increase in poverty and inequality during the recession was extremely fast. The economic recession, which was rooted in the housing and financial sectors, did not affect rural areas as much as urban areas. However, the incidence of poverty and the severity of poverty remained larger in rural than in urban areas, and the gap between both was nearly unchanged. This study raises attention on the importance of economic stability for avoiding large increases in poverty. It also calls on the importance of analyzing information as desegregated as possible, given that country averages hide important issues relevant for policy design. Desegregation is relevant among country divides, but also over time to capture the effects of economic cycles on households.

Chapter 2 investigates if multidimensional aspects of well being improved, particularly for the households below the poverty line. This chapter, based on joint work with Melanie Grosse, studies multidimensional "Pro-Poor Growth" between 1997 and 2003. One important reason for including non-income based indicators in this paper is to analyze in how far short run economic imbalances affect dimensions of well being that can have a long run impact (i.e children's education) and see if they move parallel to fluctuations in income. The investigation uses the Living Standard Measurement Survey of 1997 and 2003, due to the richness of the questionnaire, in order to construct four indices: one on asset ownership (including access to public services), one on health, another on education, and one on subjective welfare. In contrast to existing literature, the weights assigned to selected variables composing each index, (excepting those related to education) were assigned using polychoric principal components analysis as suggested by Kolenikov and Angeles (2009) instead of traditional principal component analysis, since the latter is not appropriate for categorical variables and yields misleading results.

The paper contributes to the literature by discussing the importance of selection of weights when creating indices of well being and compares statistical based procedures with normative weights selected by the researchers. It also discusses limitations for analysis of multidimensional poverty over time using variables that have an upper bound or that are based on subjective perceptions.

The selected non-income indicators showed minor changes between 1997 and 2003. In general, income poor households were not performing better or worst than non poor in a multidimensional setting. Education and health had no major drawbacks, which might be related to the effect of recent reforms directed to strengthen those sectors, but also because these dimensions need longer periods of time to change. Growth incidence curves and pro-poor growth rates show that mean income and mean expenditures by percentile decreased from 1997 to 2003.

To summarize results based on micro-data, the Colombian experience shows that the economic contraction lead to a drastic increase in income poverty and inequality. On the contrary, once the recession was over, economic growth periods had a marginal impact on poverty and inequality. Education, health and asset ownership had low variation and did not move in the same direction as income and expenditures.

Chapter 3 and 4 offer a macro-data perspective of disparities in Colombia, and are based on joint work with Boris Branisa Caballero. The macroeconomic essays are concerned with the fact that regional disparities are large and that the stable country averages hide important distributive problems. These essays ask if those disparities persisted over time, or on the contrary if they diminished. Two issues motivated research undertaken in these chapters. First, international literature found frequently ambiguous results on convergence in output, particularly when using cross country data, but suggested that convergence inside a country is more plausible. Existent research in this area in Colombia is not conclusive. Some authors argue for convergence and other for persistence or even for an increase in regional disparities. Second, cross country literature shows that even when there is no convergence of output, there is convergence in living standards, due partly to redistributive policies but also to dissemination of sanitation and health practices worldwide. While convergence studies in Colombia using production by department are contradictory and depend on the method of analysis used as well as on the data source, convergence analysis of social indicators is almost inexistent.

Analysis of convergence in production by department and in disposable income by department between 1975 and 2000 is presented in Chapter 3. The data used reflects differences in convergence on the production by department, and convergence in what households (aggregated by department) receive after discounting for net payments and adding up transfers.

The paper presents two of the most known approaches to test for convergence: the regression approach and the distributional approach. It compares both methods as a robustness check and to discuss whether they yield different results. This paper contributes to the literature by revising data issues leading to contradiction in research on convergence in Colombia, and by testing empirically convergence using time series cross sectional data. For this purpose, we used different degrees of pooling the information in order to test if there is homogeneity in the parameters of the regression for all departments, or if there is convergence among certain groups.

Results of this essay show that Colombia had no convergence in gross departmental product, and slight improvements in the distribution of gross disposable income. Basically departments remained in the same position relative to the national average in 2000 compared to the position they had in 1975. Concerning the division of the production sectors along the country, they did not change, except for some departments that discovered important mineral resources. We did not find solid evidence of convergence among groups of departments, nor evidence of parameter heterogeneity.

In spite of lack of convergence in production and mild convergence in income, we want to test if there is convergence in living standards. We investigate in Chapter 4 changes in non-income indicators across Colombian departments from 1973 to 2005. The contribution of this paper is to present the first complete and detailed analysis of convergence in social indicators in Colombia and discuss the importance of reducing disparities in health and education related indicators. The variables of analysis are literacy rate, infant survival rate, life expectancy at birth and nourishment. Convergence analysis of these variables is done using the classical regression approach to convergence, and also the distributional approach through bivariate Kernels. Using literacy rate as a proxy for education, we find regional convergence between 1973 and 2005. We find persistence in the distribution between 1975 and 2000 when we use infant survival rate and life expectancy at birth as proxies for health. Additionally, we find convergence between 1995 and 2005 in the rate of children that are well-nourished.

The central conclusion of the macroeconomic analysis, is that in the last quarter of the twentieth century, Colombia did not manage to reduce regional disparities in either gross departmental product or social indicators, except for literacy rate. Although the levels increased, particularly in social indicators, the relative outcomes of departments to the national average remained almost unchanged. It is important to emphasize that these disparities did not increase, and that there was some mobility in gross personal disposable income.

Many policy implications can be derived from these results. First, there it is necessary to revise economic linkages and spillovers between lagging departments with leading ones for achieving higher growth at the national level. Second, if poverty reduction is a key development priority in the country, it is necessary to create poverty alleviating programs focused at the departmental level, not only considering the urban and rural divide. Third, if inequality is also a goal, regional disparities need to be explicitly addressed by public policies.

Other policy implications of this collection of studies is the relevance of macroeconomic stability for poverty. Even if growth is slow and inequality anchored at different country divides, it is necessary to avoid economic crises because they lead to large increase in deprivation and disparities. For the same reason, it is necessary to enforce mechanisms to reduce high disparities in Colombia. One important mechanism to achieve this goal is to foster universal quality education, as it is the most powerful way to influence returns to labor over long periods and allows people to move from lagging to leading regions. It is also necessary to revise and enforce decentralization reforms to achieve fiscal equalization and foster regional convergence. Particular attention is needed concerning infant survival rate, in which which regional disparities are quite large and improvements very low in lagging departments relative to the national average.

Economic growth alone was clearly not sufficient in Colombia to achieve convergence and poverty reduction, on the contrary it was just enough to maintain the same distribution over time. Colombia appears like a country where reforms have not been successful to reduce disparities and foster growth. On the contrary, it is a country where disparities seem to be anchored and immobile over time.

Concerning the data, lack of consistent time series at the departmental level and absence of panel data at the household level represent major constraints for empirical research on poverty and growth, limiting the extent to which researchers can suggest policy interventions. It is urgent for the statistical office to undertake projects in this direction and, particularly, to design methodologies consistent over time.

1

Application of Income Indicators for Pro Poor Growth

Abstract

Using income data from the Colombian household surveys, this study evaluates whether or not growth in Colombia was pro-poor from 1996 to 2005 by drawing growth-incidence curves and calculating the pro-poor growth rate for different subperiods to capture separately the effects of the economic slowdown, crisis, and recovery years. Calculations are done cumulatively, as well, taking 1996 as the base year and comparing each of the subsequent years with it to see how income growth evolved over the period as a whole. Results show that when comparing only the initial and ending years, growth was very slow and was not averse to the poor, relative to the non-poor, leading to an almost unchanged incidence of poverty in comparison to the level observed in 1996. However, analysis by subperiod as well as cumulative analysis indicates that the crisis had a strong adverse effect on the income of the poorest population percentiles.

1.1 Introduction

The objective of this study is to examine whether economic growth reduced poverty in Colombia between 1996 and 2005 and the extent to which the poor participated in economic growth. The period of analysis is of great interest; it was a time when economic expansion ended with a drastic output contraction, reversing achievements in poverty reduction and returning poverty to 1988 levels, and was then followed by a slow recovery process. The paper examines how the poor experienced the negative effects of this crisis, as compared to the non-poor, and investigates whether they shared equally in the benefits of growth.

In order to measure the extent to which growth reduced poverty, (that is, whether growth was pro-poor), this study will apply the methodology developed by Ravallion and Chen

recent years, as well as the evolution of poverty and inequality indicators. Section 4 analyzes the resulting growth-incidence curves, and Section 5 concludes.

1.2 Defining and Classifying Pro-Poor Growth (PPG) by Concepts and Measurement Techniques

The relationship between growth and poverty is a familiar and important topic of debate among development economists and policymakers. Perspectives on this issue have changed in the last two decades after sweeping economic reforms and drastic policy shifts (ranging from import subsituting industrialization to economic liberalization) failed to produce the desired trickle-down growth effects or to reduce poverty in many developing countries—including several in Latin America (Birdsall and Szekely, 2003). A variety of studies have emerged on how to evaluate the effects of growth on poverty, sparking discussion of how to measure whether growth is good for the poor and can thus be considered "pro-poor". Although consensus has not been reached on a definition of pro-poor growth (PPG), many studies treat it as the economic growth path that benefits the poor population as much as or more than the non-poor population, decreases inequality, and reduces poverty (Duclos and Wodon, 2004).

While this general definition appears straightforward, measuring PPG is more complicated since it needs to tackle questions of the extent to which growth can be considered pro-poor and whether pro-poor growth is necessarily accompanied by decreased inequality. Other challenges are differentiating economic growth paths to determine which one is the most pro-poor and why, as well as determining what proportion of poverty reduction can be explained by growth. Measurement tools to cope with these questions are based mainly on the income dimension of poverty and use household surveys or Living Standard Measurement Surveys (LSMS) as data sources. Very few studies focus on non-income dimensions like health, education, and nutrition (Klasen, 2008).

There are basically two ways of classifying studies on PPG: first, according to their approach (general or strict), and second, according to specific features of the measurement methodologies (complete/full or partial). For the general (also called weak) approach, any growth path leading to poverty reduction is considered pro-poor. In contrast, the strict approach considers growth to be pro-poor only when both poverty and inequality decrease. This approach (also called strong, see Kakwani et al. (2004)) is based on the identity that decomposes reductions in poverty into changes in mean income or growth effect, and changes in the distribution of income, called the distributional effect (Datt and Ravallion, 1992).

The strict approach to pro-poor growth can be further subdivided into strict-relative or strict-absolute. The relative approach focuses on proportional changes in income between

(2004) by drawing growth-incidence curves (GIC) and calculating the pro-poor growth rate (PPGR) for the nation as a whole, for the urban/rural divide, and for each region. One of the central contributions of this paper is its detailed examination of the effects of economic recession on income by percentile. The subdivision of the period into three sub-periods in accordance with the country's growth cycle between 1996 and 2005 presents a broader picture of the recession's effects, as well as of how quickly incomes recovered post-recession.

The data sources for this study are the Encuesta Nacional de Hogares (ENH) 1996 to 2000, and the Encuesta Continua de Hogares (ECH) 2001 to 2005, conducted annually by the National Administrative Department of Statistics (DANE). Although the main objective of these household surveys is the construction of labor market indicators, they are also used to calculate the incidence of poverty, since they are the only surveys providing yearly information on household incomes.

Results show that by interpreting the aforementioned methodology strictly, growth in Colombia between 1996 to 2005 was pro-poor, since the PPGR was higher than the mean growth rate (0.94 versus 0.43). Nevertheless, the difference of these two magnitudes is too low and the methodology of pro-poor growth analysis does not indicate how large the difference between both magnitudes needs to be in order to conclude that growth was truly beneficial to the poor, relative to the non-poor. A more balanced conclusion would be that growth was very slow and was not averse to the poor (relative to the non-poor), leading to an almost unchanged incidence of poverty in comparison to the level observed in 1996.

Analysis by sub-periods show a different picture. In 1999 income of percentiles below the poverty line was 12 percent lower than in 1996, while mean income for all percentiles decreased three percent. Average income losses were larger in rural areas. Between 1999 and 2002, growth was pro-poor, as shown by the PPGR. This result is influenced by a statistical effect of income moving back to the levels observed before the economic crisis. In the period 2002 to 2005, average income increased five percent and average income of the percentiles below the poverty line by seven percent. Economic growth in this sub-period was pro-poor in urban and rural areas, as well as for Colombia as a whole.

Subdivision of results by the four regions included in the household surveys, and evaluating the years 1996 and 2005, shows small differences between the average income of percentiles below the poverty line and those above for all regions except for the Oriental Region. In this region, growth was slightly more favorable to the poorest percentiles.

This paper is divided into five sections. Section 2 present a classification of pro-poor growth and how it is measured, briefly discussing the strengths and weaknesses of the two most widely used methodologies, namely, those proposed by Ravallion and Chen (2004) and Kakwani et al. (2004). Section 3 reviews the history of economic growth in Colombia in poor and non-poor and considers growth pro-poor when relative inequality, defined as the ratio of individual incomes to the mean, decreases. This is only possible if incomes of the poor rise by a higher proportion than incomes of the non-poor. For the absolute approach, growth is pro-poor if absolute income gains of the poor are as much or more than those of the non-poor, meaning that absolute inequality (defined as the absolute difference in income between the poor and non-poor) decreases.[1] One important critique of the strict-relative approach is that in a recession, large income drops among the rich can give a pro-poor picture even if the poor are not gaining at all. Similarly, a pro-rich distributional shift during a period of overall economic expansion may result in large absolute gains for the poor without the growth path being considered pro-poor (Ravallion and Chen, 2004). Furthermore, and as explained by Klasen (2008), pro-poor growth in the strict-absolute approach is almost impossible to achieve in practice, given that absolute income gains of the poor are usually much lower than those of the non-poor. As shown by Klasen (2008), this concept makes good sense however when analyzing the non-income dimension of poverty.

PPG measures can be classified into partial or complete types. Partial measurement uses neither a concrete measure of poverty nor a poverty line, while complete measurement requires a poverty line to compare different growth paths and the degree to which they are pro-poor. The growth incidence curve developed by Ravallion and Chen (2003) and the poverty growth curve proposed by Son (2003) can both be categorized under the partial type of measurement. In contrast, the indices of McCulloch and Baulch (2000), Kakwani and Pernia (2000) and Ravallion and Chen (2003) are categorized under the full approach because the growth processes are judged from a rate or an index of pro-poor growth that requires defining a poverty line (Kakwani et al., 2004). Given that an exhaustive comparison of all existing methodologies is beyond the scope of this paper, in the next section we will summarize two selected methodologies: that of Kakwani et al. (2004), which has been applied in two previous studies on Colombia, and that of Ravallion and Chen (2003) which will be used in the present study.

[1]An example given by Ravallion and Chen (2004) illustrates the difference between changes in relative and absolute inequality better Consider only two households: a poor one with an income of $1,000 and a non-poor one with an income of $10,000 in the first period. After an income increase of 100 percent for both households in the second period, the poor household earns $2,000 while the non-poor one earns $20,000. In this case, the distance from each household to the mean remains unchanged and thus relative inequality does not change. According to the strict approach, growth would have been neither pro-poor nor anti-poor. But since the absolute difference between the two households increases from $9,000 to $18,000, absolute inequality rises sharply and growth can be considered anti-poor in the strict-absolute sense.

1.2.1 Growth Incidence Curves (GIC) and the Absolute Rate of Pro-Poor Growth

When using the absolute approach mentioned above, the growth incidence curve (GIC) graphs the rate of growth of real income (or real expenditure) (shown at the y axis) for each percentile of the distribution (shown at the x axis with increasing order by income) between two periods of time. A curve below 0 at all points of the distribution indicates that all households suffered income losses. The contrary indicates income gains for all percentiles and consequently a poverty decrease compared with the initial period. An upward-sloping curve indicates that rich households (the richer income percentiles) benefited more than others, while a downward-sloping curve indicates the poor benefited more, giving evidence of pro-poor growth in a relative sense (i.e., that relative inequality has fallen). The GIC is formally derived from the following equations:

$$y_t(p) = F_t^{-1}(p) = L_t'(p)\mu_t \quad \text{with} \quad y_t'(p) > 0 \tag{1.1}$$

$$GIC : g_t(p) = \frac{y_t(p)}{y_{t-1}(p)} - 1 \tag{1.2}$$

$$g_t(p) = \frac{L_t'(p)}{L_{t-1}'(p)}(\gamma_t + 1) - 1, \tag{1.3}$$

where p is the corresponding percentile, F_t^{-1} is the inverse of the cumulative distribution function at the p^{th}percentile (which gives the income of that percentile), $L_t(p)$ is the Lorenz curve (with slope $L_t'(p)$) and $\gamma_t = \frac{\mu_t}{\mu_{t-1}} - 1$ is the growth rate in the mean (GRIM) of income (or expenditure) per capita. The GIC can be defined as the growth rate in income of the pth percentile as shown in equation 1.2 or as shown in equation 1.3 after replacing 1.1 into 1.2. If all percentiles exhibit the same growth rate, then the Lorenz curve does not change, inequality remains unchanged and $g_t(p) = \gamma_t$ in equation 1.3 for all p. Should the ratio between the growth rate of the pth percentile to the GRIM increase over time (i.e., $\frac{y_t(p)}{\mu_t} > \frac{y_{t-1}(p)}{\mu_{t-1}}$), then the growth rate of the pth percentile is higher than the GRIM, $g_t(p) > \gamma_t$. Following this, inequality falls if $g_t(p)$ is a decreasing function for all p (Ravallion and Chen, 2001).

The graphical analysis of the GIC would not demand using a poverty line to determine whether growth was beneficial to the poor. However this is only possible when the slope of the curve has a clear trend. First-order dominance of the distribution at date t over $t-1$ exists when the GIC is above 0 for all percentiles, a conclusion that cannot be drawn if the GIC crosses 0. In practice, the GIC often has different slopes at different points and switches along percentiles, making it impossible to draw clear conclusions. To be able to do so, Ravallion and Chen (2004) proposed (based on the GIC) the rate of pro-poor growth (PPGR) as the area below the GIC up to the selected poverty line of the initial period. This area equals total income growth of the poor. The PPGR is equivalent to the ordinary rate of growth times a distributional correction given by the ratio of the actual change in poverty over time (using the Watts index) to the poverty change that would have been observed if growth had not affected the income distribution. If the PPGR is higher than the GRIM, growth is pro-poor, while the opposite result indicates that distributional changes negatively affected the poor. Formally this is defined as follows:

$$PPGR = g_t^p = -\frac{dW_t}{dt} = \frac{1}{H_t}\int_0^{H_t} g_t(p)dp, \tag{1.4}$$

where

$$W_t = \int_0^{H_t} \log[\frac{z}{y_t(p)}]dp \tag{1.5}$$

is the Watts poverty measure, z is the poverty line, and H_t is the headcount ratio H at time t.

1.2.2 Pro-Poor Growth Index (PPGI) and Poverty Equivalent Growth Rate (PEGR)

Kakwani and Pernia (2000) argue that poverty reduction depends on the growth rate of income as well as its distributional shift. For PPG to exist, both rates need to decrease. The authors propose the pro-poor growth index (PPGI) as the relationship between total poverty reduction and the amount of poverty reduction that occurs when growth does not affect the distribution at all. For calculating this ratio, the authors use the ratios of total poverty elasticity to the growth elasticity of poverty (Son, 2003).

$$\phi = \frac{\delta}{\eta} \tag{1.6}$$

where δ is the total elasticity of poverty and η is the growth elasticity of poverty. δ is decomposable into changes in poverty due to growth (holding inequality constant) and changes in poverty due to variations in inequality (holding growth unchanged). Formally:

$$\delta = \eta + \zeta \tag{1.7}$$

Where ζ is the poverty elasticity to inequality. Note that η is always negative, given that any increase in growth (assuming that the benefits of it are equally distributed among all population) is associated with a decrease in poverty (Nuñez and Espinosa, 2005). If ϕ is higher than one (i.e., $\delta > \eta$) growth is pro-poor because both poverty and inequality fall (Son, 2003). If the PPGI is higher than zero but lower than one, growth is pro-poor using the general definition but not the strict one. As this index does not address the actual rate of growth, it does not satisfy the monotonicity axiom, i.e., it is not a monotonically increasing function of the growth rate (Son, 2003).

With the aim of considering observed growth rates in measuring PPG, Kakwani and Son (2008) built the poverty equivalent growth rate (PEGR):

$$PEGR = \gamma^* = (\delta/\eta)\gamma = \phi\gamma \tag{1.8}$$

Where $\gamma = d\ln(\mu)$ is the average growth rate and $\phi = (\delta/\eta)$is the PPGI. The PEGR can be interpreted as the growth rate that would result in the same poverty reduction as the one generated by the actual growth rate had growth been distributionally neutral, i.e., if all individuals had received proportionally equal benefits of growth (Sarmiento et al., 2005b). For determining if growth was pro-poor by using the PEGR, the following criteria are used:

- If $\gamma^* > \gamma$ growth is pro-poor
- If $0 < \gamma^* < \gamma$ there is a trickle-down process: poverty decreases but growth is accompanied by increases in inequality
- If $\gamma^* < \gamma$ growth is not pro-poor

1.2.3 Applications to Colombia

When comparing the two methodologies, the reader is most interested in the desirable properties of a pro-poor measure: namely the focus axiom (the measure is invariant to changes in incomes of the non-poor), the monotonicity axiom (any increase in income of a poor person decreases poverty), and the transfer axiom (poverty decreases by transfers from poorer to less poor).

According to the monotonicity axiom, a desirable pro-poor growth measure should move in line with the poverty indicator it enhances, i.e., whenever poverty decreases (increases), the pro-poor growth measure should be positive (negative) (Ravallion and Chen, 2001). In their paper, Kakwani et al. (2004) argue that Ravallion's PPGR does not fulfill this axiom as it focuses on the headcount index in the initial period and does not take into account the incidence of poverty in the final period. But, should one incorporate the headcount index from the second period into the methodology, it would violate the focus axiom. The fact that the Watts Index is calculated using the headcount of the initial period explains why, in some cases, the PPGR can be positive (negative) although the headcount in the second period is higher (lower) than in the first.[2] Thus, the PPGR of Ravallion fulfills the monotonicity axiom restricted to both the initially poor and to the Watts Index.

[2]The typical example is when people just above the poverty line in the first period fall below it in the second, becoming poor: the amount of persons below the poverty line (headcount) increases in the second period although in the first period the incomes of the poorest rose.

As with Kakwani's methodology, it satisfies the monotonicity axiom for the Foster, Greer and Thorbecke (FGT) group of poverty measures, given that any reduction in poverty according to that type of poverty measure is a growing function of the PEGR.[3] Compared to the GIC, results in terms of elasticities are harder to interpret, as this methodology does not reveal changes in income throughout the whole distribution. Furthermore, in practice, it is difficult to separate poverty changes into growth and inequality holding one or the other constant, given that they usually happen simultaneously.

Two empirical studies using Kakwani's methodology have been done for Colombia in the period 1996-2004. The first one, Sarmiento et al. (2005b), analyzes the PEGR using the poverty gap as a poverty indicator for seven years from 1996 to 1999 and 2001 to 2004. Of these years, only 1997, 2002 and 2003 showed a positive mean income growth rate. Results show that growth was pro-poor only in 1997 and 2003 when poverty as well as inequality fell and that the PEGR was positive and higher than the observed mean income growth rate. In 1997 the fall in poverty is explained by improvements in inequality rather than in income, while in 2003 the growth effect was larger than the inequality effect. In 1999 the non-poor exhibited higher income losses than the poor, meaning that inequality decreased. The authors argue that in that year, although the poverty gap index rose, the recession was pro-poor because that increase would have been higher had inequality not improved.

The study of Nuñez and Espinosa (2005) also follows the methodology developed by Kakwani et al. (2004), uses the mean income growth rate of the household surveys, and is based on the incidence of poverty to calculate the PEGR between 1997 and 2004. His results show that economic growth for total Colombia was not pro-poor, mainly because higher incomes in the urban sector and lower in the rural increased inequality. When calculating the PEGR, the author concludes that in only two years of the period analyzed, namely 2000 and 2003, was growth pro-poor. Both years exhibit PEGR larger than observed income growth rates as well as poverty reduction. When decomposing poverty changes into growth and inequality, Nuñez and Espinosa (2005) finds that in all years other than 1999, the growth effect alone helped reduce poverty each year by about 1 percent, but that the inequality effect counteracted the growth effect in almost the entire period 1996– 2004. The author's simulations indicate that had growth been neutral, the incidence of poverty would have decreased from 50.8 to 45.9 percent between 1996 and 2004, instead of having increased to 53.3 in 2004.

The contribution of the present study is the application of Ravallion's methodology to the period 1996 to 2005, concentrating on how economic recession affected the incomes of the initial poor. The subdivision of the period into three sub-periods in accordance with the coun-

[3]For a comprehensive review of the FGT indices see Foster et al. (1984)

try's growth cycle between 1996 and 2005 presents a better picture of the recession's effects, as well as of how fast incomes recovered from it. As explained above, by drawing GIC it is possible to clearly observe changes in income by percentiles, derive conclusions about the income distribution, and provide a measure of pro-poor growth in a relative sense. Besides this, using Ravallion's methodology reveals possible data weaknesses. As is well known, income surveys have more severe problems than expenditure surveys due to the fact that people tend to omit more information or underreport it. Drawing GIC places high demands on the surveys in terms of data quality, and may also be a very useful tool to see how prices affect poor and rich households differently.

1.3 Data Sources and Constraints

As mentioned in the introduction, data are taken from the Colombian household surveys, which consist of four basic chapters: i) identification variables, ii) characteristics of the households (physical characteristics and available services), iii) education, and iv) labor force information, the latter including income data.[4] Between 1990 and 2000, the survey "Encuesta Nacional de Hogares" (ENH) was conducted quarterly, and only the identification and labor force information were included in all four quarters. Only the third quarter, which is used in this study, is representative at the national level for the rural/urban divide, for four regions, and for some labor indicators at the department level.

Starting in 2001, the methodology changed to a continuous one (Encuesta Contínua de Hogares, ECH), which means that the information is collected year-round by dividing the sample size on a weekly basis (for details on methodological changes, see Lasso Valderrama (2002)). Results are presented monthly and need to be aggregated depending on the desired degree of representativeness. For calculating poverty with the ECH, the usual procedure is to aggregate information corresponding to the third quarter.

Non-response and underreporting are important problems in Colombian household surveys, which are conducted using indirect reporting.[5] The National Planning Department (DNP) applies three correction steps: in the first, they estimate missing income using human capital models based on Mincerian equations, in the second, they adjust incomes to the national accounts to correct for underreporting, and in the third, they also rectify under-reported income of homeowners (DNP, 2006). This study uses the final corrected income variable produced by the DNP, which is the basis for official calculations of poverty. After all corrections,

[4]The household survey has specific modules introduced occasionally to investigate specific aspects of the household like household property, informality, and health.

[5]In 1996 monetary income was missing for 4 percent of persons of working age. This percentage increases up to 8 in 2003. Together with all other sources of income, the cases (persons) with missing income were 5.5 percent in 1996 and 13 percent in 2003 (DNP, 2004) of the working age population.

there remain very low and high fluctuating incomes in the first percentiles of the distribution as well as about 1 to 1.5 percent of households with an income equal to zero. When calculating standard poverty and inequality indicators, all information is taken into account. To draw the GIC, the first and last two percentiles of the distribution are not shown to facilitate reading the curves, given that high fluctuations in these percentiles may still be due to problems in the data rather than to true changes in income. Calculation of real income is done using the implicit deflators of the poverty line in its 2005 version (called M 2005), which updates the poverty lines by using the consumer price index for low-income groups.[6].

1.4 Economic Background in Colombia

1.4.1 Economic Growth and Production Structure

The main components of GDP in Colombia are agriculture (14 percent of GDP), manufacturing (15 percent), mining (5 percent), and construction (5 percent). The most dynamic industrial sectors in the country are processed food, beverages, textiles, clothing, and chemicals. Cattle and coffee are the most important agricultural products, accounting for 44 and 13 percent of total agricultural GDP (Departamento Administrativo Nacional de Estadística, (DANE), 2008).[7] Other key agricultural products are tropical fruits, bananas, rice, vegetables, potatoes, palm oil, and sugarcane (Vélez et al., 2001).[8] Regarding services, construction accounts for 4.5 percent of GDP, financial services represent 5.4, and retail commerce accounts for around 7.4. Telecommunications, a sector that has been expanding rapidly in the last decade, makes up 3 percent of total GDP.

Colombian GDP growth has been praised for its stability compared to other Latin American countries due to lower fluctuations in private consumption.[9] During the 20th century, growth was almost uninterrupted and fell only twice: once in 1931, when GDP contracted

[6]Poverty lines are available for each of the 13 metropolitan areas, for the rest of the urban areas, and for rural Colombia (DNP, 2006).

[7]Coffee production fell substantially during the nineties, as did its share of exports (from 18 percent in 1992 to 6 in 2004), explained by low coffee prices, large stocks worldwide, and a higher supply from new producing countries. Furthermore, increasing participation of manufacturing after trade liberalization fostered export diversification away from coffee.

[8]In the eighties, agriculture accounted for 22 percent of GDP while industry for less than 21. Total participation of these sectors in GDP has decreased since the mid-eighties in favor of services and mining. Discovery of important mineral sources like nickel and coal in the Caribbean departments of Córdoba and La Guajira respectively, and petroleum in the lowlands of Arauca and Casanare, both in the northeast of the country on the border to Venezuela, have played a central role in this development.

[9]Prudent management of coffee export revenues helped maintaining low external debt at the beginning of the eighties when the country entered the so-called "lost decade" in a favorable position compared to its neighbors. The sudden stop in capital flows due to the overall debt crisis in Latin America initially led to a reversal of some trade liberalization policies undertaken up to that point which were eased after 1986, when the coffee boom improved external sector (Ocampo et al., 1998).

by 2 percent, and once in 1999 when growth fell 4 percent (see Figure 1.1). After using an import-substituting economic development model for almost 40 years and up to 1990, the country introduced a comprehensive reform package, including state modernization, a constitutional reform, and key changes in the labor, financial, and exchange rate markets.[10] Barriers to foreign direct investment as well as to capital exports were removed and the exchange market liberalized by eliminating controls to the foreign currency trade (Parra and Salazar, 2000).

The liberalization efforts fostered a surge of foreign capital flows from almost nothing in 1989 to 7 percent of GDP in 1996 and translated into a credit boom channeled by banks to the private non-tradable sector (Tenjo Galarza and López Enciso, 2003).[11] The consumption boom, together with higher capital flows and oil prices, led to an annual average growth rate of 5 percent from 1992 to 1995. The saving-investment deficit of the private sector rose while the public sector saving-investment surplus increased (1991-1996) due to higher taxes and revenues from privatization.[12] The direction of monetary policy changed starting in 1994, when interest rates increased and aggregate demand as well as growth slowed down due to political uncertainty, falling coffee revenues, and recession in the neighboring country of Venezuela. Growth slowed down and aggregate demand declined. The boom in real estate markets began to wane, housing prices fell, and borrowers began facing difficulties in paying their debts due to the previously generated asset mismatch (Tenjo Galarza and López Enciso, 2003).

After a short reactivation in 1997, capital flows to the country collapsed as result of the difficulties facing international financial markets due to the Asian and Russian crisis. The reversal of flows led to a breakdown of the credit channel and evidenced the already existing fragilities in the domestic private sector. These included high levels of borrowing (36 percent of GDP in 1999), deteriorated balance sheets sensitive to increases in the interest and exchange rates, mismatches in asset prices, and extremely low saving rates (Tenjo Galarza and López Enciso, 2003). In 1997, the Central Bank increased active interest rates up to 50 percent to defend the target zone from a speculative attack, contributing to the sharp deterioration in portfolio indicators and balance sheets in the financial system. The crisis was triggered at the end of the year, when the government declared the economic emergency and

[10]Average tariffs decreased from 44 percent beginning 1990 to 11.8 in March 1992

[11]Especially the construction sector benefited from higher credit supply and the real estate market experienced a period of rapidly increasing prices between 1991 and 1995.

[12]Household savings as a percentage of GDP fell from 14 percent in 1991 to less than 5 percent in 1997 while business savings went from 15 percent to 5.

intervened in several financial institutions. The credit supply collapsed and the recession reached its peak in 1999.[13]

The immediate effects of the crisis were bankruptcies, reorganizations of firms, and increased unemployment. The financial sector became extremely risk-averse regarding credit to the private sector and redirected credit to the public sector instead. Deposits in 2000 remained higher than loans and the financial sector became a net debtor, investing more in bonds and public securities than in credit to the private sector.

From 2000 to 2002, economic growth remained low (2.1 percent), unemployment high, and public spending as well as credit to the private sector constrained. Real currency depreciation undermined contributions of the external sector to growth, and a weak agricultural sector offset stronger growth in manufacturing, telecommunications, and construction. This period coincided with a marked escalation of internal conflict after a failed process of peace talks between the government of Andrés Pastrana (1998-2001) and the FARC (Revolutionary Armed Forces of Colombia).[14] Parallel to this, confrontations between paramilitaries and guerrillas worsened considerably, as did drug-related violence.[15]

One of the most comprehensive studies of the National Planning Department (DNP) regarding the cost of conflict in Colombia estimated its overall costs at 7.4 percent of GDP in 2003 (Pinto Borrego et al., 2005). The majority of the cost burden is borne by the private sector due to kidnapping, forced displacement (approximately 2 million persons in 2002), and crimes against private property.[16] Increased military spending is estimated to make up

[13]According to Posada (2004) the economic recession marked one of the most intensive business cycles experienced in Colombia, and was more a correction to the long-term growth path exacerbated by a sudden stop in capital inflows due to the Asian crisis.

[14]The current internal conflict began almost 50 years ago with the emergence of leftist guerrilla groups whose root motivations were mainly ideological. Up to 1980, the military capacity of these groups was limited and concentrated in marginal areas of the country. Parallel to them, paramilitary groups developed slowly in the eighties to defend isolated areas from guerrilla attacks. During the coca bonanza (bonanza coquera) and the consolidation of drug trafficking in the eighties, illegal armed groups found new ways of financing operations and expanding through the control of areas where illegal crops where grown as well as territories rich in natural resources, particularly oil (Díaz and Sánchez, 2004).

[15]According to UNODC (2006a) estimations, illegal crops account for about 5 percent or of total agricultural areas (ca.121,000 hectares) the main one being coca leaf. Colombia is currently the main supplier of coca leaf worldwide with about 70 percent of total production in 2004 with a dramatically increase in plantation from 1990 to 2004 (UNODC, 2006b). Estimated repatriated earnings are around US$5 billion a year or 4 to 6 percent of GDP every year.

[16]From 1998 to 2001, the number of homicides was approximately 20 thousand each year, rising annually to reach almost 28 thousand in 2001, of which 18 percent were considered of a political nature. Observatorio de Derechos Humanos (2003). According to Fuentes (2005) adjusting life expectancy in Colombia to take into account its high homicide rate has led to the estimate that life expectancy during the nineties was reduced by between one and a half and two years.

25 percent of the total costs of violent conflict, diverting important public budget resources away from education and health.[17]

A change in policy has taken place under the administration of President Alvaro Uribe (in office since 2002), whose efforts have concentrated on fighting the guerrillas directly while negotiating the disarmament of paramilitary groups.[18] This strategy has been successful in significantly reducing homicides, kidnapping, piracy on roads, attacks on small towns, and terrorist attacks, but its success in reducing drug trafficking is still low. Increased confidence due to the security policy, favorable international conditions given by high oil and commodity prices, as well as low interest rates in developed countries have revived capital flows and reserves, raising private investment and easing credit. Annual growth averaged 4.6 percent in 2003– 2005, private consumption accelerated, and in 2005 unemployment decreased to 12 percent. Similarly to the boom experienced in the early nineties, one of the most dynamic sectors in this reactivation phase has been construction.

1.4.2 Poverty and Inequality

From 1978 to 1995, Colombia managed to reduce the incidence of poverty by ten percentage points. This reduction reversed during the crisis, however, with poverty almost returning to 1988 levels (see Figures 1.2 and 1.3). The impact of the recession on household incomes was visible in per capita income falling continuously (even before 1999) and in high unemployment rates. Income losses began in 1996 and ended up in a 9 percent drop in real household income by 2001 (see Figures 1.4, 1.5 and 1.6). The u-shaped per capita income graph gives evidence of recovery since 2002-also in regard to the incidence of poverty, which decreased to 49 percent by 2005. All poverty indicators (incidence, gap, and FGT2) show a similar trend, increasing up to 1999, briefly slowing down from 2000 to 2001, rising again in 2002, and improving since then. By 2005, poverty and inequality indicators at an aggregate level as well as real income had achieved the levels of the early to mid-nineties, or even better (see Table 1.4).

The rural/urban divide shows that at least during the recession, poverty and indigence in rural areas increased much more than in urban areas, widening the gap between them. The incidence of poverty in rural areas (with 68 percent of the population under the poverty line

[17]Other studies consider long-run GDP losses due to the conflict, varying from 0.5 percent to 2 percent. Military expenditures in Colombia have grown significantly over the last fifteen years, from around 2 percent of GDP in 1990 to over 5 percent in 2005.

[18]The strong policy of Uribe has been sponsored by the "Plan Colombia" intended to fight coca production and narcotrafics by strengthening police and military forces through a US$7.5 billion program (U.S. Department of State). The outcomes of this policy are under discussion. Although it seems to have weakened guerrillas, and different indicators point to improvements in security, there is no clear result regarding reduction of coca crops and narcotrafics.

in 2005) is more than one and a half times the urban incidence, and the rural poverty gap is twice the urban (34 percent versus 17 percent in 2005), indicating that the percentage of poor people in rural Colombia is larger and that they are much poorer than those in urban Colombia.

Although rural poverty decreased more than 10 percentage points from 1999 to 2003, it began escalating again since then (see Figures 1.2 and 1.3). Falling rural wages and employment in non-agricultural activities as well as decreasing agricultural productivity explain this behavior. It is important to note that rural income is on average 30 percent of urban income, a proportion that saw no major changes from 1996 to 2005 (see Figures 1.5 and 1.6).

Regarding unemployment, labor market indicators point to a moderate increase from 1996 to 1997, when growth slowed down. From 1997 to 2002, employment conditions deteriorated sharply. Unemployment moved from 10 percent in 1997 to 17.1 in 1999 and 15.8 in 2002. Although unemployment began decreasing in 2002 in line with economic cycles, in 2005 it was still higher than in 1996 with lower utilization of the labor force, higher underemployment (from 17.1 percent in 1997 to 37.4 in 2005) and higher part-time employment (see Figure 1.7). Weak improvements in real incomes, especially for skilled workers, and decreasing formal wage employment explain this trend (Farné et. al 2006).[19]

Analysis using non-income indicators like the Unmet Basic Needs Index (NBI) and the Life Conditions Index (ICV) show significant improvements in welfare from 1985 to 2004.[20] According to the former indicator, poverty decreased between 1985 and 2003 when the percentage of population lacking one of these basic needs decreased by about 50 percent. Similarly, the living conditions of the Colombian population reflected by the ICV have improved considerably since 1985, particularly in the non-urban areas.[21] Although effects of the crisis are not directly visible in these indicators, which measure infrastructure conditions, they are evident in the stagnating pace of improvements in the second half of the nineties.

Regarding income inequality, the data shows that it is quite high and has been worsening during the last two decades. With a GINI coefficient of 0.58 in 2005, Colombia's income inequality is extreme in the international context, although relatively moderate in comparison to the Latin American context, where it ranks just above the median (see Figure 1.8).

[19]According to official statistics, unemployment in rural areas is much lower than in urban (7.1 percent vs. 13.6 in 2005) but as explained above, low incomes help maintain high poverty rates.

[20]The Unmet Basic Needs Index mainly captures infrastructure conditions at the urban level, including variables like inadequacy of housing conditions, homes without basic sanitary facilities, crowding, school absenteeism, and economic dependency. It assumes that people are poor if they lack one of their basic needs, and extremely poor if they lack two or more.

[21]This index is a multidimensional indicator, ranking from 0 to 100, with the latter representing the highest possible welfare. It captures in a single measure variables corresponding to quality of housing, access to public services, education as a measure of human capital, and the size and composition of the household.

According to Nuñez and Espinosa (2005), income inequality decreased in the sixties and seventies, remained stable between 1978-1988, and reversed thereafter. Furthermore, since 1988, the dynamics of inequality seemed to have been asymmetric in the rural and urban areas, improving in the former and deteriorating in the latter.

According to the World Bank's Poverty Report (2002) under almost any possible measure, inequality deteriorated during the 1980s and 1990s. The GINI coefficient increased over the entire period, as did the share of the top income quintile of the distribution relative to the poorest 20 percent. From 1996-1999, these trends intensified when different inequality indicators deteriorated. As can be seen in Table 1.6, the GINI coefficient increased to 63 at the peak of the crisis in 1999.

1.5 Growth Incidence Curves

1.5.1 GIC in the Rural vs. Urban Divide

GICs are drawn from 1996 to 1999, 1999 to 2002, and from 2002 to 2005 to capture the effects of the economic slowdown, crisis, and recovery periods separately. Calculations are undertaken as well taking 1996 as base year (cumulatively) and comparing each of the following years with it to see how income growth evolved in the period as a whole.

Figure 1.9 shows results for the nation as a whole from 1996 to 2005. As can be seen, income gains were very close to zero for almost all percentiles of the distribution except the first five, giving evidence of the poor income performance. While in urban areas the GIC is rather flat, around zero (almost all percentiles had very low income growth rates and the PPGR is negative), in rural areas the curve has a clear negative slope indicating that growth was pro-poor. This is confirmed by the PPGR, which is higher than the mean growth rate (see Table 1.1). For total Colombia, the PPGR was just above the mean growth rate, influenced by results in rural areas. The behavior in rural areas would suggest a fall in inequality, confirmed by decreases in all inequality indicators except Atkinson e=2. The GINI coefficient moved from 0.51 to 0.47 and the Theil entropy measure from 0.54 to 0.47. Urban inequality decreased from 0.57 to 0.55. The poverty gap and inequality among the poor fell in both areas as well as at the national level.

Growth incidence curves for the period 1996-1999 show that the economic slowdown affected the poor much more than the non-poor (see Figure 1.10). The positive slope of the GIC, which is below the zero axis for almost all percentiles of the distribution, confirms that the poorer the household, the larger the impact of the economic slowdown on income. In urban areas the income drop was larger for the extreme poor, where extreme poverty increased to 16.2 percent and the poverty gap widened. In rural areas the rise in poverty indicators was larger, with per capita income falling more than in urban areas (-7.9 percentversus -2.5 percent). Extreme poverty (which is three times that in urban areas) jumped to 48 percent of the population and the poverty gap to 49 percent.

Between 1999 and 2002, the GIC has a positive slope and growth was pro-poor as shown by the PPGR. This result should be interpreted cautiously as it is strongly influenced by a statistical effect of income moving back to the levels observed before the economic slowdown and by large income increases for the poor in rural areas (see Figure 1.11). If compared with 1999, poverty indicators improved, for the nation as a whole, urban, and rural areas, but if compared with the base year 1996 they almost all worsened. It is important to underline that although incomes of the poor population in rural areas increased up to 60 percent, the incidence of poverty decreased only slightly, from 78 percent to 75.1 percent. The poverty gap, in contrast, showed a larger decrease from 49.3 percent to 39.4 percent, indicating a decrease in the severity of poverty. In urban Colombia, the poverty gap remained close to 23 percent while the incidence of poverty decreased slightly.

It was in years 2003 and 2004 that favorable international commodity prices helped the rural sector achieve higher incomes and reduce poverty, a dynamic that did not hold on into 2005. Rural areas seem to have followed their own dynamics, which, although not completely isolated from domestic growth conditions, had different roots. In contrast, economic recession had a direct effect on urban households, which had been major recipients of real estate credit in the boom period between 1991 and 1995. When incomes fell and the bubble in the real estate market burst, urban households were directly affected than rural households, which are more dependent on external price conditions, demand from urban areas, and climate conditions.

In the period 2002 to 2005, growth was pro-poor in both urban and rural areas and consequently at the national level. As can be seen in Figures 1.12 and 1.16, for Colombia as a whole and for urban Colombia, incomes of the extreme poor increased more than for the rest of the population. In contrast, the inverted u-shaped form of the rural GIC shows the poorest five percentiles of the population and the richest ten as exhibiting the largest income losses.

Summarizing, between 1996 and 2005, the recession affected the poor population more than the non-poor in relative terms. Although economic recovery was pro-poor, when analyzing the period as a whole it is important to notice that from 1996 to 2005 there was only a very slight progress in poverty and inequality indicators and that the population remains still very vulnerable to changes in economic conditions. Reversal in GDP growth drove the country back to 1989 poverty levels, having a major effect on the population. Adverse consequences on unemployment and income lasted longer in urban Colombia, where growth was not pro-poor. Rural areas recovered more rapidly due to external factors affecting agricultural prices.

The aforementioned results are consistent with Figure 1.21, where the PPGR and the mean growth rate are calculated for each year compared to 1996 (i.e., cumulatively). The cumulative PPGR was negative up to 2003 and below the mean growth rate (which was also negative), except in 2001. These results give evidence of income losses for the entire population but more than proportionally for the poor in comparison to the non-poor. Starting in 2003, growth becomes pro-poor due to income gains in rural areas (see Table 1.2)

Urban data show that both the mean growth rate and the PPGR were negative in all years (See Figure 1.22. Growth was anti-poor in all years if compared with 1996, and only in 2003 did the situation stop worsening and income losses diminished. In 2005, the urban mean growth rate and the PPGR were very close and just above zero, indicating that the population began benefitting from growth. In rural Colombia, growth was anti-poor until 2001 and the mean growth rate was negative up to 2002 (See Figure 1.23) while growth was favorable to the poor starting in 2001.

1.5.2 Regions

In order to identify regional differences in the pattern of pro-poor growth, we draw GICs for the five regions covered by the household surveys: Atlántico, Oriental, Central, Pacfic and Bogotá.[22] Atlántico, on the Caribbean Coast is home to about 21 percent of Colombian population and the largest coastal cities in the country: Barranquilla (1.3 million), Cartagena de Indias (1 million) and Santa Marta (434,000 million). This region comprises departments whose economies are primarily based on agriculture and cattle farming (like Sucre and Magdalena) as well as departments with significant mineral resources in La Guajira and Cesar, which is also one of the poorest departments in the entire country. In this region, the mean growth rate from 1996 to 2005 was negative (-0.67) but the poorest 20 percent of the population had income growth rates up to 6 percent and the PPGR was also close to zero (0.36) (see Table 1.3).

The Central region accounts for 25 percent of the population and is mixed in its production structure as well. It combines important coffee-producing departments (Caldas, Risaralda and Quindío) with large industrial areas in Antioquia and around its capital city Medellín. It also

[22]Since the 1991 Constitution, Colombia is divided into 32 departments (nine more than under the old constitution) and a capital district (Bogotá) Furthermore, the country is divided into five geographical regions. The departments are divided into "Municipios" which according to the 1991 Constitution are the smallest territorial entities with governmental and administrative functions. The household survey groups the departments into four regions plus Bogotá and does not include eight of the new departments, namely: Arauca, Casanare, Vichada, Guainía, Guaviare, Vaupés, Amazonas and Putumayo which represent 3 percent of Colombian population.

consists of the departments of Tolima, Huila and Caquetá, located in the south, which base their income mainly on agriculture. In this region, the growth incidence curve from 1996 to 2005 was almost flat, around a mean growth rate of 0.62, pointing to stagnation in incomes for almost all percentiles of the population. The small gains in growth were distributed almost equally among the population.

In the Oriental region, growth was more favorable to the poorest percentiles and pro-poor overall. This region includes important industrial manufacturing and commerce activities around Cundinamarca that have evolved due to the close proximity to the capital city. In the Pacific region the growth rate in mean was 1.1, and the PPGR 0.4. Growth rates were larger the higher the percentiles and the GIC is upward-sloping suggesting lack of pro poor growth in relative terms. This region encompasses extreme contrasts: it includes the poorest department in the country (Chocó) as well as one of the most developed (Valle). In Bogotá , the capital district with 15 percent of the Colombian population, the PPGR was just slightly above the mean growth rate and both rates were close to zero. The change in slope of the GIC indicates that the population closest to the poverty line showed the worst income growth.

In summary, GICs at a regional level from 1996 to 2005 presents similar results for all regions and growth was pro poor in absolute terms. Growth incidence curves drawn by region do not give evidence of important improvements in income in any of the regions. According to the criteria established by Ravallion's methodology but using this criterion alone, it is not possible to give precise information on the extent of pro-poor growth. The mean growth rate and the PPGR differ only slightly from each other and are both near the zero axis. The comparison indicates that in 2005 incomes are only now recovering slowly after the slowdown and crisis period at the end of the nineties.

1.6 Conclusions

When using the methodology of Ravallion and Chen, one could conclude that from 1996 to 2005, growth in Colombia was pro-poor according to the weak and relative approaches, since the GIC was above zero for all percentiles and the PPGR was higher than the mean growth rate (0.94 vs. 0.43). Nevertheless the difference is very small and the methodology does not indicate anything about how large this distance needs to be to conclude pro-poor growth. A more balanced conclusion in this case would be that growth was very low and was not adverse to the poor in comparison to the non-poor, leading to an almost unchanged incidence of poverty in comparison to that observed in 1996.

There are some important shortcomings to keep in mind when interpreting results. One is that application of this methodology poses high requirements on data quality. Ideally one should use panel data to be able to track the same households over time which can lead to a very different assessment of pro-poor growth as was shown by Grimm (2007). Household survey panel data are rarely available in developing countries, due to the high cost of collecting information but also because it is much harder to trace people over time, particularly poor households which are quite mobile. In the case of Colombia, interpretation of results is restricted to the fact that the sample is not the same, thus there can have been mobility across percentiles particularly when considering a period of economic turbulence.

Another constrain is that results are extremely sensitive to the base and end years chosen and thus subject to the economic context of those years. Comparisons between two distant years can hide important issues and lead to results that hold only for those two selected years, but that do not contribute to the analysis of the period as a whole nor to formulate adequate policy interventions. This issue was proved by selecting different starting and ending years and showing how interpretation changes.

To overcome this problem this paper proposes fixing the starting year, which should be the earliest possible according to data availability, and calculate the pro-poor growth rate and the growth rate in mean for each subsequent year. These results were shown in Figure 1.21 and indicate that household income losses were larger for the poorest percentiles in all years since 1996 excepting in 2005. Alternatively one could repeat this exercise comparing each year with the immediate year before to capture the effect of short run business activity.

In spite of the above mentioned shortcomings, general results are in accordance to the economic background. Household income in Colombia was quite sensitive to labor market and macroeconomic conditions, and variability was larger the lower the percentile, particularly in the peak of the recession when average income of the poorest percentiles decreased considerably. This can be corroborated also when comparing household growth rates by decile over time with growth rate of per capita GDP as shown in Figure 1.24. Contraction of income between 1996 and 1999 was compensated by expansion in 1999 to 2002. In the years between 2002 and 2005 where economic growth stabilized, the variability of per capita income growth rates by percentile diminished. As a result, comparison of the starting and ending years (1996-2005) show a quite stable result, given that the contraction and expansion effects compensated each other.

Concerning the urban vs. rural divide, from 2002 income growth for the poorest percentiles in rural areas was much higher than in urban areas, leading to reductions in the poverty gap. In the year 2005, a more stable economic environment emerged, fostering favorable conditions in rural areas and leading to a reduction of extreme poverty. Between 1996 and 2005 growth was pro-poor in relative terms in rural Colombia, while in urban areas growth was pro-poor according to the weak approach. The small income gains observed were similar for all percentiles. The overall effect is influenced by results in urban areas, where 75 percent of the population lives. Results of the FGT measures shows that the largest amount of poor people live in urban areas, but the percentage of poor, the depth and the severity of poverty are higher in rural.

Disaggregating results by regions makes it difficult to determine whether growth was more pro-poor in one region than in another given the similarity of growth incidence curves (for the period 1996 to 2005 as a whole) as in the cases of the Oriental and Central regions. It was only in Pacfic that growth was clearly more favorable to the rich according to the relative approach, while in the other regions, the results for the nation as a whole hold: low growth rates and small differences between the mean growth rate and the PPGR.

Once again, aggregation plays a significant role here. On the one side due to the selection of the initial and final years, on the other the composition of regions themselves which is based on geography and proximity, not on economic criteria. For instance, the Pacific region is composed by four departments: one of them belongs to the richest in the country and the others to the poorest. As a result aggregated figures are not precise enough to derive policy implications at the regional level.

Several policy implications emerge from this study. While progress in income poverty reduction in Colombia is a slow process accompanied by mild reductions in inequality, economic crisis reverse in a very short time progress achieved. This suggests that the speed of growth to affect poverty is not the same in boom and bust cycles. Thus, economic stability, which depends also on external conditions, some of them out of scope for policy makers, is of extreme importance to achieve pro poor growth. It is essential to design mechanisms that allow applying counter cyclical policies to promote rapid increases in employment and as a consequence in income sources for the poor during recessions.

A second implied policy is the need to analyze the relation between poverty and economic growth in the highest possible desegregated way. Averages, over time as well as over geo-political divisions can lead to wrong interpretations. Concerning the different country divides, two issues emerge. The high rural incidence of poverty as well as the large gap between average incomes in urban and rural Colombia needs special attention, and can explain why in absence of opportunities, rural population can easily involve in illegal activities as a source of income.

1.7 Tables

Table 1.1: Rate of Pro-Poor Growth for Three selected Periods

	1996-2005	1996-1999	1999-2002	2002-2005
	Total national			
Growth rate in mean	0.43	-3.03	-0.56	5.24
Growth rate at median	0.31	-5.48	0.83	5.97
Mean percentile growth rate	0.71	-6.88	4.74	6.47
Rate of Pro Poor Growth	0.94	-11.84	7.89	7.53
	Urban (Cabecera)			
Growth rate in mean	0.24	-2.56	-2.11	5.64
Growth rate at median	-0.07	-4.23	-1.04	5.45
Mean percentile growth rate	0.14	-5.17	-0.03	6.82
Rate of Pro Poor Growth	-0.02	-9.55	2.02	8.06
	Rural (Resto)			
Growth rate in mean	0.49	-7.9	6.86	3.04
Growth rate at median	1.08	-12.5	12.13	4.38
Mean percentile growth rate	1.49	-12.65	18.25	3.69
Rate of Pro Poor Growth	1.92	-16.3	19.65	4.1

Source: Own calculations based on ENH and ECH DANE

Table 1.2: Cumulative Income Pro-Poor Growth from 1996 to 2005

	1997	1998	1999	2000	2001	2002	2003	2004	2005
Total national									
Growth rate in mean	-0.63	-2.42	-3.03	-1.85	-1.60	-1.8	-0.14	-0.12	0.43
Growth rate at median	-3.81	-4.43	-5.48	-2.5	-2.14	-2.38	-0.1	-0.63	0.31
Mean percentile growth rate	-3.28	-4.37	-6.88	-2.27	-1.54	-2.04	0.29	0.06	0.71
Rate of Pro Poor Growth	-6.37	-6.20	-11.84	-2.71	-1.48	-2.25	0.62	0.13	0.94
Urban (Cabecera)									
Growth rate in mean	0.65	-2.24	-2.56	-2.12	-2.24	-2.34	-0.85	-0.64	0.24
Growth rate at median	-1.65	-4.28	-4.23	-2.71	-2.78	-2.65	-0.95	-1.13	-0.07
Mean percentile growth rate	-1.01	-3.55	-5.17	-2.98	-2.58	-2.89	-1.07	-1.03	0.14
Rate of Pro Poor Growth	-3.62	-5.09	-9.55	-4.33	-3.00	-3.83	-1.55	-1.61	-0.02
Rural (Resto)									
Growth rate in mean	-8.63	-5.51	-7.9	-1.77	-0.47	-0.79	2.07	0.96	0.49
Growth rate at median	-9.46	-6.67	-12.5	-1.09	-0.41	-0.95	2.91	0.98	1.08
Mean percentile growth rate	-11.36	-7.62	-12.65	-1.08	0.11	0.15	3.46	2.33	1.49
Rate of Pro Poor Growth	-13.08	-8.89	-16.3	-0.72	0.14	0.42	4.07	2.60	1.92

Source: Own calculations based on ENH and ECH DANE

Table 1.3: Rate of Pro-Poor Growth by Regions from 1996 to 2005

	Atlántico	Oriental	Central	Pacífico	Bogotá
Growth rate in mean	-0.67	0.49	0.56	1.16	0.42
Growth rate at median	-0.38	0.47	0.34	1.00	0.18
Mean percentile growth rate	-0.08	1.16	0.67	0.86	0.48
Rate of Pro Poor Growth	0.36	1.71	0.81	0.44	0.68
Headcount Index (1996)	54.00	52.00	58.00	54.00	29.00

Source: Own calculations based on ENH and ECH DANE

Table 1.4: Colombia: Poverty Measures by Area from 1996 to 2005

	Poverty Line			**Extreme Poverty Line**		
Total National	**FGT0**	**FGT1**	**FGT2**	**FGT0**	**FGT1**	**FGT2**
1996	50.6	23.3	14.4	17.1	7.7	5.2
1997	52.4	25.0	15.7	18.2	8.4	5.6
1998	54.8	26.5	16.8	20.4	9.3	6.2
1999	57.1	30.8	21.1	25.2	13.0	8.9
2000	55.0	26.4	16.5	19.0	8.3	5.3
2001	55.2	25.9	15.9	18.7	7.8	4.8
2002	57.0	27.5	17.1	20.7	8.9	5.6
2003	50.7	22.8	13.7	15.8	6.6	4.1
2004	52.7	24.0	14.2	17.4	6.5	3.6
2005	49.2	21.7	12.8	14.7	6.1	3.7
Urban	**FGT0**	**FGT1**	**FGT2**	**FGT0**	**FGT1**	**FGT2**
1996	42.8	17.8	10.1	10.6	4.3	2.8
1997	44.0	18.7	10.7	11.1	4.3	2.7
1998	47.1	20.4	11.7	13.1	4.8	2.9
1999	49.1	23.6	15.0	16.2	7.6	5.1
2000	48.2	21.8	13.0	13.5	5.6	3.6
2001	49.4	21.6	12.5	13.4	5.1	3.0
2002	50.2	23.0	13.9	15.5	6.5	4.0
2003	46.3	20.2	11.8	12.6	5.0	3.0
2004	47.4	20.9	12.1	13.7	4.9	2.7
2005	42.4	17.4	9.7	10.2	3.8	2.2
Rural	**FGT0**	**FGT1**	**FGT2**	**FGT0**	**FGT1**	**FGT2**
1996	70.1	37.1	25.0	33.2	16.2	11.0
1997	73.7	41.0	28.3	36.4	18.8	13.0
1998	74.8	42.4	29.9	39.3	20.9	14.8
1999	78.0	49.3	36.9	48.5	26.8	18.8
2000	72.8	38.5	25.6	33.2	15.4	9.9
2001	70.5	37.4	24.7	32.7	14.8	9.7
2002	75.1	39.4	25.7	34.5	15.3	9.8
2003	62.9	29.9	18.8	24.5	10.9	7.1
2004	67.6	32.7	20.2	27.5	10.8	6.2
2005	68.2	33.6	21.3	27.5	12.4	8.0

Source: Own calculations based on ENH and ECH DANE

Table 1.5: Mean of Income by Deciles from 1996 to 2005

Decile	1996	1997	1998	1999	2000	2001	2002	2003	2004	2005
1	20885	18432	18726	10306	19223	21401	20829	25680	26510	28025
2	49392	44754	44326	30147	43828	45463	43247	52955	49882	54770
3	70378	64889	63905	51320	63846	65410	62017	74148	69485	76817
4	92569	85884	84147	74076	83967	85541	81042	94750	90037	99204
5	117381	110609	108035	98260	107310	108321	103920	118207	114044	125659
6	148520	143173	137533	129012	136592	136986	133874	149246	144827	158207
7	189799	186132	178527	171427	176422	174645	174063	192202	189383	202247
8	253355	252910	244299	236315	238639	235459	235864	258341	258188	273463
9	371575	379036	371559	366945	361715	358639	353216	383108	390017	410543
10	843382	865265	851798	850095	820391	810560	791166	848791	880533	915480
Mean	215724	215108	210285	201790	205193	204242	199924	219743	221290	234442

Source: Own calculations based on ENH and ECH DANE

Table 1.6: Atkinson Inequality Measures from 1996 to 2005

	Total Colombia			**Urban Colombia**			**Rural Colombia**		
Year	$\varepsilon = 0.5$	$\varepsilon = 2$	**Gini**	$\varepsilon = 0.5$	$\varepsilon = 2$	**Gini**	$\varepsilon = 0.5$	$\varepsilon = 2$	**Gini**
1996	0.31	0.94	0.59	0.28	0.96	0.57	0.23	0.66	0.51
1997	0.31	0.92	0.60	0.27	0.94	0.56	0.23	0.69	0.51
1998	0.31	0.81	0.60	0.27	0.65	0.57	0.26	0.79	0.54
1999	0.34	0.99	0.63	0.29	0.77	0.58	0.34	0.99	0.62
2000	0.29	0.76	0.59	0.26	0.70	0.56	0.21	0.67	0.49
2001	0.29	0.74	0.58	0.26	0.66	0.56	0.23	0.69	0.51
2002	0.31	0.81	0.60	0.28	0.73	0.57	0.29	0.79	0.56
2003	0.27	0.68	0.56	0.25	0.67	0.55	0.20	0.54	0.47
2004	0.29	0.71	0.59	0.27	0.68	0.57	0.21	0.58	0.49
2005	0.28	0.76	0.58	0.25	0.66	0.55	0.20	0.71	0.47

Source: Own calculations based on ENH and ECH DANE

1.8 Figures

Figure 1.1: Gross Domestic Product Growth Rate (Real). Total and Per Capita. 1978-2005

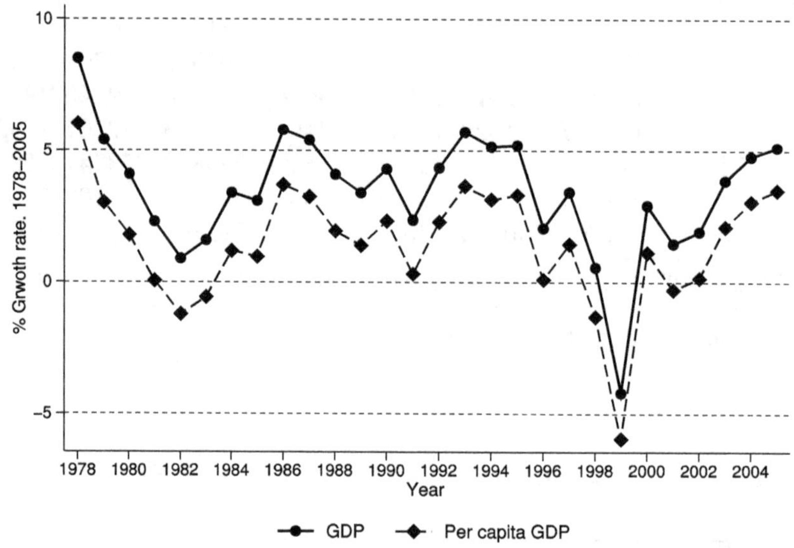

Source : Own Calculations based on data from National Accounts. DANE.

Figure 1.2: Headcount Index by Areas. Moderate Poverty Line. 1996-2005

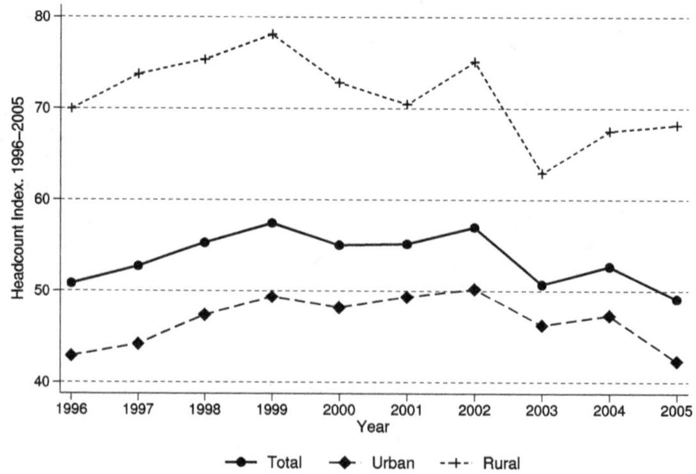

Source : Own Calculations based on Encuesta de Hogares and Encuesta Contìnua de Hogares. DANE-DNP.

Figure 1.3: Headcount Index by Areas. Extreme Poverty Line. 1996-2005

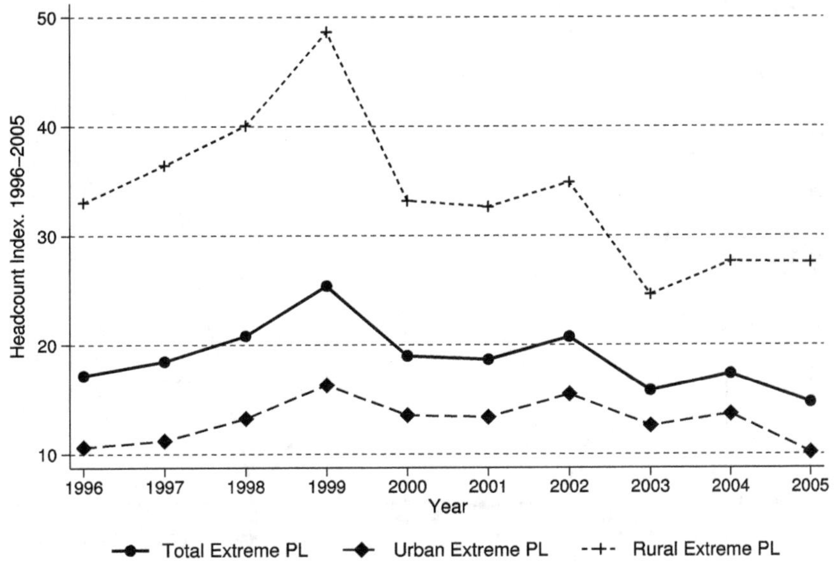

Source : Own Calculations based on Encuesta de Hogares and Encuesta Contìnua de Hogares. DANE-DNP.

Figure 1.4: Average Household Income (Real Prices of 1998). Total Colombia 1996-2005

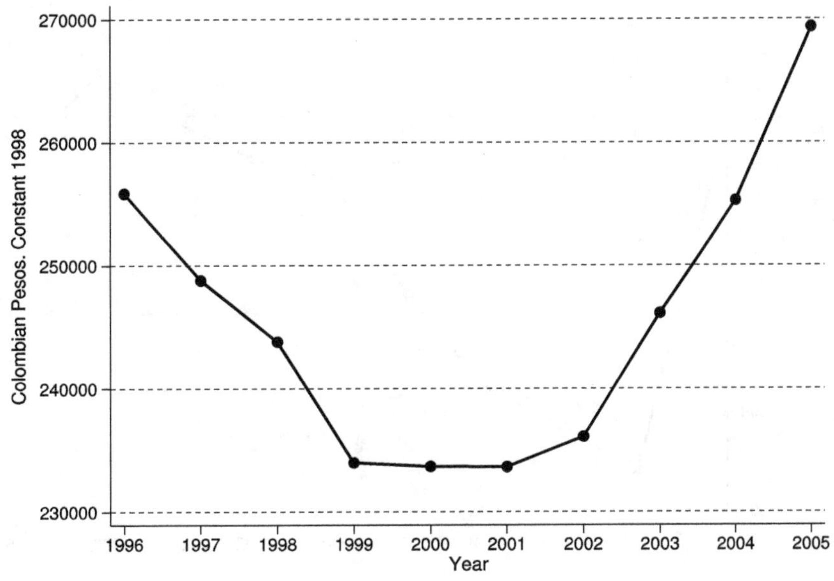

Source : Own Calculations based on Encuesta de Hogares and Encuesta Contìnua de Hogares. DANE-DNP.

Figure 1.5: Average Household Income (Real prices of 1998). Urban Colombia 1996-2005

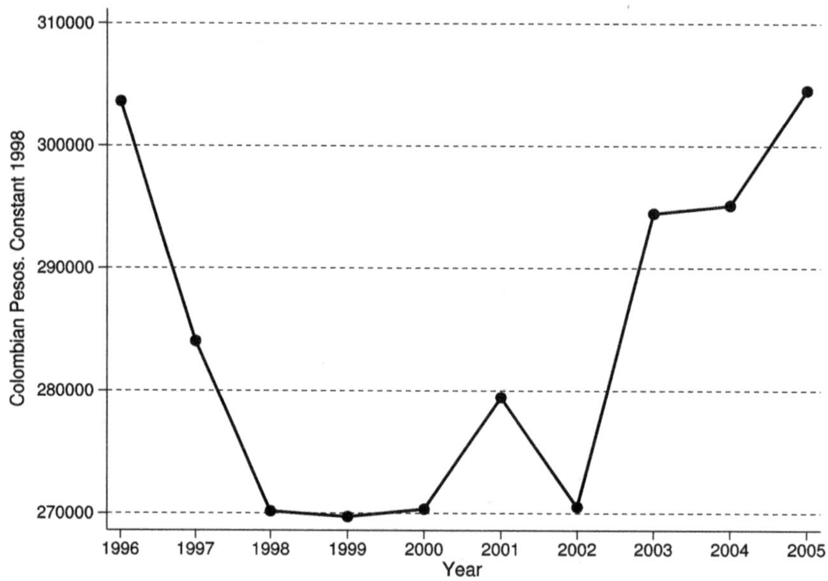

Source : Own Calculations based on Encuesta de Hogares and Encuesta Contìnua de Hogares. DANE-DNP.

Figure 1.6: Average Household Income (Real prices of 1998). Rural Colombia 1996-2005

Source : Own Calculations based on Encuesta de Hogares and Encuesta Contìnua de Hogares. DANE-DNP.

Figure 1.7: Unemployment Rate by Areas. 1996-2005

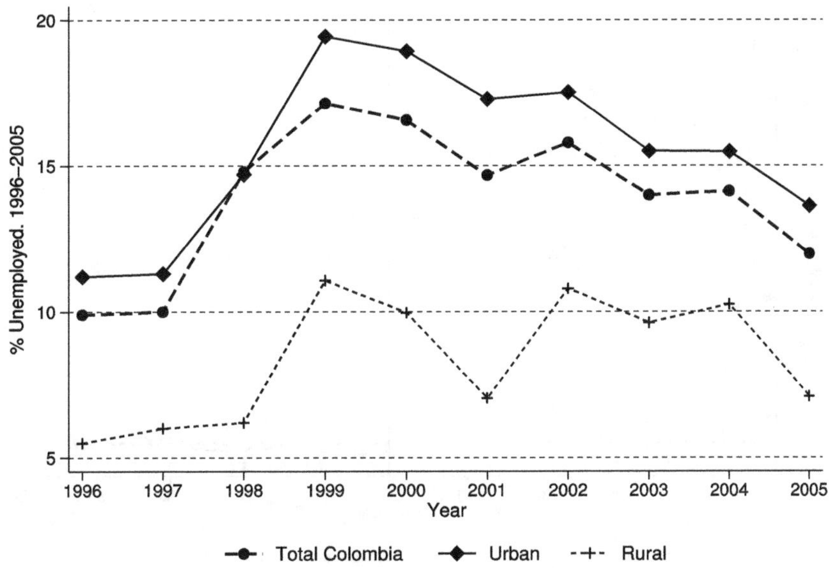

Source : DANE-DNP.

Figure 1.8: GINI Coefficient. Total Colombia 1996-2005

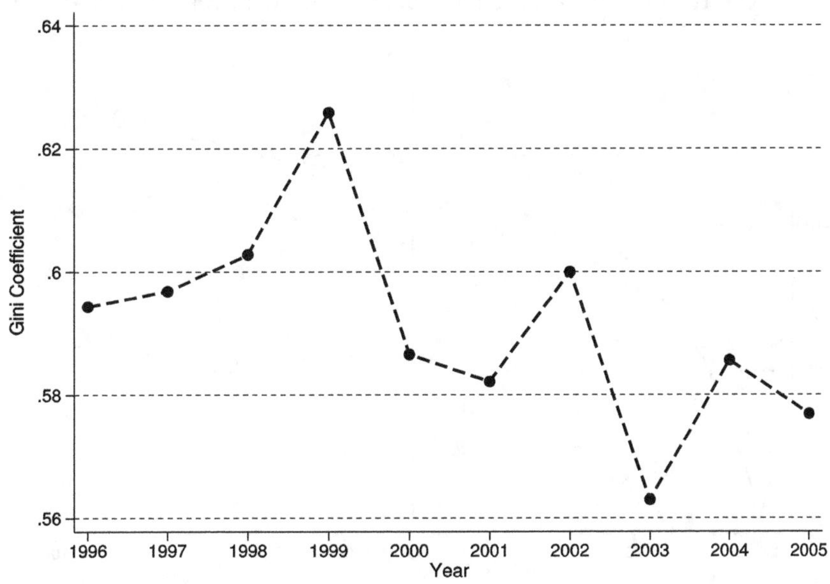

Source : DANE-DNP.

Figure 1.9: Growth Incidence Curve. Total Colombia. 1996-2005

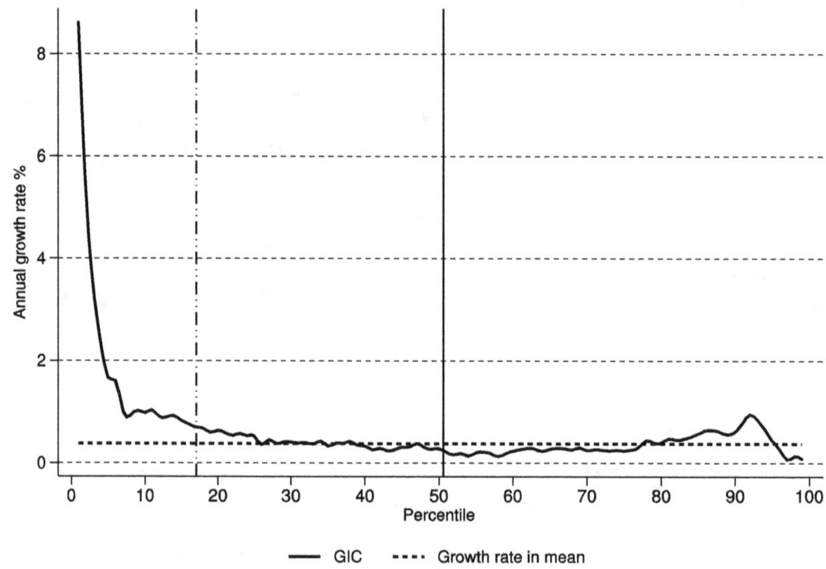

Source : Own Calculations based on Encuesta de Hogares and Encuesta Contínua de Hogares. DANE-DNP.

Figure 1.10: Growth Incidence Curve. Total Colombia. 1996-1999

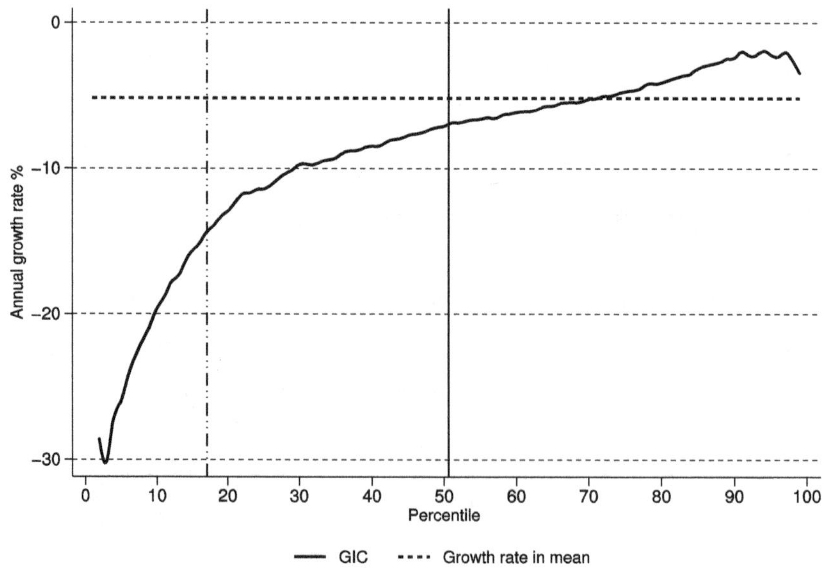

Source : Own Calculations based on Encuesta de Hogares and Encuesta Contínua de Hogares. DANE-DNP.

Figure 1.11: Growth Incidence Curve. Total Colombia. 1999-2002

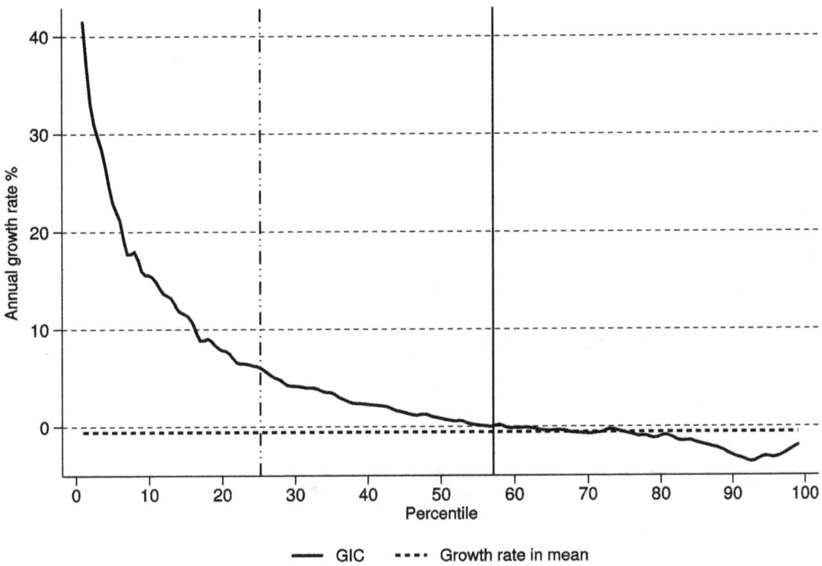

Source : Own Calculations based on Encuesta de Hogares and Encuesta Contínua de Hogares. DANE-DNP.

Figure 1.12: Growth Incidence Curve. Total Colombia. 2002-2005

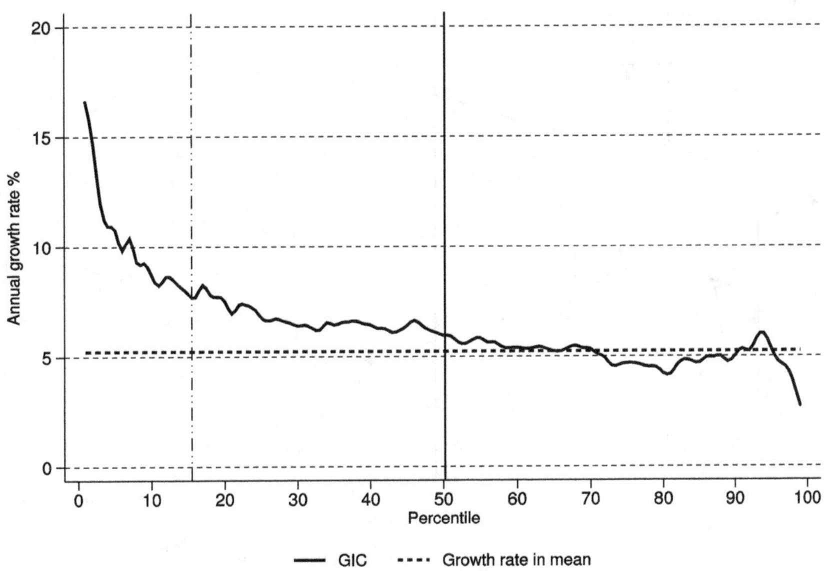

Source : Own Calculations based on Encuesta de Hogares and Encuesta Contínua de Hogares. DANE-DNP.

Figure 1.13: Growth Incidence Curve. Urban Colombia. 1996-2005

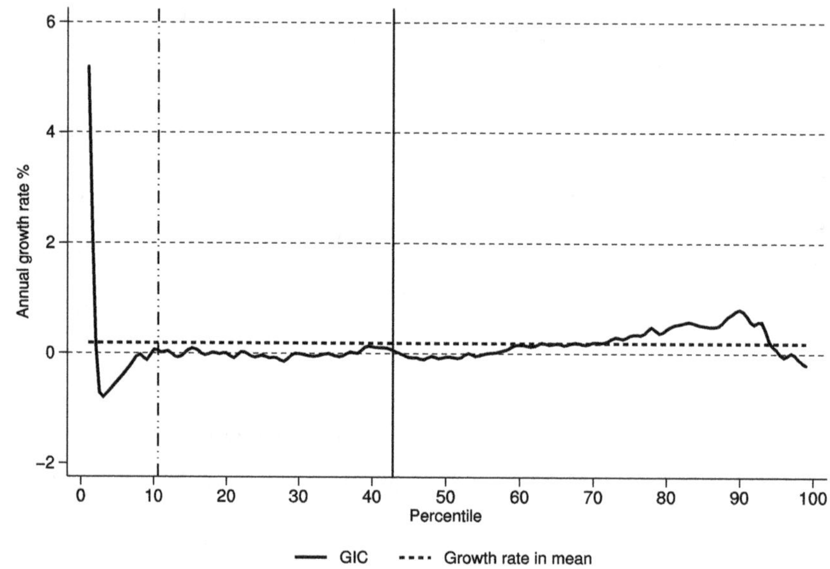

Source : Own Calculations based on Encuesta de Hogares and Encuesta Contínua de Hogares. DANE-DNP.

Figure 1.14: Growth Incidence Curve. Urban Colombia. 1996-1999

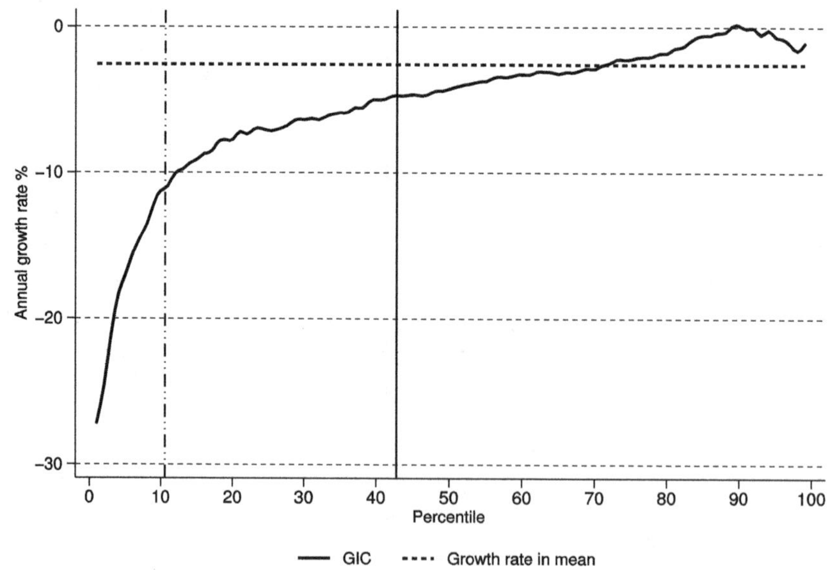

Source : Own Calculations based on Encuesta de Hogares and Encuesta Contínua de Hogares. DANE-DNP.

Figure 1.15: Growth Incidence Curve. Urban Colombia. 1999-2002

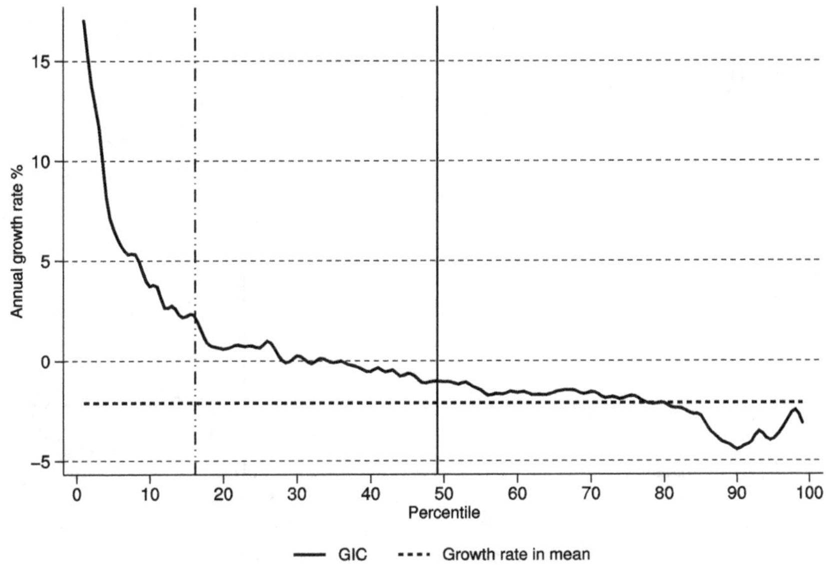

Source : Own Calculations based on Encuesta de Hogares and Encuesta Contínua de Hogares. DANE-DNP.

Figure 1.16: Growth Incidence Curve. Urban Colombia. 2002-2005

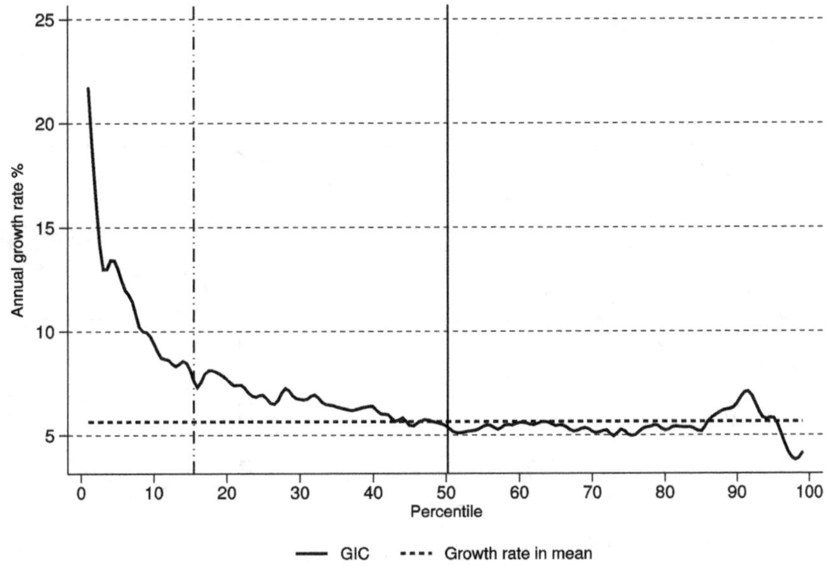

Source : Own Calculations based on Encuesta de Hogares and Encuesta Contínua de Hogares. DANE-DNP.

Figure 1.17: Growth Incidence Curve. Rural Colombia. 1996-2005

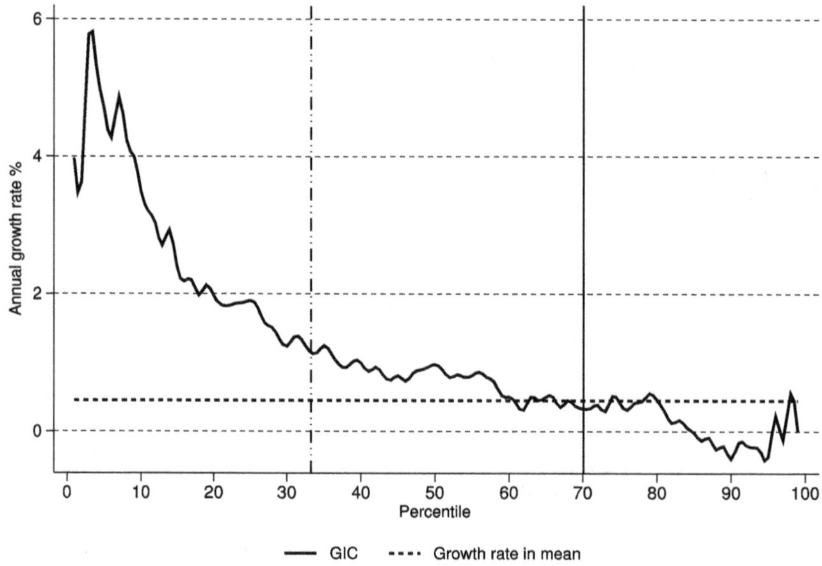

Source : Own Calculations based on Encuesta de Hogares and Encuesta Contínua de Hogares. DANE-DNP.

Figure 1.18: Growth Incidence Curve. Rural Colombia. 1996-1999

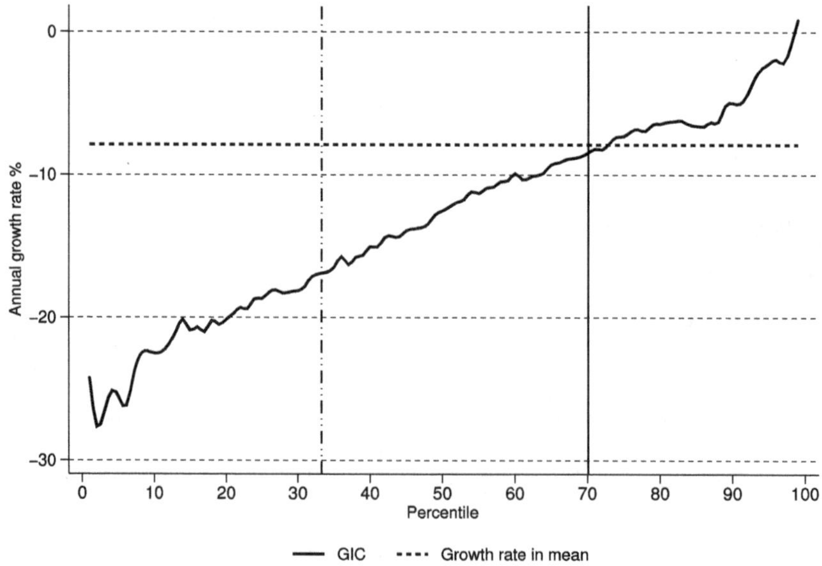

Source : Own Calculations based on Encuesta de Hogares and Encuesta Contínua de Hogares. DANE-DNP.

Figure 1.19: Growth Incidence Curve. Rural Colombia. 1999-2002

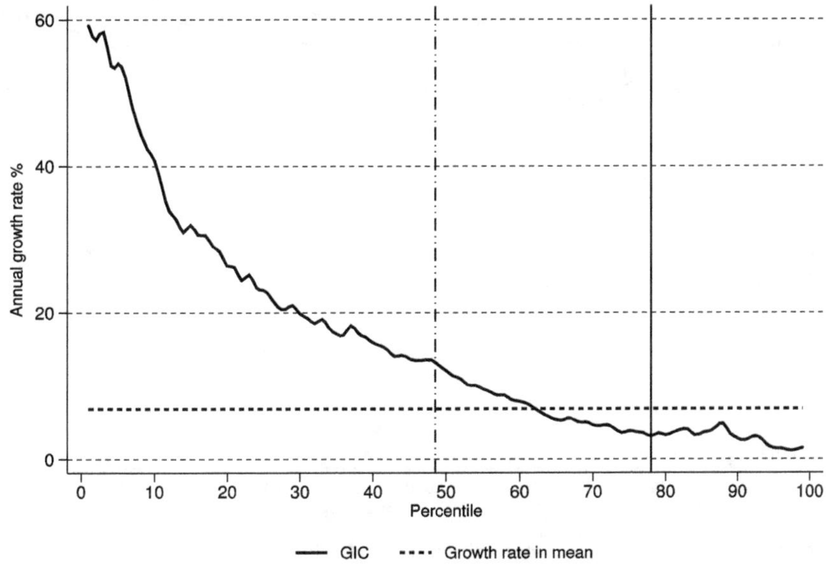

Source : Own Calculations based on Encuesta de Hogares and Encuesta Contínua de Hogares. DANE-DNP.

Figure 1.20: Growth Incidence Curve. Rural Colombia. 2002-2005

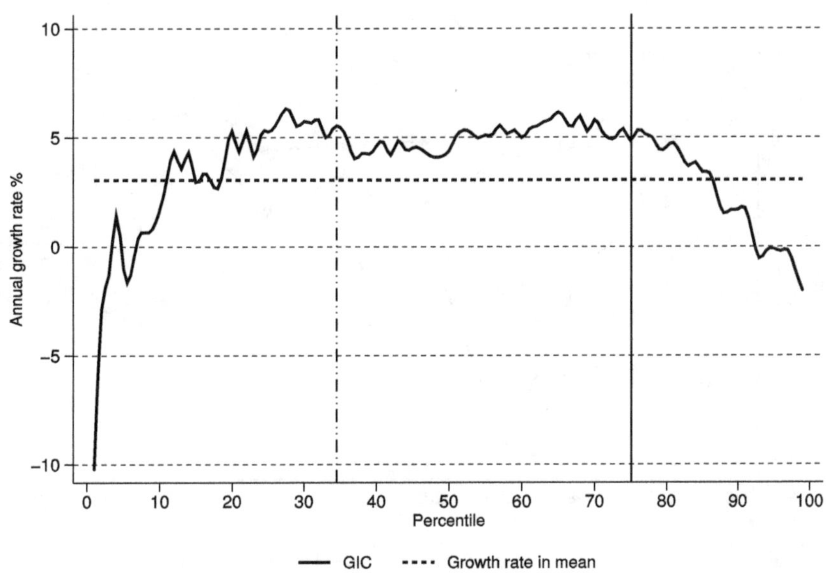

Source : Own Calculations based on Encuesta de Hogares and Encuesta Contínua de Hogares. DANE-DNP.

Figure 1.21: Cumulative Results of Growth Incidence Curves. Total Colombia. 1996-2005

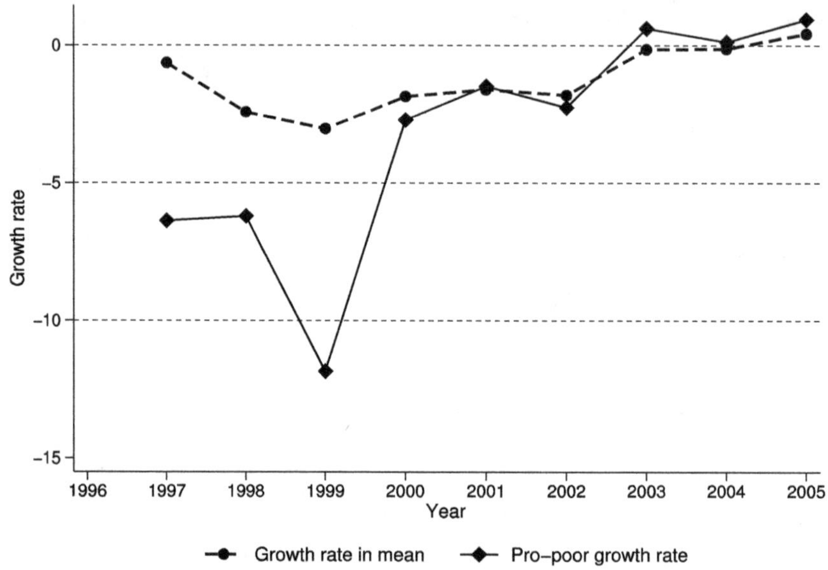

Source : Own Calculations based on Encuesta de Hogares and Encuesta Contínua de Hogares. DANE-DNP.

Figure 1.22: Cumulative Results of Growth Incidence Curves. Urban Colombia. 1996-2005

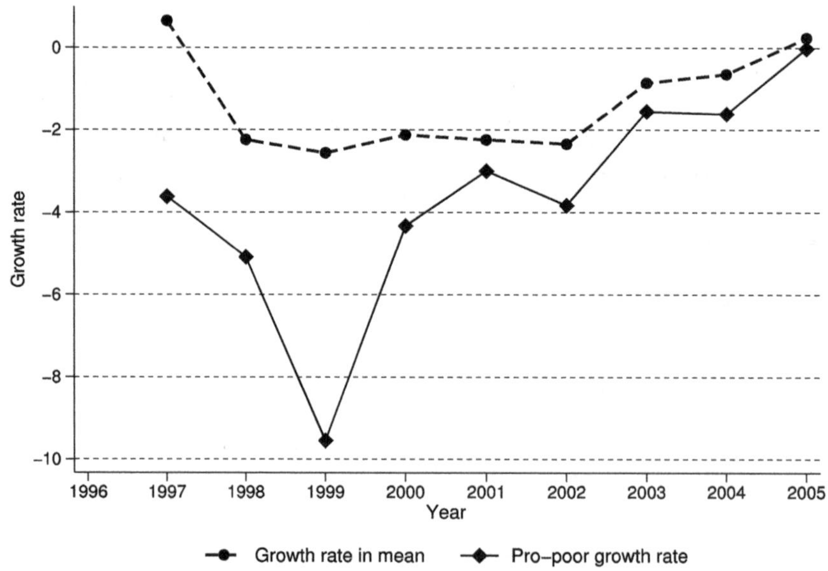

Source : Own Calculations based on Encuesta de Hogares and Encuesta Contínua de Hogares. DANE-DNP.

Figure 1.23: Cumulative Results of Growth Incidence Curves. Rural Colombia. 1996-2005

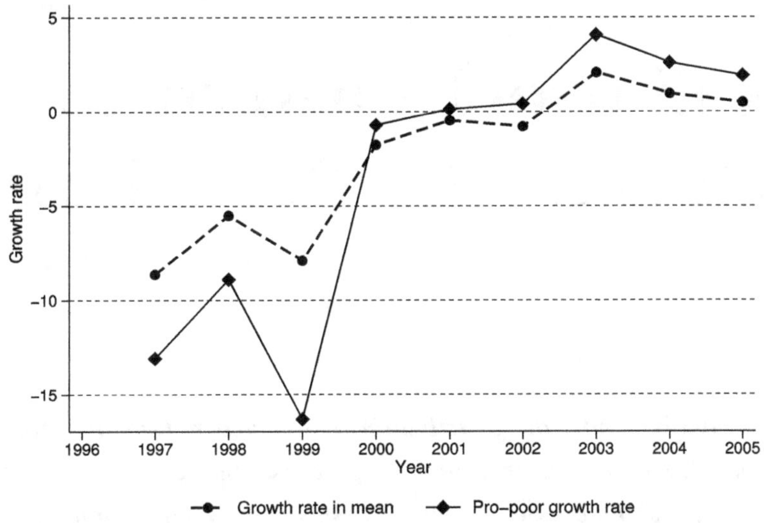

Source : Own Calculations based on Encuesta de Hogares and Encuesta Contínua de Hogares. DANE-DNP.

Figure 1.24: Average Decile Household Per Capita Growth Rate vs. GDP Per Capita Growth Rate. 1996-2005

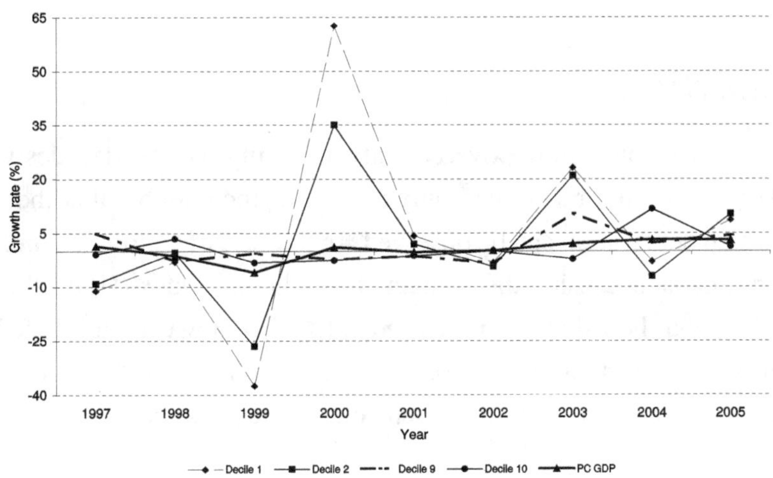

Source : Own calculations based on EH, ECH and National Accounts from DANE.

2

Application of Non-Income Indicators for Pro Poor Growth

Abstract

*In this paper, we analyze how the distribution of selected non-income welfare indicators changed between 1997 and 2003 in Colombia. We use multidimensional pro-poor growth measurement techniques and create indices for assets, health, education, and subjective welfare using two alternative weighing techniques: polychoric principal components and normatively selected weights. Results show that while income and expenditures fluctuated according to economic growth, reflecting the effects of the 1999 economic crisis, non-income indicators show minor changes. While income and expenditures decreased for all income percentiles, and relatively more for the richest, the non-income dimensions stagnated and remained in 2003 as unequally distributed as in 1997.**

2.1 Introduction

One of the major issues concerning poverty analysis during the last decades was the recognition that poverty should not be defined only as lack of income, but that there are multiple dimensions by which deprivation can be observed. In the case of Colombia, multidimensional poverty has been approached using the Human Development Index (HDI), the Unmet Basic Needs Index (NBI), and the Life Conditions Index (ICV).[1] However, all three have methodological and conceptual shortcomings. Moreover, research on the effects of macroeconomic growth, stagnation, or recession on multidimensional poverty is scarce.

---

*Based on joint work with Melanie Grosse

[1]NBI and ICV are the abbreviations in Spanish, which we will keep in this document.

The objective of this paper is to analyze how the distribution of particular dimensions of welfare in Colombia changed between 1997 and 2003, and if there was a relation between changes in income and non-income dimensions. We create indicators reflecting human and physical capital (education and assets), health status, and subjective welfare and track relative and absolute changes in those indicators along quantiles of the population, for example deciles and vintiles.

By applying the recently developed methodologies on multidimensional pro-poor growth (Klasen, 2008) to the Colombian Living Standard Measurement Survey (LSMS) we discuss whether changes in assets, education, health, and subjective welfare were more beneficial to the poor than to the non-poor.

For constructing indices, we select a subset of variables and apply principal component analysis (PCA) in a recently modified version known as polychoric PCA, suggested by Kolenikov and Angeles (2009) to define weights. This methodology allows to correctly calculate the correlation matrix before applying traditional principal components analysis, diverging from the standard procedure used up to now in the literature. Results are compared to the same indicators using normatively selected weights to enrich the discussion about the right weighting procedure.

Although the time span is short and covers a turbulent economic period with a large recession, it is quite relevant because it gives an insight into how it affected non-income dimensions like education, health, assets ownership, and access to public services. We find that multiple dimensions of welfare might contradict each other in the short run, particularly when they depend on public policies.

Public spending can thus play an important role for counteracting the depth of economic crisis like the one experienced in Colombia in 1999. We also find that even though infrastructure conditions and access to education improved due to reforms and higher public spending, self reported welfare perception was largely driven by available income and thus by consumption possibilities. In contrast to the available literature on Colombia, our subjective welfare indicator does not show improvements in self reported welfare of Colombians between 1997 and 2003.

Results also show that while income and expenditures fluctuated according to economic growth, reflecting the effects of the 1999 economic crisis, non-income indicators proved to be more stable, less unequally distributed, and had minor improvements during the period of analysis. We find that income and expenditures decreased relatively more for the richest, while the non-monetary welfare dimensions stagnated and remained in 2003 as unequally distributed as in 1997.

2.2 Multidimensional Poverty Analysis: Concept and Measurement Issues

2.2.1 Concept and Use

Multidimensional poverty analysis is primarily concerned with poverty assessment in attributes different than income. Conceptually, it gained attention among academics and policy makers in the last two decades, inspired by the work of Sen (1985), who developed what is known in the literature as the capabilities approach. According to this approach, poverty is understood as deprivation of capabilities, or substantive freedoms, suggesting that poverty measures based solely on income and material status do not represent all aspects of human being, nor give information about people's capacities to achieve basic functionings. The capabilities approach also focuses on the individual's ability to participate in society, move across different spheres of life, and access markets, something that can hardly be captured by traditional income-based poverty measures (Clark, 2005).

Although there is a consensus about the existence of multiple dimensions of poverty, there is not a unique combination of dimensions to be included, and there are big debates on how to determine a threshold for judging whether an individual is poor or not. Dimensions frequently included are health, nutrition, education, and dwelling characteristics, taken as tangible outcomes that reflect functionings. However, there are many dimensions that can hardly be measured, but affect the ability of an individual to escape out of poverty. Typical examples are freedom, human rights, and violence.

Some authors argue that the different dimensions of poverty are generally weakly correlated with income (or expenditures) and that links between income and indicators such as malnutrition, mortality, and school enrollment are difficult to identify (Klasen, 2000; Günther and Klasen, 2009). Other authors affirm that multidimensional welfare indicators and income give similar overall pictures of poverty (von Maltzahn and Durrheim, 2007).[2]

An important range of studies on multidimensional poverty use variables reflecting physical, human, and social capital to create a composite index. The internationally best known indicator trying to capture multidimensional poverty is UNDP's Human Development Index (HDI), which combines indicators of longevity (measured by life expectancy at birth), education (a weighted average of the adult literacy rate and school enrollment rates), and living standards (GDP per capita converted to USD using PPP). This indicator has been criticized

[2]Using aggregated data, empirical cross-country literature focusing on non income indicators found evidence of regional convergence in such indicators, even in absence of convergence in per capita income (Kenny, 2005; Neumayer, 2003). Such studies argue for giving less attention to per capita income, but shifting it to other welfare indicators.

for having weak conceptual foundations, but has gained a key role in policy debate given its comparability across countries (Kanbur, 2002). Grimm et al. (2008) have addressed some of the critiques raised against the HDI using data for 2006. They extend the analysis from the macro level of between country comparisons, i.e., of national averages, to the micro level in breaking down the HDI for comparisons within countries. They do so by disaggregating the HDI by income quintile for a sample of 13 countries using micro-level household surveys. In doing so, the authors address one of the main critiques towards the HDI. With their approach, it has become possible to look at the distribution of multidimensional poverty within countries.

What Grimm et al. (2008) criticize (but not address themselves) is the weighting scheme by which each component gets the same arbitrary weight. In this paper, we address this critique and present two ways to avoid equal weighting. One is to define the weights based on researchers' own evaluation, thus on normative procedures, outlined in Section 2.3.2. The definition of normative weights is delicate, and thus might expose us to some discussions. However, equal weighting, despite being a popular weighting scheme, is exposed to even more discussion and critique because it also sets weights normatively, in this case equal to each other. When trying to avoid equal weighting, the researcher can assign normative weights according to her own criteria of the welfare each item provides, a procedure which might be questionable, but allows to control for different valuations according to the household's environment, for example the use of a bicycle as transportation vehicle in rural areas versus its use in urban areas (Moser and Felton, 2009).

Another way to define weights is to use statistical procedures to generate an overall index. Particular attention has been given to aggregation and weighting procedures of asset indices, often used to proxy for socio-economic status in the absence of income or expenditures information, i.e., to evaluate long-term wealth independently of short-term or cyclic income fluctuations. The most widely used technique in recent research is principal component analysis (PCA), which extracts the linear combinations between variables that best explain their variance and covariance structure. Intuitively, it allows aggregating several variables into a single dimension, giving each one a weight resulting from the eigenvalues and eigenvectors of the covariance matrix.[3]

The use of PCA for creating asset indices as proxy measures for socioeconomic status was suggested by Filmer and Pritchett (2001). The authors transform selected categorical

[3]An alternative to weight selected variables is to use the price of assets and value them in terms of the monetary welfare they provide. This is only possible if prices, quantities, and the current monetary value of each item are available, which is not the case for our data.

variables into binary ones, splitting each category into a set of dummy variables before using PCA. The resulting asset index for each household is defined as:

$$A_j = \frac{f_1 * (a_{j1} - a_1)}{s_1} + ... + \frac{f_N * (a_{jN} - a_N)}{s_N}, \tag{2.1}$$

where f_1 is the scoring factor for the first asset as resulting from the first principal component, a_{j1} is the jth household's value for the first asset and a_1 and s_1 are the mean and standard deviation of the first asset variable over all households.[4]

As discussed by Kolenikov and Angeles (2009), PCA is suitable when variables are multivariate normal, an assumption that does not hold when data are discrete. Breaking down categories into dummy variables results in perfectly negatively correlated variables, introducing spurious correlations. Additionally if the majority of the data points are concentrated in a single category, the method assigns larger weights to the most skewed variables and creates a biased correlation matrix. The authors propose using polychoric correlations in order to estimate the correlation matrix before using PCA. Polychoric PCA assumes that the observed ordinal variable has an underlying continuous variable and uses maximum likelihood to calculate how that continuous variable would have to be split up in order to produce the observed data. The resulting polychoric correlation matrix is used to calculate the eigenvectors. This procedure is particularly useful for ordinal data as it allows maintaining the original valuing and ordering of categories. Moreover it allows computing weights not only on owning but also not owning an asset (Moser and Felton, 2009) and it generates a larger percentage of explained variance by the first component as shown by Kolenikov and Angeles (2009).[5] Our study is the first to apply polychoric PCA in empirical research on multidimensional poverty in Colombia.

2.2.2 Multidimensional Poverty Dynamics: Pro-Poor Growth

Evident from above is the point that poverty is a multidimensional phenomenon that should be measured by one or several multidimensional indices. Furthermore, the within- and between-country distribution of multidimensional welfare is an important point having gained more attention in the last years. The HDI by income quintile of Grimm et al. (2008) is a one-time, static snapshot on this point. The next point is to look beyond statics and turn to dynamics, thus at multidimensional poverty and inequality over time.

Since the early 2000s, the concept of pro-poor growth has gained attention in research and policy. The term pro-poor growth refers broadly to economic growth that benefits the

[4]Other authors using this procedure are for example Ram (1982), Sahn and Stifel (2000, 2003), and Klasen (2000).

[5]An alternative to overcome the problem of using PCA for discrete data is multiple correspondence analysis (MCA), see for example the application of Booysen et al. (2008).

poor, and has been measured empirically mainly through household income or consumption expenditures changes, i.e., in the traditional income-based dimension of poverty. Studies on pro-poor growth can be classified according to their approach (weak or strong), and according to specific features of the measurement methodologies (complete/full or partial). For the weak (also called general) approach, any growth path leading to poverty reduction is considered pro-poor, so any positive income growth is defined as being pro-poor. In contrast, the strong (also called strict) approach considers growth to be pro-poor only when both poverty and inequality decrease.

The strong approach to pro-poor growth can be further subdivided into relative or strong absolute. The relative approach focuses on proportional changes in income between poor and non-poor and considers growth to be pro-poor when relative inequality decreases. This is only possible if incomes of the poor rise by a higher proportion than incomes of the non-poor. For the strong absolute approach, growth is pro-poor if absolute income gains of the poor are higher than those of the non-poor, meaning that absolute inequality (defined as the absolute difference in income between the poor and non-poor) decreases.[6]

As shown by Grosse et al. (2008a) and Klasen (2008) for Bolivia, it is possible to extend pro-poor growth measurement to non-income variables such as education or health by specifying non-income growth incidence curves (NIGIC). The income-based growth incidence curve (GIC) graphs the rate of growth of real income (or real expenditure) (shown at the y axis) for each percentile of the distribution (shown the x axis with increasing order by income) between two periods of time.

A curve below 0 at all points of the distribution indicates that all households suffered income losses. The contrary indicates income gains for all percentiles and consequently a poverty decrease compared with the initial period. An upward-sloping curve indicates that rich households (the richer income percentiles) benefited more than others, while a downward-sloping curve indicates that the poor benefited more, giving evidence of pro-poor growth in a relative sense (i.e., that relative inequality has fallen). Following Ravallion and Chen (2004), the GIC is formally derived from the following equations:

$$y_t(p) = F_t^{-1}(p) = L_t^{'}(p)\mu_t \quad \text{with} \quad y_t^{'}(p) > 0 \tag{2.2}$$

$$GIC : g_t(p) = \frac{y_t(p)}{y_{t-1}(p)} - 1 \tag{2.3}$$

[6]An example given by Ravallion and Chen (2004) illustrates the difference between changes in relative and absolute inequality. Consider only two households: a poor one with an income of USD 1,000 and a non-poor one with an income of USD 10,000 in the first period. After an income increase of 100 percent for both households in the second period, the poor household earns USD 2,000 while the non-poor one earns USD 20,000. In this case, the distance from each household to the mean remains unchanged and thus relative inequality does not change. According to the strict approach, growth would have been neither pro-poor nor anti-poor. But since the absolute difference between the two households increases from USD 9,000 to USD 18,000, absolute inequality rises sharply and growth can be considered anti-poor in the strong absolute sense.

$$g_t(p) = \frac{L_t'(p)}{L_{t-1}'(p)}(\gamma_t + 1) - 1, \tag{2.4}$$

where p is the corresponding percentile, F_t^{-1} is the inverse of the cumulative distribution function at the pth percentile (which gives the income of that percentile), $L_t(p)$ is the Lorenz curve (with slope $L_t'(p)$) and $\gamma_t = \frac{\mu_t}{\mu_{t-1}} - 1$ is the growth rate in the mean (GRIM) of income (or expenditure) per capita.

The GIC can be defined as the growth rate in income of the pth percentile as shown in Equation (2.3) or as shown in Equation (2.4) after replacing (2.2) into (2.3). If all percentiles exhibit the same growth rate, then the Lorenz curve does not change, inequality remains unchanged, and $g_t(p) = \gamma_t$ in Equation (2.4) for all p. Should the ratio between the growth rate of the pth percentile to the GRIM increase over time (i.e., $\frac{y_t(p)}{\mu_t} > \frac{y_{t-1}(p)}{\mu_{t-1}}$), then the growth rate of the pth percentile is higher than the GRIM, $g_t(p) > \gamma_t$. Following this, inequality falls if $g_t(p)$ is a decreasing function for all p (Ravallion and Chen, 2004).

The graphical analysis of the GIC would not demand using a poverty line to determine whether growth was beneficial to the poor. However this is only possible when the slope of the curve has a clear trend.[7] In practice, the GIC often has different slopes at different points and switches sign along percentiles, making it impossible to draw clear conclusions. To overcome this problem Ravallion and Chen (2004) suggest calculating the rate of pro-poor growth (PPGR) as the area below the GIC up to the selected poverty line of the initial period. This area equals total income growth of the poor. The PPGR is equivalent to the ordinary rate of growth times a distributional correction given by the ratio of the actual change in poverty over time (using the Watts index) to the poverty change that would have been observed if growth had not affected the income distribution. If the PPGR is higher than the GRIM, growth is pro-poor, while the opposite result indicates that distributional changes negatively affected the poor. Formally this is defined as follows:

$$PPGR = g_t^P = -\frac{dW_t}{dt} = \frac{1}{H_t}\int_0^{H_t} g_t(p)dp, \tag{2.5}$$

where

$$W_t = \int_0^{H_t} \log[\frac{z}{y_t(p)}]dp \tag{2.6}$$

is the Watts poverty measure, z is the poverty line, and H_t is the headcount ratio H at time t.

The extension of applying GIC to non-income indicators is particularly interesting to depict changes in variables expressing non-income welfare (or functionings of households) by income percentiles, i.e conditional on income, and thus investigating how the progress was distributed over the income distribution (Grosse et al., 2008a). It is particularly useful

[7]First-order dominance of the distribution at date t over $t-1$ exists when the GIC is above 0 for all percentiles, a conclusion that cannot be drawn if the GIC switches sign.

to analyze absolute changes in non-monetary indicators, which is additionally informative to using only growth rates. In the framework of pro-poor growth analysis, such changes are defined through the following set of equations:

$$GIC_{absolute}: c_t(p) = y_t(p) - y_{t-1}(p). \tag{2.7}$$

$$PPCH = c_t^p = \frac{1}{H_t}\sum_{1}^{H_t} c_t(p) \tag{2.8}$$

$$CHIM = \delta_t = \mu_t - \mu_{t-1}. \tag{2.9}$$

Equation (2.7) expresses absolute changes of the selected indicator for each percentile (in this case as example income y), Equation (2.8) defines the pro-poor change (PPCH) as the average absolute change of the poor, and Equation (2.9) is the change in mean (CHIM). If the PPCH exceeds the CHIM, growth is pro-poor in the strong absolute sense. Thus it is possible to measure pro-poor growth using the three definitions of weak absolute, weak relative, and strong absolute introduced above. It is also useful to present results conditional to income (sorted by income percentiles) and unconditional, which means quantiles are created based on the non-income variable itself (e.g., from the education-poor to the education-rich).

As mentioned already, we concentrate on selected variables reflecting dwelling characteristics and asset ownership, education, health, and subjective welfare. For constructing an asset index we follow the methodology proposed by Kolenikov and Angeles (2009). We do not intend to assess the magnitude of poverty in the selected non-income dimensions, i.e., we do not define poverty lines for each dimension. Our goal is rather to compare the distribution along percentiles in our proposed non-income indicators with the same distribution according to the income dimension and particularly of people classified as income poor. Interpretations are done, thus, using the moderate and extreme income poverty lines as will be explained in detail in Section 2.3.2.

2.3 Application to Colombia

2.3.1 Macroeconomic Issues and their Expected Relation to Multidimensional Poverty

At the beginning of the 1990s, Colombia undertook several political and economic reforms by which the economic model moved from an import substituting to an open and liberalized one. Several changes in the labor, financial, and exchange rate markets were undertaken, together with drastic reductions in average tariffs and the removal of barriers to foreign direct investment and capital exports (Cardozo-Silva, 2008).

The role of the state in providing education and health was also modified. The constitution of 1991 accelerated the fiscal decentralization process. The new model increased the responsibility of departments and municipalities in the administration of resources and placed them as primary providers of basic services to the population, particularly in education and health (Sánchez, 2006; Bès et al., 1998). Reforms were expected to increase public spending efficiency through participation of local governments that are much more aware of population needs.

Decentralization had positive effects on access to basic services, although not in the expected magnitude. Changes in the education system contributed to progressive increases of gross enrollment rates, particularly concerning secondary education, but the quality of public education continued to be very low and even weakened, showing dramatic differences compared to private schools.[8]

In the health sector coverage increased, especially after further reforms undertaken in 1993,[9] moving from 20 percent of the total population in 1993 to 32 in 1995 and 75 in 2004 (Sánchez, 2006). However, the goal of achieving universal health coverage by 2000 as well as equal access for all individuals was not reached, and quality of services remained largely dependent on the purchasing power of the households.[10]

At the end of the 1990s, the economic and political environment became particularly difficult due to the combination of the second largest recession experienced during the 20th century and the dramatic escalation of the armed conflict. Large unemployment rates due to the crisis as well internally forced displacement due to violence increased poverty to levels last observed in 1985. The economic downturn that started in 1996 and lasted until 2001 achieved a peak in 1999 with a contraction of -5.52 percent in per capita GDP. All poverty indicators increased up to 1999 (headcount of 57 percent), slowed down from 2000 to 2001, rose again in 2002, and improved since then. By 2005, national poverty and inequality indicators as well as real income had returned to the levels of the early to mid-1990s, but unemployment remained higher than in 1996, at around 12 percent (Cardozo-Silva, 2008).

The temporary effects of the recession on households were certainly channelled through unemployment, and thus reduction of income. It is not clear in how far that affected non-

[8] Access to pre-school education increased from 51 percent in 1995 to 88 percent in 2006; and gross enrollment rates in middle and secondary education also rose, although there is still an important lag in achievements of secondary schooling, especially in rural areas, where even though gross enrollment rates almost doubled since 1995 they were only 55 percent in 2006 (Sánchez, 2006). Widespread primary education explains high literacy rates (of 98 percent) among the youth.

[9] Law 100 of 1993.

[10] Recent studies show that only 48.1 percent of population in the 1st quintile of the income distribution are covered by the health system, compared to 83.7 percent of the 5th quintile (Jazmín et al., 2004) and that public spending in health benefits the richest 4th and 5th quintiles (González, 2001).

income dimensions, particularly those in which the government was increasing public spending. The final outcome on other dimensions of poverty might have depended on the counteracting effect of reforms at that time. One could expect households in the upper quintiles of the income distribution to have overcome the crisis easily, restructuring expenditures towards maintaining education and health status but reducing luxurious expenditures. The effect on middle income groups is much harder to be predicted: the most vulnerable might have become at least temporarily poor, others might have turned to using more public services, particularly in education, as suggested by Barrera and Domínguez (2006). Finally, income related deprivation of the poorest quintiles might have accelerated drop out of students, reduced asset ownership, and slowed down the pace of improvement in access to public services (Sarmiento et al., 2005a).

Periodic analysis of multidimensional poverty in Colombia is done using the Human Development Index (HDI), the Unmet Basic Needs Index (NBI) and the Life Conditions Index (ICV) as proxies. The NBI includes five basic needs: inadequate dwelling, dwellings without basic services, households being overcrowded, no attendance to school, and high economic dependence. It classifies a household as poor if it lacks one of these basic needs, and extremely poor if it lacks two or more. Using Census data, the NBI can be calculated at the municipal level (the smallest administrative unit) and is used to determine distribution of transfers from the central government (for example to infant primary health care and education (DNP, 2008)), to target social programs, and also to create poverty maps, thus to assess the geographical distribution of poverty. This indicator has several well known shortcomings. The selection of the included basic needs is subjective as well as the fact that they have the same weight. Thus, two households are equally poor if one lacks good dwelling characteristics and if schooling-age members of the other do not attend school. Moreover, it does not allow to make assessments on the depth of poverty nor judgements on the amount of poor persons as it is calculated by household, making the classification dependent on the demographic characteristics of it. Finally, components of the NBI are strongly oriented towards infrastructure conditions, some of which are not relevant to measure poverty in urban areas due to nearly full coverage of service infrastructure there (DNP (2006); Feres and Mancero (2001)).

The ICV ranks from 0 to 100, with the latter representing the highest possible welfare. It captures in a single measure variables corresponding to quality of housing, access to public services, education, and the size and composition of the household. The corresponding weights are calculated using PCA. This index has become an important tool for targeting of social programs, but is criticized for leaving completely aside the income dimension, and being built based purely on statistical procedures.

Recent research on multidimensional poverty has been done by Vélez and Robles (2008), who apply axiomatically derived poverty indices to three socio-economic dimensions: consumption, education, and security, in order to explain improvements of welfare perceptions by Colombians between 1997 and 2003. The authors apply seven types of three-dimensional poverty indicators[11] to the mentioned dimensions and test four types of normative weights among them using data from the Colombian Living Standard Measurement Survey (LSMS) in 1997 and 2003.[12] Consumption is calculated in two ways: excluding and including subsidies, education corresponds to years of education of the household head, security to a dichotomous variable on how the person feels in the neighborhood, and welfare to the person's perception of the household's current economic conditions. The authors conclude that the negative effects on welfare induced by the lower per capita consumption due to the economic recession of the late 1990s were more than compensated by the increasing progressiveness of subsidies due to social programs and the improvement in the educational endowments of household heads. However, conclusions are very sensitive to the chosen normative weights among dimensions, and the relation with improvement in self-reported welfare cannot be directly derived from the resulting reduction in the multidimensional poverty indices.[13]

2.3.2 Non-Income Indicators

Our approach consists of creating indices reflecting four key areas of welfare: basic assets and infrastructure endowment of the household (including access to public services), education, split up into education of children in schooling age and education of adults, and health. The fourth index is on welfare self-perception in order to discuss if welfare reported by households increased or decreased with economic conditions that deteriorated dramatically between 1997 and 2003. The indices on assets, health, and subjective welfare were created using two weighting alternatives: polychoric PCA and normative own weighting.

Constructing non-income indicators has two challenges: selection of adequate variables, constrained usually by data availability, and selection of the weighting procedure. In this study we focused on four non-income dimensions. The first one comprises durables owner-

[11]Intersection, Union, Chakravarty 1 and Chakravarty 2, Bourguignon-Chakravarty-Substitutes, Bourguignon-Chakravarty-Complements, and Bourguignon-Chakravarty-Leontief.

[12]First, equal weighting; second, 50 percent for consumption and 25 percent for education and security each; third, 50 percent for education and 25 percent for consumption and security each; and fourth, 25 percent for consumption and education each and 50 percent for security.

[13]Hernández Flórez (2007) presented at the 50 years CEDE conference on 2008 results of her Master Thesis. The author tested if progress in non-monetary dimensions substitute or complement for progress in monetary dimensions applying a two-dimensional axiomatically derived poverty index. After making pairwise comparisons between income and safety or income and education variables, she concluded that multidimensional poverty increased when considering safeness as non-income dimension, regardless of income, and that when considering education, results are mixed: poverty increased in urban areas and decreased in rural.

ship, dwelling characteristics, and access to services, combined together into what we call an asset index. This dimension is intended to reflect accumulated long-term welfare beyond fluctuations in income. Note that it is calculated at the household level, as it reflects items and services shared by all its members. Using an asset index is widely done in the literature and can be used to complement the income dimension, overcoming problems of seasonality and high variability in income, particularly of households engaged in informal markets. It is also useful to overcome income measurement error (Moser and Felton, 2009).

To construct the asset index, we selected a subset of eight basic household items, five dwelling characteristics, number of rooms per person, and access to public services (Table 2.1). Each household item and dwelling characteristic corresponds to a binary variable, in which having it is associated with higher welfare.[14] To capture overcrowding in an ordinal variable, we calculated the number of rooms per person and created five groups (at reasonable cutoffs) on it. The services variable includes access to electricity, piped gas (which is a relatively newly available service in Colombia), water, sewage, litter collection, and telephone (fixed line network). We included these services separately into the overall asset index.[15]

Normative weights were assigned according to two criteria: the importance of each item inside the corresponding sub-category composing an index (for example each durable) what we call scores, and the value inside the index, what we call weights. Due to lack of information on the amount of each of the eight selected durables a household has, as well as the value, we gave this subset of variables the lowest weight for constructing the asset index. These minimal basic items facilitate household functioning, thus the importance relies on having them, while lack of them is a clear indicator of deprivation. Floor material, wall material, and type of toilet were assigned the highest weights for constructing the asset index, followed by material used for cooking, rooms per person, and services. The same logic applies for the health and subjective welfare indices; for education, see below.

Polychoric PCA weights were calculated using the STATA routine proposed by Kolenikov and Angeles (2009). The baseline results shown here are generated using a pooled sample. For sensitivity, and due to different sample designs, sample sizes, and weighting of the 1997 and 2003 surveys we also calculated them separately for each year. Resulting weights in both years are very similar to the ones shown in Table 2.1.

With the second non-income dimension using the LSMS data we try to capture health. To construct a health index we selected six variables: reported health status of the person,

[14]We aggregated categories with very low frequencies into a single one for cooking material, wall material, floor material, and type of toilet.

[15]We did not include property of a house in the asset index, due to its large variation in value and therefore in interpretation, as well as because that information is available only for urban areas in the two survey rounds.

having or not a chronic health disease, having or not a sickness in the last month, being affiliated to a medical service, going to a health check up once per year, and having or not been to hospital last year. Although the first of these variables is subjective in nature, it is the only one available giving an overall judgement of each person's health and thus is a good proxy for health status. These variables for health are not strongly correlated to each other (the opposite could have been expected, i.e., all variables measuring the same thing), so all of them were not taken into account for the final analysis.

Third, we create a life satisfaction index, which takes into account various spheres of subjective perception: current living conditions compared to 5 years before, perception of whether income is enough for household needs, having had problems with death or serious illness of a family member in the last year, and safety perception in the neighborhood. This combination captures four important aspects: changes in the general welfare perception, subjective judgement of income, major events affecting the whole household, and a proxy for the effects of violence and criminality. For the indicators mentioned above we apply the two weighting alternatives: normatively determined weights and statistically determined weights.

The fourth and last non-income indicator we selected is education. We created separately one index for individuals not older than 20 years and one for adults older than that. The main objective of the former is to track progress of the population in schooling age taking two aspects into account: years of schooling and being in the right degree for the corresponding age. We assume that children are expected to start primary education at the age of 6, which would drive them to have completed at least 1 year of primary education by the age of 7. If the education process is continuous, at the age of 17 students must be finishing secondary education (11th degree).[16] By subtracting the age of each individual younger than 20 years from the reported years of schooling (*YOS*) we should ideally get a difference of 6, indicating the student started schooling at 6 and never repeated any degree nor stopped studying. We allow individuals up to 20 years to fall into these indicators, to capture young adults still enrolled in school. The indicator can be defined as follows:

$$E_{children} = Age - YOS. \tag{2.10}$$

Students enrolled in degrees lower than the right one for their age are considered over-aged, and would get a value higher than 6. The maximum and minimum possible values for this indicator are 4 and 20, the first one accounting for a child having started school early or

[16]According to Law 115 of 1994, all Colombians should receive a minimum of 1 year of preschool education and 9 years basic education divided into 5 of primary schooling and 4 of basic secondary schooling. Schooling grades 10 to 11 are considered as middle education degrees ending up into complete secondary schooling. Upper and lower age bounds for each degree can be defined by each school, but most of them expect children to finish mandatory preschool degree at age 5, primary at 10, basic secondary at 14 and middle education at 17.

having skipped one year and the last one accounting for an illiterate young adult.[17] Note that the same result, for instance of 15, can have different meanings for different individuals. It can be a 20 years old person with 5 years of education, or a 15 years old without education. Both are however overaged in the sense that they do not have the education expected for their age. Improvements in education through this indicator should be reflected in less students being overaged.

For adults older than 20 years, we calculate the average years of education by adult household members as follows:

$$E_{adults} = \frac{\sum YOS_{adults}}{\sum N_{adults}}. \tag{2.11}$$

The detailed overview of all variables used and their weights according to each procedure is shown in Table 2.1.[18] The normatively assigned weights in Table 2.1 correspond to weights for each index independently of the others, not to weights for an overall index which would not be interpretable given that some indices are presented at the household level and others at the individual. Inside each index, we take two steps: scores and weights. The scores are higher the higher the welfare provided by each item or possible sub-category corresponding to the same question. The weights were selected according to the relative importance we wanted that question to have in the index. The final weight is the results of multiplying both. To make this procedure clearer, look at Table 2.1 again. The asset index, for example, consists of household durables, dwelling quality (material used for cooking, wall, and floor; quality of toilet and shower; crowding), and access to public infrastructure and services. Scores show that we consider a fridge more important than a video, i.e., within the durables sub-index. Weights show how important we consider having durables compared to having high quality toilet facilities, i.e., we consider it more important to have a good toilet rather than many durables.

To transform indices into the same scale and ease comparability we normalize them from 0, the worst possible achievement, to 10, the best, following the methodology of the Human Development Index (HDI) and Grosse et al. (2008b).[19] Once normalized, results are averaged by quantile to draw the corresponding NIGIC. We draw for each indicator two types of curves: sorted by income, what we will call hereafter conditional, (e.g., education outcomes for the

[17] One might question if 4 is really better than 6 or if 4 is rather as good as 6. We suggest that 4 is better than 6 since it reflects that the child has higher abilities than others to be able to complete the educational system more quickly and to enter the labor market earlier.

[18] Education is not shown in the table because the two indicators are based on one single variable, which basically is years of schooling.

[19] $Index = 10 * \frac{1}{n}\sum_{i=1}^{n} \frac{individual_n - min}{max - min}$. Another possible standardization is dividing by the standard deviation. However, the proposed range between 0 and 10 is simple to explain and understand, and it allows the reader to intuitively and quickly see the distributional difference between each indicator.

income-poorest to the income-richest) and in their original form, or unconditional (e.g., from the education-poorest to the education-richest). Both conditional and unconditional will be presented in relative and absolute terms. Relative curves show growth rates in percentages and absolute curves show absolute differences between the two years for each indicator.

2.3.3 Data

For the current study we used the Living Standard Measurement Survey (LSMS) (Encuesta de Calidad de Vida, ECV) of 1997 and 2003, due to the richness of its questionnaire in non-income aspects compared to the yearly Household Survey (Encuesta de Hogares, EH) which focuses strongly on the labor market. Moreover, the ECV includes income and expenditures, for which we draw as well relative and absolute GIC.

Expenditures and income are presented in per capita monthly terms and reported in local currency units constant of 1997. Colombian peso is the local currency, corresponding to an average of 2000 pesos per USD in 1997. We used as deflator the consumer price index for low income groups, available separately for each of the 13 metropolitan areas, rest of urban areas, and rural areas. This same deflator is used to update the poverty lines, which exist for the same subdivisions (Official poverty lines version 2005).[20]

The total amount of observations included in 1997 is 37,735 individuals and in 2003 is 83,757. The sample of 2003 is larger because it is also representative for sub-urban areas of Bogotá and sub-regions of the department of Valle. The ECV is representative at the national, urban, rural, and regional level (five regions) in both years. Monthly household per capita expenditures include all expenditures on food, clothes, leisure, household durables, health, education, services, and finance costs but could neither be corrected for agricultural home production nor household property because this information is only partially available in the 2003 round.

A check for outliers in income and expenditures was done constructing box plots by subgroups, as well as scatter plots of income versus expenditures to track implausible values. Extreme cases where the difference between income and expenditures is large, checked using scatter plots, were double checked for consistency and possible mistakes in the original information. Outliers were finally identified as values greater or less than three standard deviations from the median of log income or log expenditures and were not used for the analysis.[21] Zeros and missing values were not taken into account to calculate the medians. This

[20]For methodological details on the poverty lines, see DNP (2006) and for details on effects of price deflators on pro-poor growth measurement see Günther and Grimm (2007).

[21]These outliers coincide with those showing large difference between income and expenditures, so no additional cases had to be excluded.

procedure skipped out of a total of 854 households in 1997 and 1476 in 2003, corresponding to 2 percent and 1.7 percent of each sample.

2.4 Results

2.4.1 Inequality and Distribution by Deciles

Table 2.1 shows a first snapshot of non-income welfare and the trends from 1997 to 2003. For all indicators (except education) we present the sample means of the variables included. Of the durables included in the assets index, TV and washing machine ownership go up, the other six go down. Stronger changes can be observed for some elements of the dwelling quality, with a strong increase of piped gas as cooking material at the expense of electricity. Minor improvements are found in wall material, toilet facility, and crowding. Hardly any change show wall material and shower facility. Public services and access to infrastructure increase for all six services.

For the variables forming the health index (which is the only one that can be evaluated at the individual level), we find an overall but minor general improvement. Concerning health status, there is an increase in those reporting having good health, and less reporting very good, regular, or bad health status. However people reporting having a chronic disease slightly increase. On the contrary temporary diseases go down, while affiliation to a medical service system improves.

The amount of households reporting that life was better than 5 years before decreased slightly. But in general, changes in the answers to this variable are minor. The share of households that consider their household income as being enough or more than enough for fulfilling their need goes down. Severe health problems or even death of a family member which affect the household as a whole go down. The strongest deterioration occurred for the safety perception which goes down more strongly.

We aggregate the variables shown in Table 2.1 to composite welfare indices and show the distribution of the aggregated indices in Table 2.2. Here we calculate for each indicator the sample deciles and means, first sorted by income (conditional) and second sorted by the indicator itself (unconditional). For each indicator, the table shows also inequality measures: the ratio of the richest to poorest decile (10:1 ratio), the Gini coefficient, and the Theil Index. Three main issues emerge in these tables: (i) indicator means calculated using normative weights and polychoric PCA are very close, (ii) there are minor improvements in almost all deciles with means staying nearly equal between 1997 and 2003, and (iii) inequality in non-income indicators is low compared to income and expenditures (Table 2.3), the latter all being higher than 0.5 for the Gini coefficient. Among non-income indicators, inequality measured by the Gini is highest for adult education (0.35 in 1997 compared to 0.34 in 2003) and assets (around 0.22 to 0.24). Inequality is lowest for children's education but increases over time (10:1 ratio, Gini coefficient and Theil index). For all other variables, the indicators show the same trends: slightly decreasing inequality.

Conditional to income, results are similar between polychoric PCA and normative weights. Unconditional results are not that similar, particularly regarding changes in the 10:1 relation for health and subjective welfare. The relation doubles when using normative weights. In general, results using both methods confirm that the 10:1 relation is much lower when percentiles are lined up by income, indicating that not necessarily the income poorest (richest) correspond to the non-income poorest (richest). As expected, we find an income gradient. This means that non-income deciles increase the higher the income decile. Such differences suggest that there are reasons beyond income facilitating or impeding access to certain assets and services. This might be of course related to geographic location, public policies, and the existence of markets for non-income indicators. Similar results are also found in Grosse et al. (2008a) and Klasen (2008) for Bolivia.

The different outcome between indicators sorted or not by income is evident in adults' education: approximately 3 versus 20 in both years (Table 2.2) for the 10:1 ratio.[22] While low inequality in children's education outcomes reflects the nearly full coverage of primary schooling, irrespective of the income decile, high inequality in adult education can be explained by the limited access to public tertiary education, thus depending on households' ability to pay for it in the private sector. It can also reflect persisting low education levels (or even illiteracy) of older cohorts, which do not catch up once they enter the labor force.

The second most unequally distributed indicator, assets, also seems to have an important relation to income, partly explained by the households' ability to pay for public services. Breaking down this indicator to track access to services, one finds low coverage rates for the first income deciles but almost full coverage for the last.

Comparison of decile means among indicators shows that children's education is (for almost all deciles) the closest one to the upper bound followed by subjective welfare, while the asset index is the most distant from the upper bound. Disparities increase the lower the income decile, indicating that poor people have access to education, at least for children, but cannot afford basic assets, good dwelling characteristics, or access to public services.

Lower inequality in non-income indicators compared to income or expenditures must be interpreted cautiously, given that those indicators have a natural upper bound while income does not. As already mentioned, inequality measures of income and expenditures are

[22]Note that the Gini and Theil inequality indicators are calculated only unconditionally, but not conditionally.

pretty high. The Gini coefficient is above 0.5 in both cases, although it decreases over time (Table 2.3). The 10:1 ratio also decreased over time. As explained by Klasen (2008), inequality in non-income indicators turns out lower, given that most likely rich households already achieved the upper limit while poor households are getting closer to it. Particularly health and children's education have an upper limit, which is 11 years for education. To summarize, there were low improvements in deciles below the income poverty line and a lack of correspondence between decile outcomes sorted or not by income. Inequality prevailed in dimensions less influenced by public policies, that are at the same time those highly correlated with income.

2.4.2 Pro-Poor Growth Analysis

Income versus Expenditures

We present in this section growth incidence curves by vintiles and show for higher accuracy the upper and lower 90 percent confidence intervals calculated using bootstrap techniques. Analysis based on growth incidence curves and pro-poor growth rates show that mean income and expenditures by vintiles decreased from 1997 to 2003. Poverty increased (Table 2.4) and means fell for the overall income distribution. However, contraction was higher for the richest in relative as well as in absolute terms (growth rates and absolute changes).

Table 2.5 shows pro-poor growth rates (PPGR) and pro-poor changes (PPCH). We present first relative results (growth rates) and then absolute (changes), both divided further into unconditional and conditional to income. The table shows that growth rates in mean (GRIM) for income and expenditures were negative, but contraction was stronger in income (-3.65 versus -2.45). We present PPGR using two different poverty lines: moderate (PPGR mod.) and extreme (PPGR extr.). Both PPGR were higher than the GRIM but still negative, confirming the contraction of income and expenditures for households below the poverty line. Results indicate that, on average, households below the extreme poverty line were affected to a lesser extent from contraction in income and expenditures than those up to the moderate poverty line. In absolute terms, the change in mean income (CHIM) was -38,118 Colombian pesos (monthly per capita real of 1997). If considering only households up to the moderate poverty line, the PPCH was -6,939. Once again, absolute losses for households up to the extreme poverty line are lower, but proportional to their initial income of a higher magnitude.

As a result, when analyzing income and expenditures, growth was not pro-poor according to the weak (general) nor to the absolute approach. However, losses were lower for the poor relative to the non-poor. The richest vintiles of the distribution experienced the hardest contraction, while households below the extreme poverty line seemed to be less affected by the 1999 economic recession in absolute and relative terms.

The graphical analysis confirms these results. Figure 2.1 shows the GIC based on income and on expenditures. On the left hand scale we present the relative GIC and on the right absolute changes. Growth rates are below 0 for almost all income vintiles and the GIC is downward sloping, indicating higher rates of income falls the richest the household. Although relative losses of the poor were less than those of the non-poor, negative growth rates for almost all percentiles point to an increase in poverty. As can be seen in Table 2.4 the incidence of poverty (FGT0) increased from 55 to 60 percent between 1997 and 2003. The absolute GIC is also decreasing by vintile and below the 0 axis, showing large absolute losses for the richest. Relative and absolute GIC for expenditures are also downward sloping and below 0 for all vintiles. It is not surprising to observe larger absolute decreases in expenditures the higher the vintiles, given that poor households have less scope for reducing expenditures.

Income losses were more severe for urban than for rural households (Figure 2.2). The GRIM was around -2.0 for rural, while the urban GRIM was around -4.0. Also in absolute terms, losses were much higher in urban areas, which can also be explained by higher mean incomes in the former. The urban GIC is clearly downward sloping, thus showing higher losses for the richer, while the rural GIC is u-shaped with higher losses for the middle part of the distribution.[23]

Assets, Health, and Subjective Welfare

Figures 2.3 and 2.4 show relative GIC for assets, health, and subjective welfare. The left figure corresponds to indicators using normative weights, while the right figure to those using polychoric PCA weights. Concerning growth rates and sorted by income (Figure 2.3) the evolution of asset ownership is pro-poor according to the weak approach (GIC above 0). According to the relative approach, growth can also be declared to be pro-poor since growth rates are higher for income-poorer households, even though there is no clear downward sloping trend for the first half of the distribution, but growth is clearly higher than for the second half. For health, although the shape of the curves is similar regardless of the weighting system, the GIC is above 0 when using normative weights and below when using PPCA weights. The subjective welfare GIC is nearly always below 0 and the trend downward sloping when using normative weights, but above 0 for approximately the first half of the distribution and

[23] As an exercise we compared results for the same years using the EH. Overall, growth rates are also negative at the national level, but to a lesser degree in EH results. While the national GIC shows basically the same picture, just shifted upward, the GIC for urban areas is clearly different with strongly negative growth rates for the poorest. Even stronger are differences in rural areas. The growth rates are positive for the whole rural population and there is also a clear downward sloping trend compared to the flat part in the middle of the distribution of the rural ECV data. These differences can be explained by sampling issues, questionnaire design, as well as by adjustments to national accounts undertaken in the income variables of EH.

then changes sign to negative for richer households in the case of PPCA weights, also having a downward sloping trend.

In Figure 2.4 we present results sorted only by the non-income indicator. In the case of assets, GIC are downward sloping regardless of the weighting system, although with some differences for the first few vintiles. However according to both systems growth is pro-poor according to the weak and relative approaches. As observed when sorting by income, the unsorted GIC of health show opposite results. One is above 0 (normative weights) and the other close to 0 or below it (PPCA weights). Concerning subjective welfare, there are positive but volatile growth rates for the first 7 (normative weights) or 10 (PPCA weights) vintiles.

A more rigorous analysis is possible using pro-poor growth rates, presented in Table 2.5. For comparison purposes we use the percentiles derived from the moderate and extreme head-count index based on income poverty lines to calculate PPGR: 54 percent (corresponding to vintile 11) for moderate and 18 for extreme (corresponding to vintile 4) poverty. The GRIM are overall rather low, in the range of -0.21 (health using normative weights) and 0.42 (assets using PPCA weights).

For assets, PPGR for percentiles below the moderate and extreme poverty lines are higher than the GRIM for both weighting systems and also for conditional and unconditional, indicating that the poor exhibited larger increases in assets. For health we obtain two different results depending on the weighting scheme: using normative weights we find pro-poor growth, using PPCA weights we find anti-poor growth, the latter less clearly so for the conditional case.

The GRIM for the subjective welfare indicator is slightly below 0 using normative weights and at 0.20 using polychoric PCA weights. For both weighting schemes, the poorest have positive growth rates, thus PPGR above GRIM in the unconditional case, whereas the income-poorest percentiles have negative growth rates using normative weights. For PPCA weights, the result for conditional pro-poor growth depends on the poverty line: anti-poor for the moderate poverty line and pro-poor for the extreme poverty line.

To summarize, asset ownership improved independent of weighting and sorting. Subjective welfare seems to have clearly improved for the unconditional case and less clearly for the conditional case. For health, results more strongly depend on the weighting system. Overall, growth rates correspond to rather low absolute changes. They are highest for assets, showing an inverted-U-shape, and close to 0 for the other indicators (Figures 2.5 and 2.6).

Education

As a lagged result of the economic crisis in the late 1990s, gross enrollment rates declined by 2001. The largest fall was in pre-school enrollment rates, followed by secondary education.

There is also evidence of decreases in net enrollment of the poorest quintiles in secondary education, as well as higher demand from middle income households for public education (Barrera and Domínguez, 2006).

Figures 2.7 and 2.8 show the GIC for children's education. Observing results lined up by income, children being overaged is clearly the more relevant the poorer the household. However, between 1997 and 2003 one observes minor but positive growth rates for the income-poorest percentiles, in contrast to the falls observed in the unconditional case. As a consequence, inequality between the first and last income deciles of the distribution decreased. The PPGR confirms these results (Table 2.5). The GRIM and the CHIM are both positive but very close to 0 (0.07 and 0.03) with the conditional PPGR and PPCH slightly above them. The unconditional relative and unconditional absolute GIC show large decreases for the education-poorest children (up to the extreme income-poverty headcount). This is reflected in a PPGR of -3.15 when using the extreme poverty line and confirms higher overage rates for households sorted in the lowest percentiles in 2003. All other percentiles show no major variation but growth rates slightly above 0.

The puzzling result of the educational poorest regardless of income raises the question about their socioeconomic characteristics. The generational effect of improvement in access to education in recent years can be seen in higher average years of schooling for younger generations, where those adults between 18 and 45 years show the largest average years of education compared to the elderly. However, educational outcomes are still much better for those ranking higher in the income distribution. While the poorest 10 percent of households have on average just 3 years of education (including children and adult education) the richest achieve up to 11. Although this average increased slightly from 1997 to 2003, differences between poor and rich remained the same.[24]

Figures 2.7 and 2.8 also show relative and absolute GIC on adults' average years of education. The relative GIC conditional to income is above 0 and downward sloping up to the 16th vintile, thus covering people below the poverty line. The PPGR is way higher than the GRIM indicating that the poorest percentiles in 2003 had higher average adult education in 2003. In absolute terms, changes in average years of education were positive up to the same vintile, but rather small and equally distributed, relativizing results obtained using growth rates. Sorted only by average years of education, the resulting PPGR is negative (-0.85 and -1.91) and less than the GRIM (-0.28), due to the sharp fall in the first few vintiles. However,

[24]Coverage of tertiary education shows a much lower participation of the poorest quintiles, with only 6 percent of the 18-25 years old students enrolled in 2003 belonging to the 1st quintile of income. New entrance to tertiary education was also affected by the crisis, when the number of new entrants from 1997 to 1999 declined by 19 percent (World Bank, 2003).

in absolute terms, this sharp decline is not reflected because it is rather driven by the first mathematically-defined growth rate which is very low. This result points to a fall in the average years of adult education for the poorest few vintiles of the distribution in 2003 compared to 1997 (Table 2.5).

Summarizing, average years of adult education went slightly down in the period of analysis, although these changes were proportionally larger for the income poor. However it is not clear in how far this result is affected by better-educated adults who became poor in 2003. Interesting to note is that growth rates for the education-poorest correspond to very small changes in absolute terms, thus their real welfare gain in terms of human capital accumulation is questionable. Further tests to explain why education seems to be anti-poor, especially for children's education in the case in the unconditional case, reveal that there might be some sampling problem. For the departments of Bogotá and Valle, the sample size was strongly increased in 2003 compared to 1997 to gain significant insights at lower geographical levels. Even with the sample weights, results are strongly influence by these departments. However, even excluding them still results in some negative growth rates for the first few vintiles, but to a lesser extend. Adults' education growth rates also increase when excluding Bogotá and Valle.

2.4.3 Discussion and Possible Limitations

Before doing a critical discussion on pro-poor growth, it is necessary to underline some limitations. The first one is that many variables are bounded due to questionnaire design and concepts. Even if the household has, for example, a large and varied set of assets, only 18 possible are listed in the survey. Thus, middle income and rich households who already have all items do not show improvements in the data set, although they might have had in real life. Similar arguments hold for dwelling characteristics. Concerning access to public services, the variables included are all bounded: It is not possible to have more than "one" access to a service.

Once having access, differences depend on the consumption and tariff paid for it.[25] Research on particular services show that coverage of water and sanitation did not show major improvements between 1993 and 2003 (Sánchez, 2006). Natural piped gas became available to households in the major cities at the beginning of the 1990s and its access increased considerably since then (Libhaber and Foster, 2003). Table 2.1 confirms these results, for example the percentage of households having access to piped gas increased from 20 percent in 1997 to 36 percent in 2003. This explains why it adds up one of the largest weights inside the asset index but it is not a major deprivation if a household does not have it. Electricity had

[25]The single variable that is unbounded, at least in the questionnaire, is number of rooms.

already in 1997 high coverage rates, thus large improvements on it between 1997 and 2003 were not feasible.

Another important issue to keep in mind is that while facing income variations and temporary draw backs during economic crisis, dwelling characteristics and access to services might not change as rapidly as income, given that the initial response of the household is to reduce expenditures, take credits (also in form of delaying debt payments), and use savings. A simple tabulation of the question on how households responded to the loss of employment or income sources during the five years previous to the 2003 survey showed that 23 percent of them opted for reducing expenditures in clothing, 21 percent in food, and 21 percent took credits. Only 10 percent confirmed having used savings, 4 percent moved to a cheaper dwelling, while 3 percent enrolled their children in a less expensive school.

These issues contextualize the resulting GIC of our asset index. Growth rates are positive for all households and downward sloping, indicating pro-poor growth. Absolute changes though are very low and equally distributed for all income percentiles reflecting rather stagnation in the asset index. In light of privatization and decentralization reforms undertaken in the early 1990s, designed to improve coverage and efficiency in the provision of basic services, one would have had expected higher improvements in the asset index. However the combined effect of implementation problems and the economic crisis slowed the progress, particularly due to the reduction of public funds. In this context, increases in access to public services were modest, and poor households had in 2003 almost the same coverage as in 1997 except for fixed line telephone service (Figure 2.9).

Another argument to be taken into account for assets would be to think about transforming them in per capita terms, similar to the rooms per person. It makes a difference to share a TV with one other family member or with ten. In this case, larger households would be worse off. However, the questionnaire does not ask about the amount of each asset, only about owning "one" or not, but maybe (and likely) some households have more than one. However, transforming some varialbes into per-capita terms would give a kind of lower bound. Looking at the list of varialbes included in the asset index, we would identify some, but only a few, to exhibit rivalry in consumption: TV, radio, car, video, toilet, shower, phone. For the others, rivalry is not convincingly given. Rerunning the calculation leads to no big changes, neither in weights nor in pro-poor growth findings.

Results on education and health can also be related to reforms. Provision structure of health services was transformed in 1993 from a system based on subsidies to supply (direct transfers to public hospitals) to a system based on subsidies to demand.[26] Research on

[26]Law 100 of 1993.

this area shows that the reform had a large impact on increasing health affiliation, but did not achieve the desired increase in competitiveness of public health providers and ended up doubling the sectors budget due to the coexistence of subsidies to demand and subsidies to supply. One particular disadvantage is that the system in place, composed by a subsidized and a contributive regime, has encouraged informal employment and has hampered the creation of formal one, threatening the sustainability of the system (Gaviria et al., 2006).

Our summary statistics confirmed an increase in affiliations to a medical service, but this category does not have a large weight in the index. The outcome variable, subjective health status, is the one having the largest weight. In that variable we see that the average health status had no major changes, and that most Colombians report having good health in both years. The small changes do not affect poor households more or less than rich ones, and inequality in health according to this index is low. When sorting households from the health-poor to the health-rich, this result changes. The average for the 10th decile is 5 times larger than for the 1st one (Table 2.2). This suggests a lack of relation between being income-poor and health-poor, and vice versa. However interpretation should consider that the included questions reflect perceptions, and are not supported by objective health measures like infant mortality rates, prenatal care, or nutritional status which use to be inversely correlated with income. Furthermore, the way people value their own health status and that of their family members can differ considerably from a physician's valuation.

With respect to the education indices, the low growth rates found in children's education sorted by income can be linked to stagnation in enrollment rates in primary and secondary schooling during the crisis, as well as quality deterioration leading to high repetition rates. This combined effect is stronger the higher the educational level. Thus, although gross enrollment rates increased, net enrollment (which takes into account children in the right age for the level they are doing) did not. Studies focusing on education show that public schools absorbed part of the enrollment decline of high income groups in private schools, while the lower-income students dropped out. As a consequence the educational gap between poor and rich increased, particularly due to immense quality differences between private and public schools (Velez et al., 2003).

The subjective welfare index has also some limitations. Ideally the question on current living conditions should be in the index, but this question in 2003 is not comparable to the one in 1997.[27] We used only variables that had the same response alternatives in both years, in this case how the person values the current household situation compared to that 5 years before. The three available response categories (better, equal, worse) have each a share of around

[27]The number of possible answer options changed from 3 to 4.

one-third in both years, raising doubts on whether responses are driven by each person's understanding on the question and what each one consider as "better", rather than by a conscious and comparable answer across households. One would have expected more variability as the period between 1997 and 2003 was particularly turbulent due to the economic crises, the rise in unemployment, and more problems with violence. Furthermore, there seems to be no relation between this variable and having enough income for household needs. Around 50 percent of households report that income is just enough for their needs and 40 that it is not.

2.5 Conclusion

Empirical multidimensional poverty assessment poses two important challenges: selection of indicators and weighting procedures. When looking for implementation of indices one finds a large variety and combination of variables, usually focused on education, health, and asset ownership. Few studies or indices include proxies for political and social participation, burden of violence, and environmental issues, due to lack of appropriate data among others.

In this paper we ranked households according to four indices: one on asset ownership (including access to public services), one on health, another on education, and finally one on subjective welfare. Education was calculated for two population groups: individuals in schooling age and adults. We did not combine these indicators into a single one, but analyzed them as separate dimensions of welfare. In contrast to existing indices, we applied polychoric PCA instead of "traditional" PCA, since the latter is less appropriate for categorical variables and yields misleading weights (Kolenikov and Angeles, 2009). Additionally, we compared results with normative weights for robustness check.

Several interesting issues emerged. The assets adding the highest weight for the average Colombian household using polychoric PCA are: having high quality floor, having a car, and using electricity as cooking material. Among public services, piped gas has the highest weight followed by phone connection.

The variables most diminishing the household's score are: lack of access to electricity, lack of toilet, low quality wall material, and lack of shower facility. Concerning health, the best (worst) subjective health status of the person has the largest (lowest) weight inside the index. A strong negative weight is given to having a chronic disease, having been in hospital, and having had a disease recently.

Whereas we consider it as desirable to be affiliated to a medical service and to go a health checkups frequently without being ill, this is not reflected in the PPCA weights: the signs are opposite than expected. This is also most likely the reason for the opposite results in the pro-poor growth analysis. In the subjective welfare index, not having had severe health problems and having more than enough money for household needs are the ones contributing with the largest weight, while the general perception of life being worse than 5 years ago subtracts the most.

Dynamic results using GIC shows minor changes in the indices considering people's perceptions regardless of the income percentile (health and subjective welfare). It is questionable if this result is driven by lack of comparability on how people value what they get out of goods and services. In contrast to this, the asset index had positive growth rates, and larger for the poorest. However, absolute changes relativize results and showed that changes were small. As discussed in Section 2.4.3 this can be explained by stagnation in the provision of public services and strategies undertaken by households when affronting income or employment losses which prioritize reducing expenditures in items not included in this index like clothing and food. Such reduction is confirmed with the GIC for expenditures (Figures 2.1 and 2.2).

Given that household needs as well as valuation of those needs change in time, the weights obtained by any selected procedure need to be revised regularly, particularly when using indices for selecting social program beneficiaries. An example of this is the provision of piped gas which was almost non-existing in the 1980s and has now a large weight in the asset index. Another classical example is the valuation of a black and white television 20 years ago with its value today.

Our proposed indices differ considerably from the existing ICV in the literature due to the weighting system, combination of variables, and data source.[28] The ICV uses PCA and combines in a single measure asset ownership, variables accounting for human capital, and variables on household composition. The NBI index, which is currently used to distribute government transfers to social sectors, is not comparable at all, given that it considers all categories included as having the same weight. This index underestimates poverty, particularly in urban areas, due to problems with the current irrelevance of the included categories since most categories show nearly full coverage in urban Colombia.

Other plausible alternatives for selecting variables to be included in each index exist as well as weighting procedures. We offered here two opposed methodologies to calculate weights: one based on statistical procedures and the other based only on the researchers' criteria. Depending on the variables, results are very close when analyzing growth rates by percentile. Graphs have similar scales and shapes, with some exceptions when calculating absolute changes in each indicator. A limitation is that the time period of analysis is too short for indicators that might need even generations to exhibit significant changes. Low variability is a possible explanation for the similar results obtained, as well as the large sample size.

[28]Detailed documentation on how the ICV is currently calculated is not available. We base our description on DNP (2006) and internal unpublished documents of DANE and DNP (see for example: unstats.un.org/unsd/methods/poverty/RioWS-Colombia.pdf).

Although non-income indicators are easier to measure and less prone to error as discussed by Günther and Klasen (2009), low variation, the existence of upper boundaries, and the fact that some of them depend on public policies are challenging for interpreting them. However, our results are consistent with previous analysis on multidimensional pro-poor growth using longer time spans (Grosse et al., 2008a): inequality in non-income indicators is lower than income indicators and they change little as time passes.

2.6 Tables

Table 2.1: Composition of Variables of Non-Income Indices

	1997	2003	Normative weights			PPCA
	mean	mean	Score	Weight	Final	pooled
ASSETS						
Household durables						
Fridge	65.4	63.9	5	2	10	0.13
No	34.6	36.1	0	0	0	-0.23
Mixer	75.4	67.8	1	2	2	0.10
No	24.6	32.2	0	0	0	-0.25
Color TV	69.5	73.0	3	2	6	0.11
No	30.5	27.0	0	0	0	-0.29
Radio	43.4	40.9	2	2	4	0.19
No	56.6	59.1	0	0	0	-0.15
Car	12.7	10.1	8	2	16	0.32
No	87.3	89.9	0	0	0	-0.04
Oven	21.5	17.5	7	2	14	0.28
No	78.5	82.5	0	0	0	-0.07
Washing machine	19.3	23.1	6	2	12	0.29
No	80.7	76.9	0	0	0	-0.10
Video	17.2	13.8	4	2	8	0.32
No	82.8	86.2	0	0	0	-0.07
Dwelling quality						
Cooking material						
Electricity	19.5	10.5	4	5	20	0.33
Gas tube	18.8	35.0	3	5	15	0.12
Gas cilinder	37.1	33.9	2	5	10	-0.06
Kerosene, coal, other, wood	24.6	20.6	1	5	5	-0.27

to be continued

Table 2.1 continued

	1997 mean	2003 mean	Normative weights Score	Weight	Final	PPCA pooled
Wall material						
Brick, block, stone, prefabricated, polished wood	76.5	81.2	4	6	24	0.08
Adobe, or compressed earth material	6.8	4.8	3	6	18	-0.21
Bahareque (combination cane + mud)	10.6	6.5	2	6	12	-0.28
Crude wood, guadua (bamboo), organic material, zinc, cardboard, residuals, plastic	6.1	7.6	1	6	6	-0.43
Floor material						
Marble, parquet, polished wood	3.4	2.6	4	7	28	0.48
Carpet	2.0	1.7	3	7	21	0.35
Vinly, sheet tiles, ceramic tiles, brick	40.2	42.2	2	7	14	0.13
Crude wood, wood planks, concrete, fine gravel, earth, sand	54.5	53.5	1	7	7	-0.18
Toilet facility						
Toilet to sewer	66.9	68.7	4	6	24	0.13
Flush toilet	12.9	14.4	3	6	18	-0.17
Toilet without conection, letrine	9.1	8.1	2	6	12	-0.27
No facility	11.1	8.9	0	6	0	-0.44
Shower facility						
Watering can in shower room	74.1	74.2	3	4	12	0.10
Shower room without watering can	12.4	14.1	2	4	8	-0.23
No Shower room	13.5	11.7	0	4	0	-0.41
Number of rooms per person						
up to one-third	16.9	12.9	1	5	5	-0.23
one-third to one-half	9.1	8.4	2	5	10	-0.13
one-half to three-quaters	26.9	27.3	3	5	15	-0.05
three-quaters to one	29.5	31.5	4	5	20	0.06
more than one	17.6	19.9	5	5	25	0.20
Access to services						
Electricity	93.5	95.4	2	4	8	0.03
No	6.5	4.6	0	0	0	-0.53
Piped gas	20.3	36.4	1	4	4	0.19
No	79.7	63.6	0	0	0	-0.10
Water	84.1	85.7	2	4	8	0.07
No	16.0	14.3	0	0	0	-0.36
Sewage	67.9	69.5	1	4	4	0.13
No	32.1	30.5	0	0	0	-0.28

to be continued

Table 2.1 continued

	1997 mean	2003 mean	Normative weights Score	Weight	Final	PPCA pooled
Litter	70.2	72.1	1	4	4	0.12
No	29.8	28.0	0	0	0	-0.31
Phone	46.3	55.9	1	4	4	0.18
No	53.7	44.1	0	0	0	-0.23
HEALTH						
Health status of the person						
Very good	12.6	9.1	4	7	28	0.90
Good	57.3	63.0	3	7	21	0.13
Regular	26.5	25.0	2	7	14	-0.55
Bad	3.7	2.9	1	7	7	-1.16
Does not have a chronic health disease	88.4	86.0	1	5	5	0.14
Does	11.6	14.0	0	0	0	-0.92
Has not been sick in the last month	83.8	88.5	1	1	1	0.08
Has been	16.2	11.5	0	0	0	-0.59
Is affiliated to a medical service	57.4	61.8	1	3	3	-0.12
Is not	42.6	38.2	0	0	0	0.21
Goes to health check up once per year	43.5	46.1	1	4	4	-0.15
Goes not	56.5	53.9	0	0	0	0.17
Has not been to hospital last year	92.8	93.5	1	2	2	0.06
Has been	7.2	6.6	0	0	0	-0.86
LIVING CONDITIONS AND SUBJECTIVE WELFARE						
Life compared to 5 years ago is						
better	36.6	33.4	3	4	12	1.19
equal	32.5	36.5	2	4	8	0.30
worse	30.9	30.1	1	4	4	-0.59
Household income is						
more than enough	6.7	6.0	3	4	12	0.65
just enough	50.3	52.5	2	4	8	-0.02
not enough	43.0	41.5	1	4	4	-0.68
Household / Household members						
had no severe health problem (last year)	86.4	92.4	1	4	4	0.08
had	13.6	7.6	0	0	0	-0.72
had not experienced a death (last year)	94.7	96.1	1	2	2	0.02
had	5.3	4.0	0	0	0	-0.53
feels save in neighborhood	77.7	73.2	1	5	5	0.09
does not	22.3	26.8	0	0	0	-0.23

Notes: PPCA stands for Polychoric principal component analysis. Final normative weights are calculated multiplying scores and weights.
Source: Own calculations. Based on Encuesta de Calidad de Vida (ECV) 1997 and 2003.

Table 2.2: Non-Income Deciles, 1997 and 2003

	1	2	3	4	5	6	7	8	9	10	10:1	Gini/Theil[a]	Mean
	Normative weights												
	Mean of the Deciles (conditional), 1997												
Assets	2.92	3.24	3.65	3.98	4.38	5.03	5.38	5.95	6.64	7.51	2.57	0.24	5.20
Health	5.75	5.88	5.97	6.05	6.17	6.36	6.43	6.70	7.01	7.34	1.28	0.16	6.42
Subj. welf.	5.25	5.33	5.40	5.61	5.82	6.03	6.08	6.35	6.70	7.31	1.39	0.19	5.93
	Mean of the Deciles (unconditional), 1997												
Assets	1.07	2.62	3.80	4.58	5.15	5.69	6.18	6.76	7.50	8.56	7.97	0.10	5.20
Health	2.98	4.40	5.27	6.09	6.20	6.90	7.04	7.69	8.06	9.30	3.12	0.04	6.42
Subj. welf.	2.26	3.88	4.22	5.40	5.56	6.33	7.04	7.07	8.49	8.93	3.96	0.07	5.93
	Mean of the Deciles (conditional), 2003												
Assets	3.40	3.72	4.27	4.75	5.19	5.64	6.03	6.45	6.98	7.86	2.31	0.22	5.31
Health	5.97	6.09	6.22	6.41	6.51	6.62	6.77	6.95	7.12	7.54	1.26	0.15	6.54
Subj. welf.	5.16	5.27	5.37	5.60	5.62	5.75	5.96	6.09	6.31	6.85	1.33	0.18	5.92
	Mean of the Deciles (unconditional), 2003												
Assets	1.25	3.01	4.10	4.79	5.31	5.76	6.20	6.70	7.37	8.57	6.87	0.09	5.31
Health	3.11	4.54	5.49	6.11	6.31	6.94	7.23	7.94	8.06	9.29	2.98	0.04	6.54
Subj. welf.	2.30	3.82	4.28	5.21	5.56	5.98	7.04	7.04	8.17	8.83	3.84	0.06	5.92

to be continued

Table 2.2 continued

	1	2	3	4	5	6	7	8	9	10	10:1	Gini/Theil[a]	Mean
						Polychoric PCA weights							
						Mean of the Deciles (conditional), 1997							
Assets	2.87	3.25	3.71	4.10	4.54	5.30	5.69	6.32	7.00	7.78	2.71	0.25	5.47
Health	7.19	7.14	7.16	7.15	7.12	7.14	7.16	7.12	7.15	7.28	1.01	0.12	7.17
Subj. welf.	4.84	4.95	5.02	5.25	5.53	5.79	5.86	6.19	6.57	7.29	1.51	0.20	5.70
						Mean of the Deciles (unconditional), 1997							
Assets	0.88	2.44	3.77	4.82	5.59	6.23	6.78	7.35	7.99	8.80	9.95	0.12	5.47
Health	3.78	5.45	6.36	6.96	7.35	7.67	7.96	8.27	8.58	9.37	2.48	0.03	7.17
Subj. welf.	2.21	3.45	4.11	4.88	5.40	6.19	6.66	7.02	8.13	8.78	3.96	0.07	5.70
						Mean of the Deciles (conditional), 2003							
Assets	3.48	3.85	4.51	5.08	5.58	6.14	6.53	6.96	7.45	8.19	2.35	0.23	5.60
Health	7.11	7.12	7.10	7.08	7.08	7.02	7.00	7.01	6.98	7.06	0.99	0.12	7.08
Subj. welf.	4.90	5.07	5.20	5.44	5.50	5.66	5.90	6.08	6.32	6.95	1.42	0.19	5.77
						Mean of the Deciles (unconditional), 2003							
Assets	1.06	2.76	4.09	5.05	5.71	6.30	6.86	7.37	7.95	8.89	8.40	0.10	5.60
Health	3.54	5.42	6.28	7.03	7.36	7.37	7.96	8.02	8.57	9.00	2.54	0.03	7.08
Subj. welf.	2.52	3.50	4.44	4.96	5.49	6.09	6.42	6.92	8.07	8.75	3.47	0.06	5.77

to be continued

Table 2.2 continued

	1	2	3	4	5	6	7	8	9	10	10:1	Gini/Theil[a]	Mean
Education													
Mean of the Deciles (conditional), 1997													
Adults	1.99	2.25	2.51	2.89	3.03	3.68	4.12	4.83	5.93	6.95	3.49	0.35	4.07
Children	7.30	7.49	7.56	7.50	7.43	7.79	7.89	7.95	8.30	8.48	1.16	0.10	7.85
Mean of the Deciles (unconditional), 1997													
Adults	0.44	1.39	2.07	2.78	3.37	4.08	4.91	5.81	6.90	8.79	20.02	0.20	4.07
Children	4.33	6.36	7.17	7.66	8.05	8.47	8.67	8.89	9.30	9.51	2.20	0.02	7.85
Mean of the Deciles (conditional), 2003													
Adults	2.49	2.63	2.96	3.42	3.84	4.17	4.67	5.19	5.65	6.33	2.54	0.34	4.00
Children	7.49	7.61	7.73	7.76	7.76	7.90	8.02	8.08	8.13	8.18	1.09	0.12	7.88
Mean of the Deciles (unconditional), 2003													
Adults	0.42	1.42	2.10	2.75	3.30	4.07	4.83	5.65	6.70	8.56	20.32	0.20	4.00
Children	3.55	6.15	7.12	7.71	8.15	8.65	8.87	9.20	9.33	9.69	2.73	0.03	7.88

Source: Own calculations Based on Encuesta de Calidad de Vida (ECV) 1997 and 2003.

Notes: [a]Gini Index can be found in the conditional parts of the table. The Theil Index can be found in the unconditional parts.

Notes: [a]This does not mean, however, that the indices are calculated conditionally or unconditionally.

Table 2.3: Income and Expenditures Deciles, 1997 and 2003

	1	2	3	4	5	6	7	8	9	10	10:1	Gini	Mean
	Mean of the Deciles (conditional). 1997												
Income	20.475	39.453	55.324	72.106	92.013	117.017	151.575	207.655	319.473	797.519	38.95	0.55	190.829
Consump.	46.837	47.963	59.693	69.972	80.585	101.088	115.867	169.757	239.465	445.803	9.52	0.53	145.226
	Mean of the Deciles (unconditional). 1997												
Consump.	16.927	32.310	44.896	58.569	75.566	96.123	123.701	164.278	245.499	569.579	33.65	0.53	145.226
	Mean of the Deciles (conditional). 2003												
Income	19.797	36.154	49.141	63.585	80.274	101.008	129.481	171.521	256.454	641.587	32.41	0.52	152.712
Consump.	41.406	44.954	54.027	67.474	82.143	95.045	117.737	151.754	212.926	430.511	10.40	0.51	125.143
	Mean of the Deciles (unconditional). 2003												
Consump	15.783	29.695	41.632	54.054	67.691	84.566	108.538	145.532	212.960	502.475	31.84	0.51	125.143

Notes: Income and expenditures are in 1000 Pesos.
Source: Own calculations based on Encuesta de Calidad de Vida (ECV) 1997 and 2003.

Table 2.4: Poverty and Inequality Measures by Area 1997–2003

	Moderate poverty line			Extreme poverty line			Inequality measures		
	FGT0	FGT1	FGT2	FGT0	FGT1	FGT2	Gini	Theil	Pop Share
Income based using ECV data									
National									
1997	54.06	24.85	14.64	18.02	6.40	3.29	0.55	0.59	100
2003	60.34	27.85	16.28	20.53	6.83	3.32	0.52	0.52	100
Urban									
1997	46.46	20.23	11.59	13.11	4.65	2.41	0.53	0.53	72.14
2003	55.37	24.75	14.25	16.66	5.45	2.67	0.51	0.47	73.61
Rural									
1997	73.71	0.37	0.23	30.72	10.96	5.56	0.45	0.39	27.86
2003	74.19	36.81	22.53	31.32	10.65	5.13	0.44	0.38	26.39
Expenditure based using ECV data									
National									
1997	55.18	25.55	15.09	19.05	6.63	3.28	0.53	0.52	100
2003	63.13	30.62	18.50	23.83	8.56	4.27	0.52	0.49	100
Urban									
1997	45.41	18.25	9.76	10.44	3.09	1.39	0.49	0.44	72.14
2003	57.10	25.74	14.75	43.16	17.08	9.05	0.48	0.42	73.61
Rural									
1997	80.47	44.44	28.87	41.33	15.81	8.19	0.45	0.38	27.86
2003	79.95	44.24	28.97	16.89	5.55	2.56	0.47	0.41	26.39

Notes: Own calculations based on ECV.

Table 2.5: Mean Growth Rates, Mean Absolute Changes, Pro-Poor Growth Rates, and Pro-Poor Changes

	Relative NIGIC 1997-2003					Absolute NIGIC 1997-2003				
		(unconditional)		(conditional)			(unconditional)		(conditional)	
	GRIM	PPGR mod.	PPGR extr.	PPGR mod.	PPGR extr.	CHIM	PPCH mod.	PPCH extr.	PPCH mod.	PPCH extr.
Income (ECV)	-3.65	-1.73	-0.82	-1.73	-0.82	-38,118	-6,939	-1,646	-6,939	-1,646
Consumption (ECV)	-2.45	-1.56	-1.26	-1.18	-1.91	-20,082	-5,568	-2,089	-4,044	-4,737
	Non-income indices using normative weights									
Assets	0.35	0.77	2.11	1.98	2.51	0.11	0.10	0.28	0.50	0.51
Health	0.32	0.42	0.91	0.65	0.67	0.12	0.11	0.20	0.23	0.23
Subjective welfare	-0.02	0.07	0.76	-0.52	-0.17	-0.01	-0.02	0.14	-0.18	-0.05
	Non-income indices using PPCA weights									
Assets	0.42	0.92	2.36	2.46	3.14	0.14	0.13	0.27	0.66	0.65
Health	-0.21	-0.29	-0.47	-0.24	-0.12	-0.09	-0.09	-0.09	-0.10	-0.05
Subjective welfare	0.20	0.35	1.08	-0.04	0.42	0.07	0.04	0.18	-0.03	0.12
	Education									
Education of children	0.07	-0.31	-1.54	0.22	0.41	0.03	0.02	-0.26	0.09	0.17
Education of adults	-0.28	-0.85	-1.91	1.91	2.99	-0.07	-0.07	0.02	0.28	0.41

Source : Own calculations based on Encuesta de Calidad de Vida (ECV) 1997 and 2003

2.7 Figures

Figure 2.1: Growth Incidence Curve National. 1997–2003

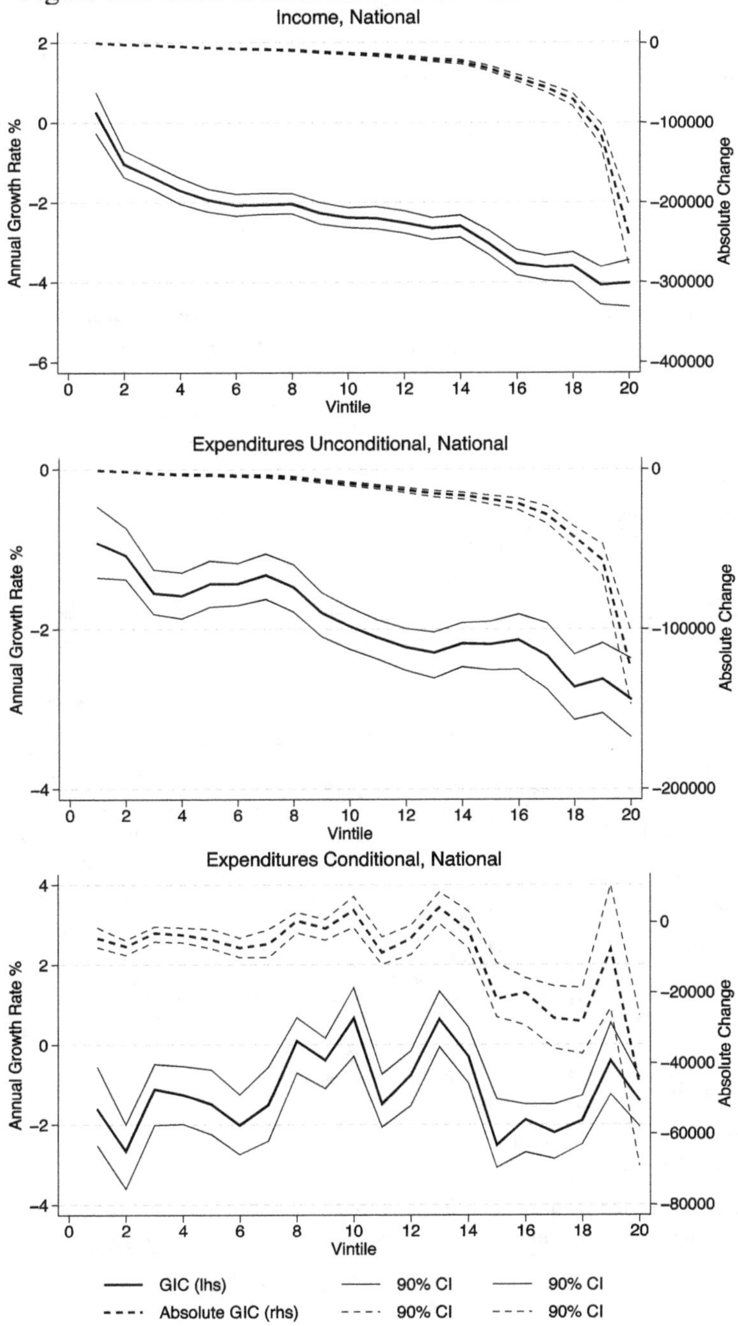

Source : Own Calculations based on data from ECV.

Figure 2.2: Growth Incidence Curve Sub-National. 1997–2003

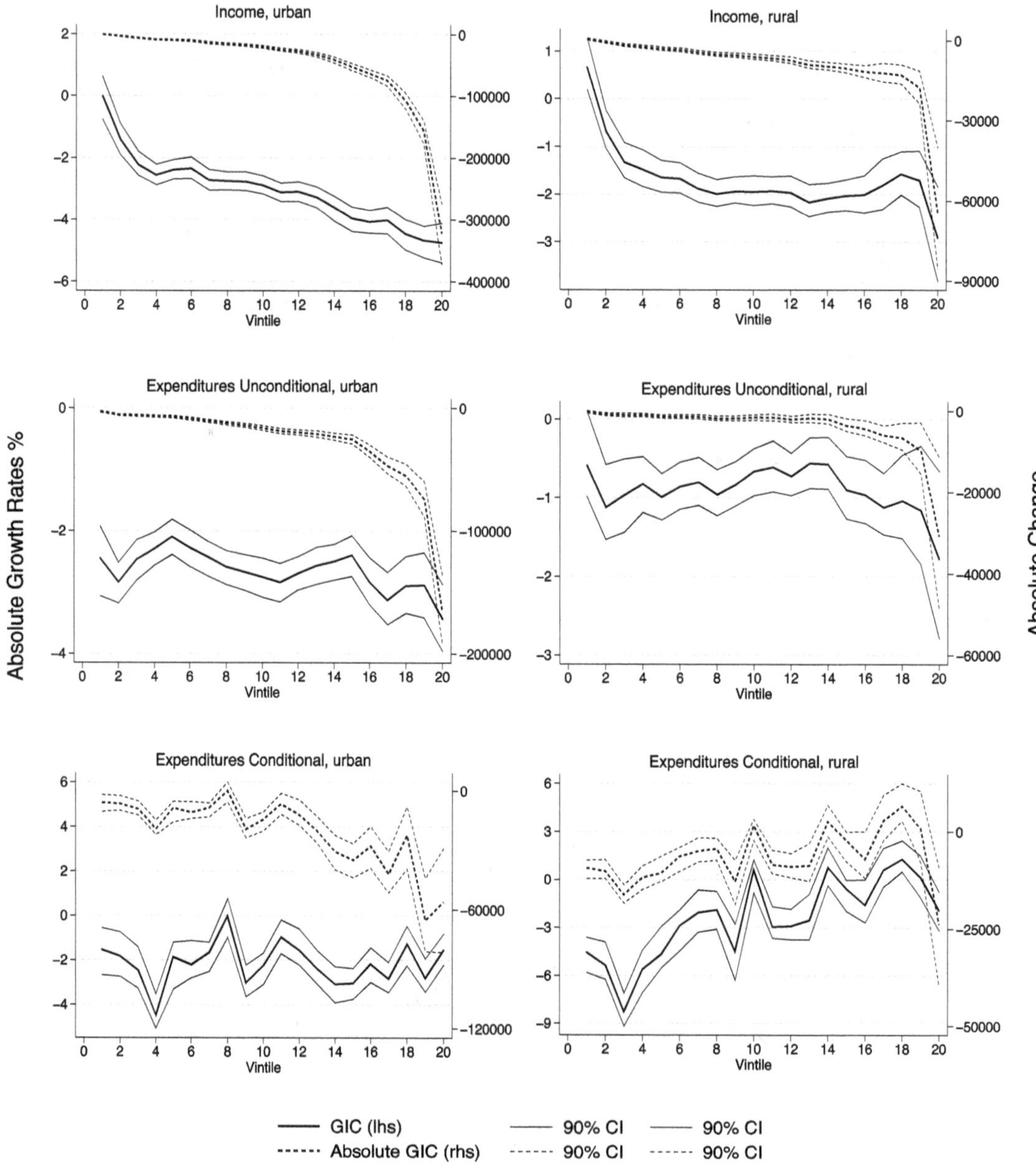

Source : Own Calculations based on data from ECV. *Note :* For each figure left vertical axis show absolute growth rates. Right vertical axis show absolute changes.

Figure 2.3: Assets, Health, Subjective Welfare: Relative Conditional NIGIC, 1997–2003

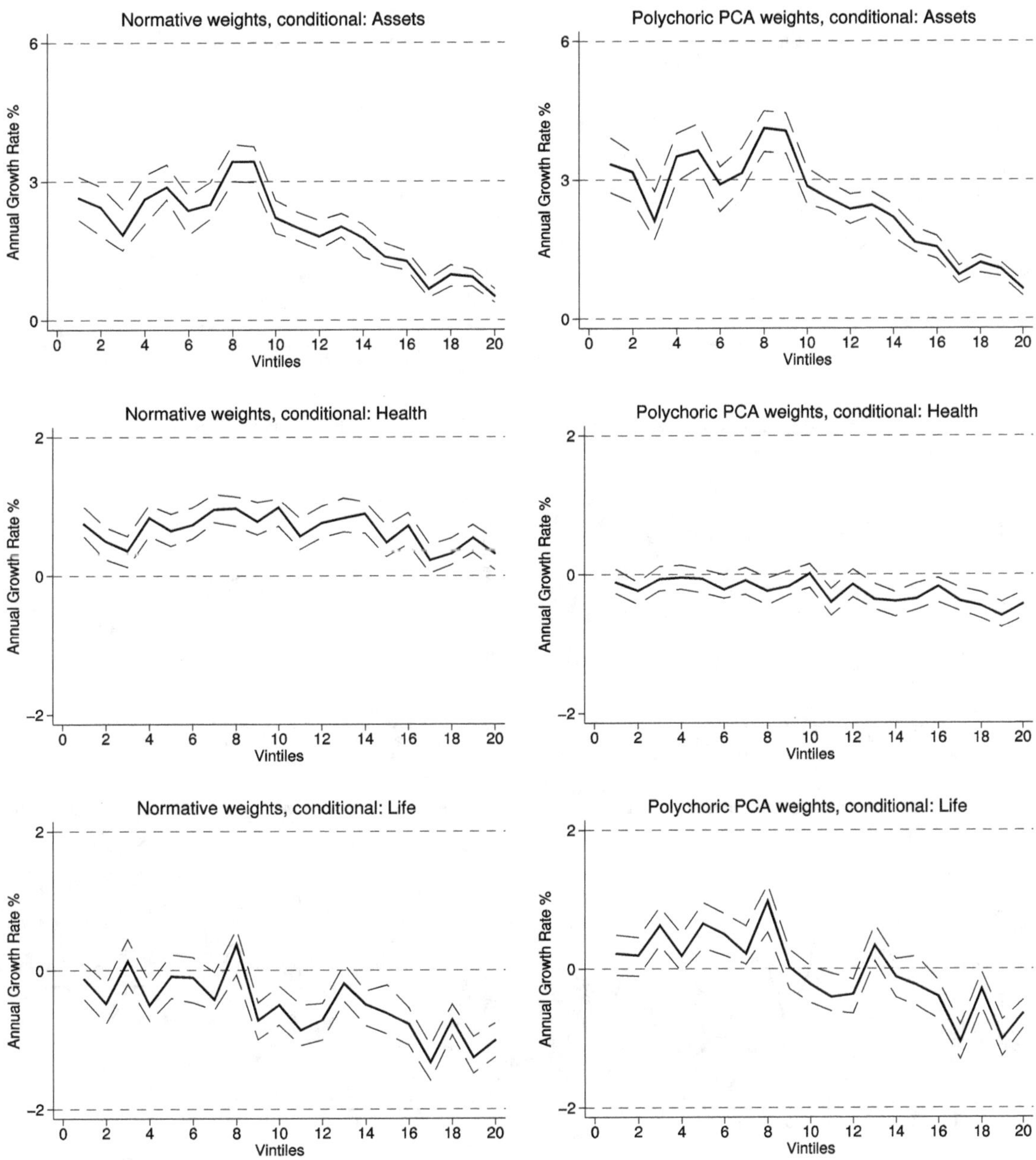

Legend: - NIGIC conditional – Confidence interval

Source : Own Calculations based on data from ECV with 90% confidence intervals.

Figure 2.4: Assets, Health, Subjective Welfare: Relative Unconditional NIGIC, 1997–2003

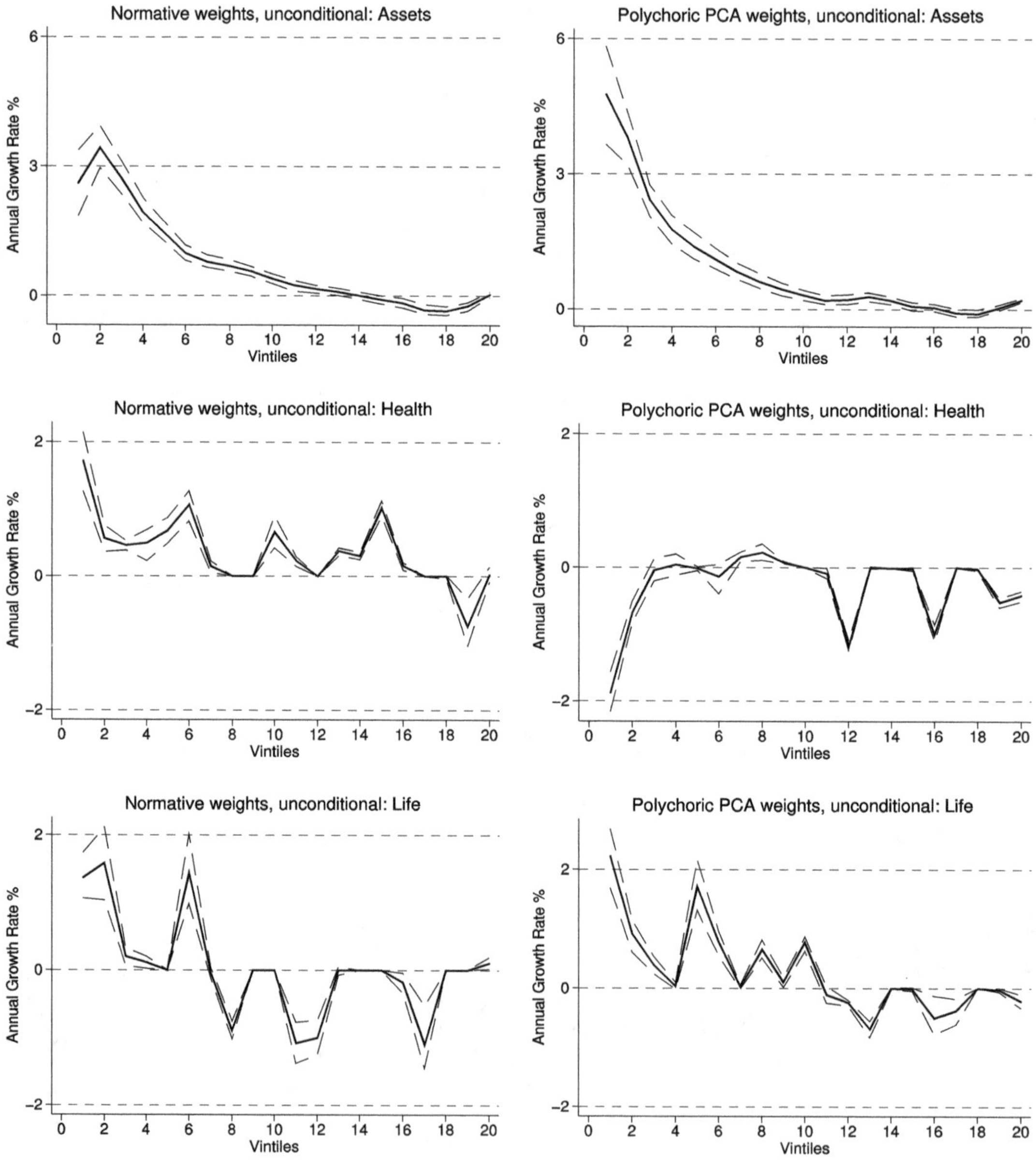

Legend: - NIGIC unconditional – Confidence interval

Source : Own Calculations based on data from ECV with 90% confidence intervals.

Figure 2.5: Assets, Health, Subjective Welfare: Absolute Conditional NIGIC, 1997–2003

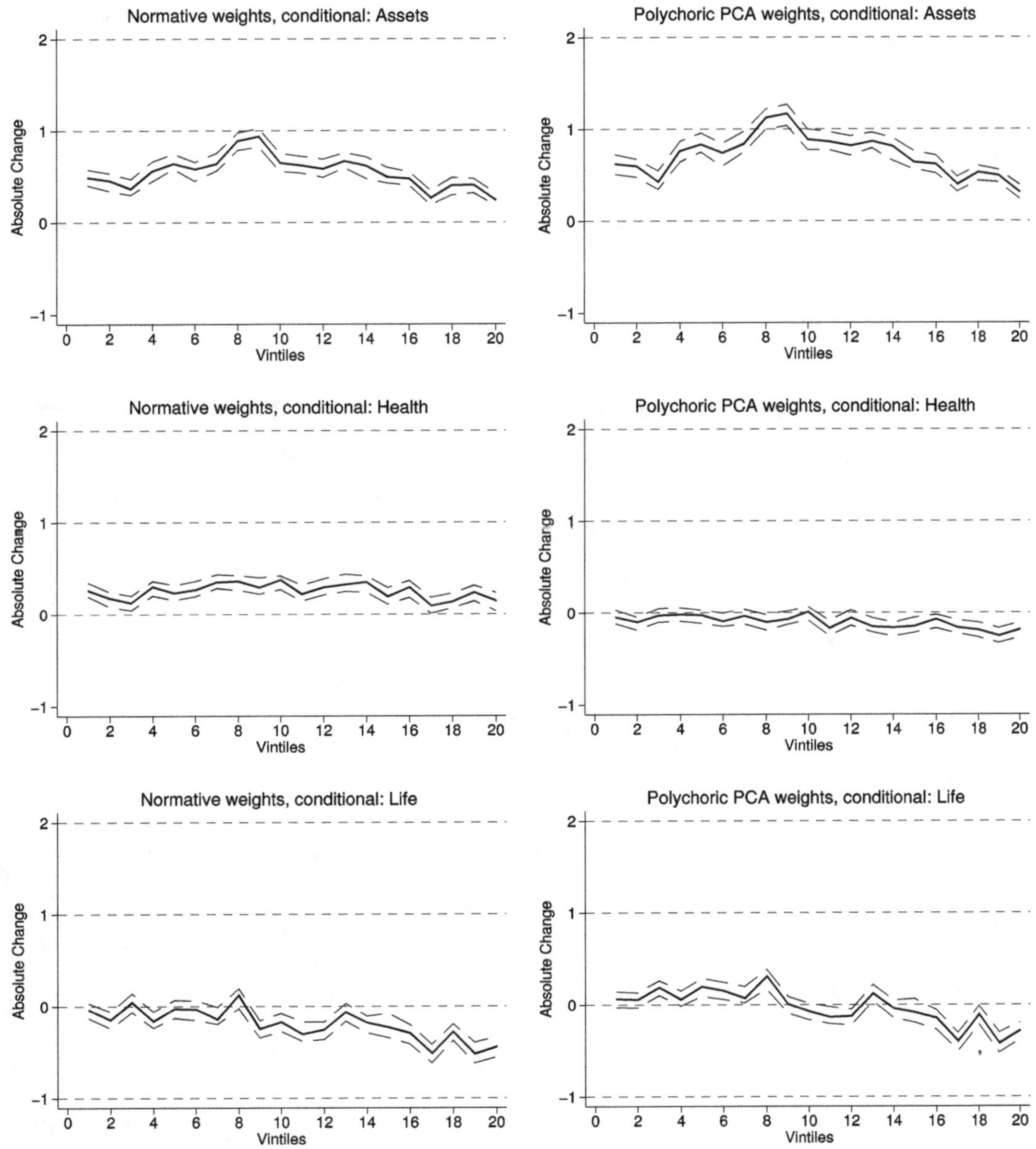

Legend: - NIGIC conditional – Confidence interval

Source : Own Calculations based on data from ECV with 90% confidence intervals.

Figure 2.6: Assets, Health, Subjective Welfare: Absolute Unconditional NIGIC, 1997–2003

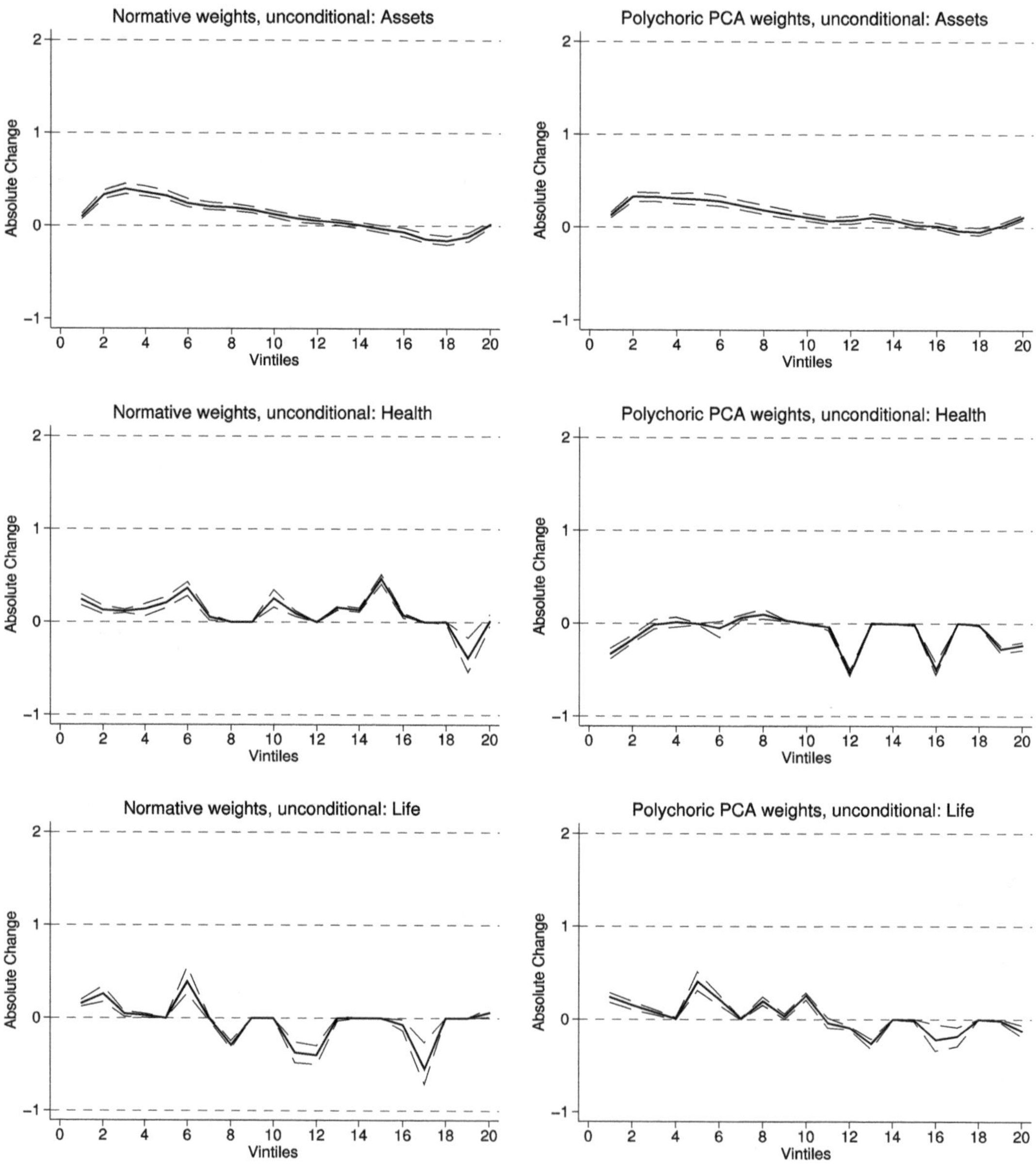

Legend: - NIGIC unconditional – Confidence interval
Source : Own Calculations based on data from ECV with 90% confidence intervals.

Figure 2.7: Education, Conditional NIGIC, 1997–2003

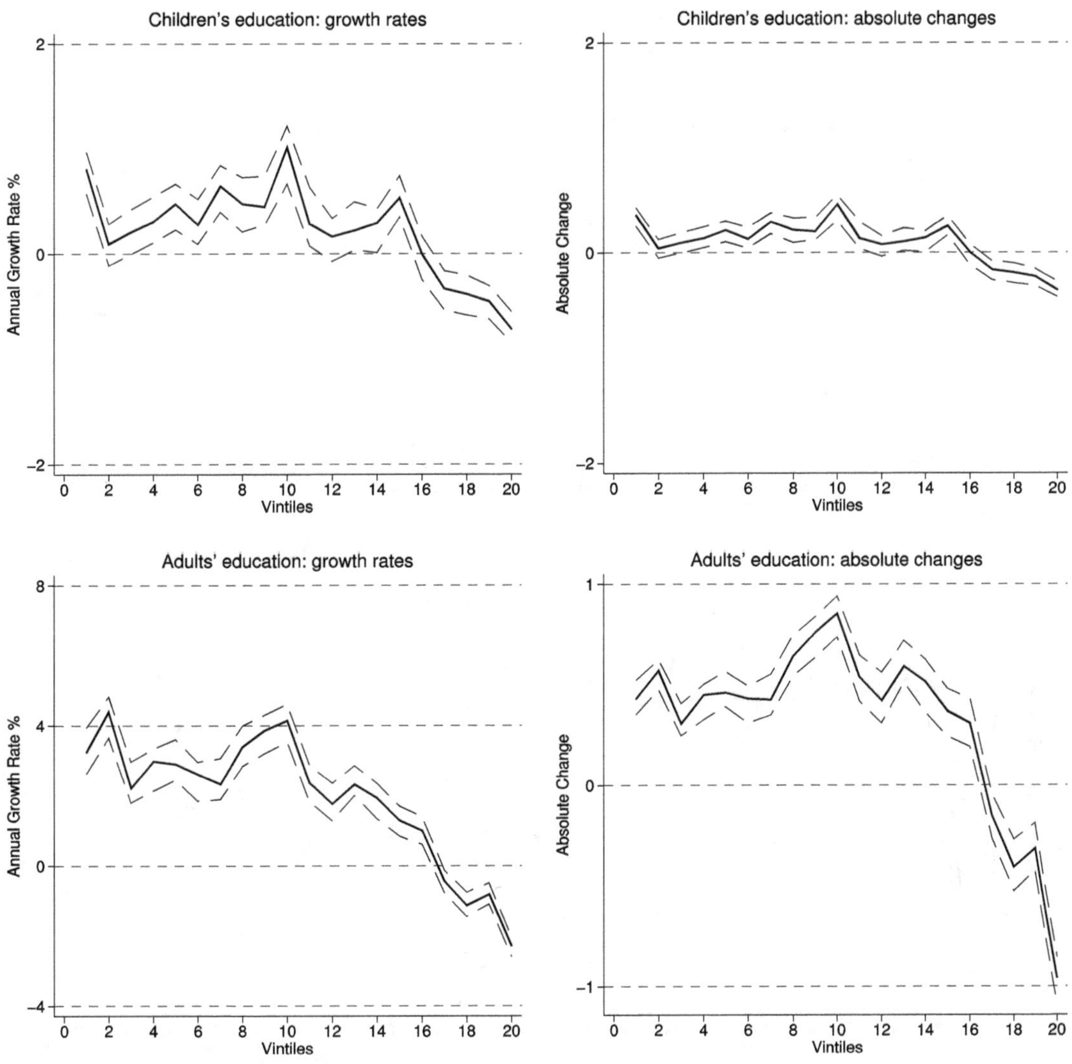

Legend: - NIGIC conditional – Confidence interval

Source : Own Calculations based on data from ECV with 90% confidence intervals.

Figure 2.8: Education, Unconditional NIGIC, 1997–2003

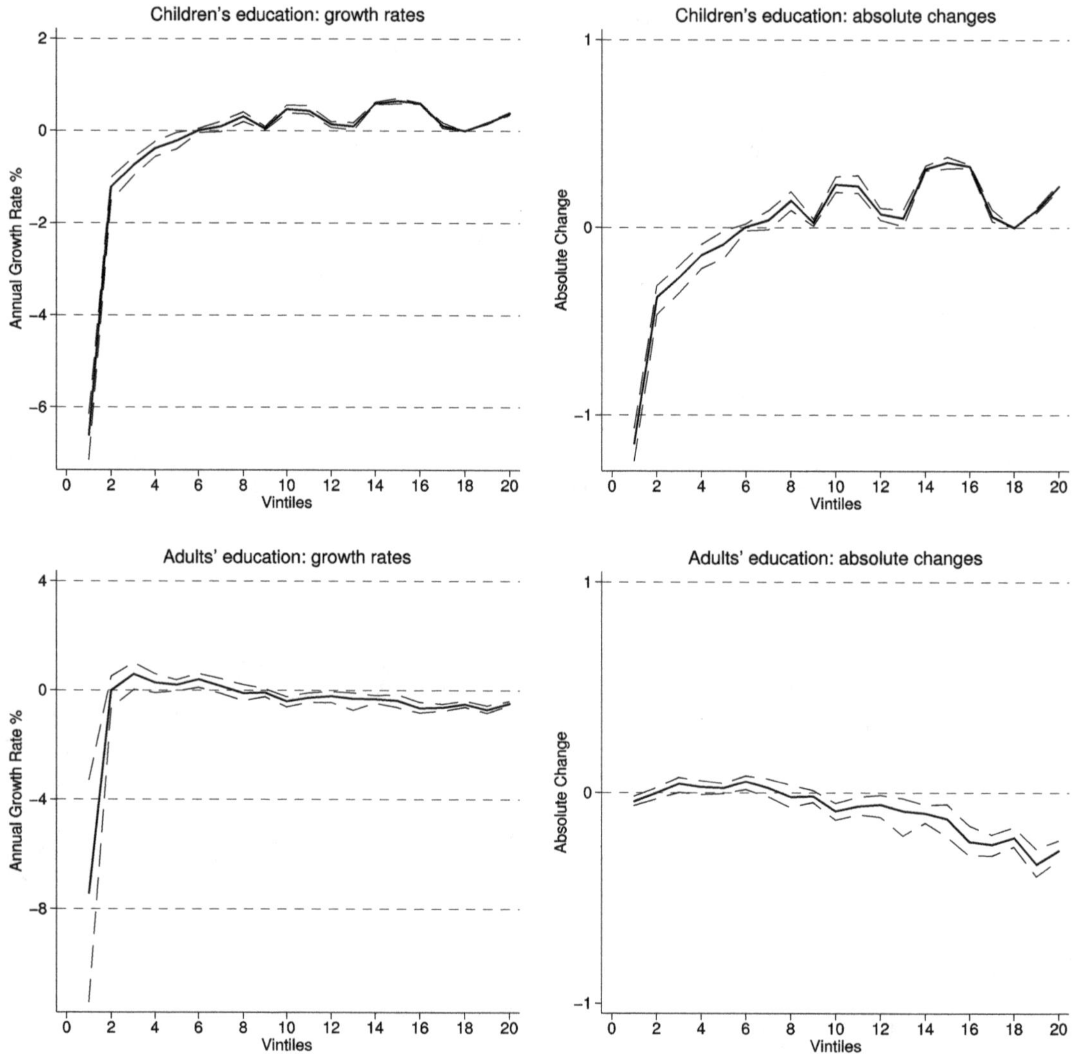

Legend: - NIGIC unconditional – Confidence interval
Source : Own Calculations based on data from ECV with 90% confidence intervals.

Figure 2.9: Households with Access to Basic Services by Income Percentile, 1997–2003

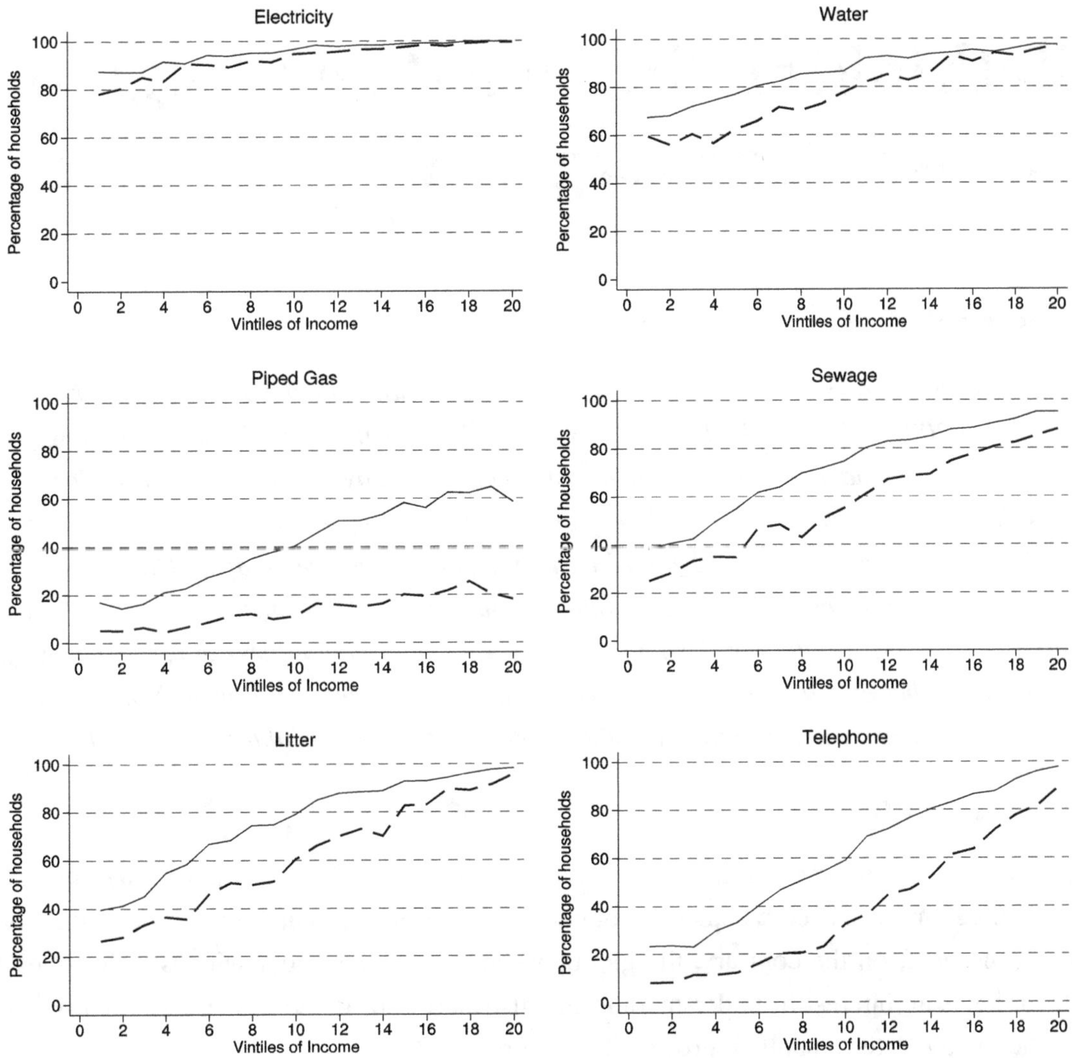

Legend: - -1997 – 2003

Source : Own Calculations based on data from ECV.

3

Rethinking the Debate on Regional Growth Convergence

Abstract

*his paper investigates growth convergence across Colombian departments during the period of 1975 to 2000, following both the regression and the distributional approaches suggested in the literature, and using two income measures computed by Centro de Estudios Ganaderos (CEGA). We also discuss issues related to data provided by Departamento Administrativo Nacional de Estadısticas (DANE) used by previous convergence studies. Our results show no evidence supporting convergence using per capita gross departmental product, but rather persistence in the distribution. Using per capita gross household disposable income, we find convergence, but only at a low speed, close to one percent per year. Furthermore, we find no evidence of the existence of different steady states for the two variables considered.**

3.1 Introduction

One of the most interesting and disputed questions in the economics discipline during the last half century has been whether or not poor countries tend to catch up with wealthier ones over time or if, on the contrary, the gap between the rich and poor widens. This question also reflects an interest in understanding the distribution of outcomes across countries and, implicitly, the determinants of growth (Durlauf et al., 2005).

Empirical research on this topic is based upon macroeconomic aggregates and has concentrated on testing the neoclassical growth model of Solow (1956) using the estimation method proposed by Barro and Sala-i-Martin (1991) to investigate whether economies with lower capital per person at a certain initial point in time tend to grow more quickly than

---

*Based on joint work with Boris Branisa Caballero

economies with higher capital per person. If this is the case, there is convergence among economies over the long run.

The convergence question has also been studied within particular countries to analyze how much regional disparities diminish over time. The difference with cross-country convergence analysis is that in such cases it is risky to make assumptions across countries on key model parameters, such as technology, savings, and population growth rates. On the contrary, within a single country, it is plausible to assume that regions exhibit similarities in these and other variables, such as language, institutions, and preferences. This presumed homogeneity has lead researchers to assume that convergence is more likely to hold within, rather than across, countries (Barro and Sala-i-Martin, 2004).

Empirical research supports regional convergence within industrial countries over the long run. Typical examples are given by Barro and Sala-i-Martin (1992b) who find convergence across U.S. states between 1880 and 2000, across Japanese prefectures between 1930 and 1990, and between regions in eight European countries between 1950 and 1990 (see also Barro and Sala-i-Martin (1992a)).

In the case of Colombia, a heterogeneous country at the department level in economic, geographic, and cultural aspects, existing research is contradictory. While some authors argue that Colombia was a successful case of convergence in the second half of the twentieth century, others argue for the persistence of regional disparities.

The objective of this study is to investigate whether or not Colombia was a case of convergence at the department level between 1975 and 2000 using two different per capita income variables: gross departmental product and gross personal disposable income. The first variable reflects production by residents in each department, while the second one reflects income received by households after subtracting taxes and net payments to the social security and adding other net current transfers. As will be argued in the next section, we consider that the second variable is more appropriate for measuring convergence in well-being.

We have two main hypothesis. First, we do not expect convergence in per capita gross departmental product between 1975 and 2000. At the beginning of the period, production factors were already concentrated around large cities. The mobility of capital faces important constraints related to geography and lack of adequate infrastructure connecting regions as well as to the domestic conflict. Moreover, it is known that the returns to scale in agriculture tend to be constant, while in manufacturing and services they tend to be increasing, fostering concentration of these two sectors close to the three major metropolitan areas.

Second, we expect convergence in per capita gross personal disposable income. One issue leading to this hypothesis is the taxing system. As shown by CEGA part of the taxing resources received by the richest departmental economies, particularly Bogotá, are transferred to other regions compensating partly their deficit. Thus, poorer regions should have got closer in terms of disposable income to the richest.

The study is constructed around three main questions. First, the study evaluates whether departments converged between 1975 and 2000 and if so, if convergence results obtained using the regression approach contradict the results obtained with the distributional approach suggested by Quah (1997), using bivariate Kernel density estimators. Second, we determine if the assumption of a common steady state for all departments holds or whether there is evidence of heterogeneity in the model parameters. Finally, the study evaluates whether the presence or absence of convergence occurs simultaneously in gross departmental product and in gross personal disposable income.

An important contribution of the study is that it tests the convergence hypothesis using time-series cross-sectional data with different specifications to check the robustness of results. The results are based upon data from Centro de Estudios Ganaderos (CEGA) because those data provide the longest time series (25 years) computed with a consistent methodology.[1]

To summarize our results, we do not find convergence in gross departmental product and find no evidence of different steady states across departments using that variable. When using gross personal disposable income, we find convergence, but a very slow one, and no evidence of different steady states. For both variables, when using the regression approach, we find that the best estimators can be achieved using pooled time-series cross-section data and assuming homogeneity in the parameters. Furthermore, considering both variables, we do not find a contradiction in results obtained using the regression and the distributional approaches. Using bivariate kernel density estimators, we find persistence in the distribution of gross departmental product and slight convergence in gross personal disposable income.

One important policy implication of our results is the need to periodically review whether or not departmental disparities diminish over time based on consistent time series constructed under a single methodology. We explicitly warn that linking different time series computed with different methodologies can lead to incorrect conclusions for interventions, such as poverty-alleviating policies and growth strategies. In keeping with previous studies on this topic (e.g. Bonet and Meisel, 2006a), we consider important the need to have an explicit regional policy in Colombia to foster growth in departments lagging behind national averages, after conducting case studies to assess which policies could be most effective in each case.

[1]CEGA was a large research center financed by a private financial institution in Colombia.

3.2 Motivation and Background

3.2.1 Economic Background

One remarkable characteristic of Colombia is the large income inequality which exists at different levels-between individuals, between rural and urban areas, and between departments. The country is currently divided into 32 departments and the capital district of Bogotá. Departments may also be grouped into 5 regions: the Caribbean Region comprising departments with access to the Caribbean Sea; the Pacific Region, with departments in the weast coast to the Pacific Ocean; the Central Region, covering the three branches of the Andes mountain chains; Orinoquia, comprising large plains to the south-east of the country; and Amazonia in the south, comprising the Colombian part of the Amazon rainforest (see the map of Colombia in Figure 3.1).

Economic growth over the last 30 years, which was low but stable compared to other countries in the region, comes together with a combination of a high incidence of poverty, inequality, and violence. In 2004, the percentage of people living below the poverty line (headcount index) was 52 percent and the Gini coefficient was 0.58. The homicide rate was 63 per 100,000 people. Evidence shows that growth slowed compared to long-term historical trends after 1970. In fact, after having achieved in 1970 a growth rate of 3.1 percent in per capita gross domestic product, growth between 1980 and 1990 occured at an average annual rate of only 1.2 percent due primarily by the adverse effects of Latin America's debt crisis. In the 1990s, the average growth rate was similar (1.1 percent), driven by a boom and bust cycle throughout the decade, which concluded in a severe recession in 1999 (per capita GDP contracted by 5.5 percent (Table 3.1). On the contrary, in the present decade, favorable external conditions, especially high commodity prices and confidence due to the easing of internal conflict, have contributed to the acceleration of the economy (Tenjo Galarza and López Enciso, 2003; Cárdenas, 2007).

The heart of economic activity in Colombia lies in the Central or Andean Region which concentrates the largest proportion of population within the major cities. Bogotá and the departments of Cundinamarca and Antioquia account for 42 percent of total GDP with Bogotá having a high level of participation in total production (22 percent). This area concentrates not only manufacturing industry and commerce near the cities, but also coffee plantations and other large-scale agricultural areas.

The GDP of departments in the Caribbean Region is based upon mining, small-scale agriculture, and cattle farming. La Guajira and Cesar are the two largest producers of coal, while Córdoba is the largest nickel producer. Despite having some departments rich in minerals, this region nevertheless has a high incidence of poverty, particularly in Córdoba and Sucre.

The Pacific Region comprises, relative to the Colombian average, three poor departments and one wealthy one (Valle del Cauca). Chocó, which is the poorest department in this region and in the country, is predominantly rural and sparsely populated, with large tropical rain forests and humid areas. It is known as the rainiest area in the country (and even one of the rainiest worldwide) and is geographically isolated from the rest of the country due to a chain of mountains to the east and the ocean to the west. Transport of population living in the department is largely done by way of its abundant rivers; road infrastructure is minimal. The scarce literature explaining socio-economic factors in this department argues that the current distribution of population and the quality of institutions may largely be explained by the early settlement of an extractive economy during colonization, at which time colonizers brought slaves to exploit gold mines but did not establish themselves in the department (Bonet, 2007). As opposed to Chocó, Valle del Cauca is the third largest departmental economy in the country after Bogotá and Antioquia and has some of the most productive agricultural areas, as well as a high level of participation in the manufacturing sector.

During the last 30 years, production was driven in some departments by the discovery of important mineral resources, as is the case for the departments of Arauca and Casanare, which have the largest oil fields in the country.[2] The same applies for La Guajira, which has the largest open coal mine in Latin America.

According to Meisel (2007b), the burden of poverty in Colombia is geographically located in the coastal departments and inequality is greater between departments than within them. Meisel argues that the urban-versus-rural divide is not the relevant dimension upon which to design poverty-alleviating programs, but the departmental one. Moreover, Meisel affirms that the already-large disparities have increased over the past 15 years and will not spontaneously disappear merely as a result of market forces.

The level of empirical research addressing regional disparities in Colombia has increased gradually since the early nineties, inspired by the international debate on convergence and the methodology proposed by Barro and Sala-i-Martin (1991). Since then, approximately 20 papers have investigated whether departments, regions, or even major cities have converged over time. Important shortcomings in this field arise due to the absence of consistent time-series data allowing for a long-term perspective. As a consequence, results frequently depend upon how the researcher combined the available time series, as well as on the methodology

[2]These departments are included in our sample as one group named Nuevos Departamentos (Nuevos), meaning new departments. The so-called New Departments are distributed in the south-east lowland plains, the Amazon Region, and the Caribbean islands. Excepting the islands, these departments are large in extension but have low population densities.

and control variables used, with no robust and undisputed evidence concerning departmental convergence.

Debate in this field in Colombia revolves around two issues: first, a methodological discussion as to whether or not to rely on the methodology proposed by Barro and Sala-i-Martin (1992a) or on the distributional approach proposed by Quah (1993b), and second, whether one should use information generated by Departamento Nacional de Estadísticas (DANE), rather than by Centro de Estudios Ganaderos (CEGA).[3]

Early studies used Barro-type regressions. The pioneer work of Cárdenas and Pontón (1995), combining early GDP data by department from the National Planning Department with those produced by DANE, concluded that between 1950 and 1990, Colombia was a successful case of convergence with a 4-percent speed of convergence, and that migration played an insignificant role in convergence. Alternative combinations of data from DANE yield different results, despite using the same methodology. For instance, Barón (2003) finds convergence during the eighties but not during the nineties. Research using kernel density estimators concluded that Colombia was a case of polarization with the existence of three groups: a wealthy one that diverges from the average national income, a middle income one that shows convergence inside the group, and a third one that grows more impoverished over time (Birchenall and Murcia, 1997). Using CEGA data, research points to polarization in favor of the capital district of Bogotá, to the detriment of departments located in the peripheries (Bonet and Meisel, 2006b). Almost all studies focus only upon convergence in income, while only three ask for convergence in living standards using social indicators.[4]

The reader is then confronted with the question of whether Colombia is a successful case of convergence or rather an example of hopeless persistence unless strong regional redistributive policies are adopted.[5]

Intuitively, when observing the different geographic conditions of the country and the agglomeration processes around the largest cities, as well as the differences in infrastructure, it is unrealistic to expect that poor departments can catch up with leading departments in terms of per capita product, given that they lack basic infrastructure and have a minor manufacturing and government presence.

However, there are mechanisms that could have promoted convergence among departments in recent years. One of them is fiscal equalization through central government transfers. Starting in the mid eighties, the government implemented a decentralization program to

[3]DANE is the official statistical agency in Colombia (http://www.dane.gov.co/).

[4]A comprehensive list of convergence studies in Colombia can be found in Aguirre (2008). We deal with regional convergence in social indicators in Colombia in a companion paper (Branisa and Cardozo, 2009a).

[5]Research using alternative methodologies and looking for linkages among regions found that Colombia has limited spatial interdependency (Haddad et al., 2008).

reduce the burden of spending by the central government. This process accelerated with the new constitution of 1991 which established a new system of transfers in order to increase the efficiency of social expenditures, as well as the supply of social services, compensated municipalities with weak financial capacities, and increased political power and the participation of local governments in the implementation of health and educational policies (Departamento Nacional de Planeación DNP, 2002; Rojas, 2003; Barrera and Domínguez, 2006). As a result, social spending increased from 7 to 15 percent between 1991 and 2001. Moreover, starting in the eighties, the model of industrialization through import substitution changed to the policy of liberalization of the economy, reduction of tariffs, and integration into the world markets in order to increase competitiveness, productivity, and economic growth. This shift also accelerated after the constitutional reform.

Another possible mechanism for convergence is migration. In general, the country underwent an important urbanization process in recent decades encouraged by industrialization around urban centers and a higher orientation towards export markets. Labor mobility was a combination between voluntary migration for economic gain (which profited from increasing returns to scale in the manufacturing sector) and forced migration due to violence, which migration helped enlarge informal markets. Migration from rural to urban areas accelerated during the twentieth century. The percentage of population which is urban changed from 59 percent in 1973 to 75 percent in 2005 due not only to a transformation from a predominantly agriculture-based economy to a services and industry-based one, but also due to conflict, violence, and a lack of opportunities in rural areas (Murad R., 2003).

In this context, the substantive question we try to empirically answer in this study is whether or not Colombia was a case of convergence at the department level between 1975 and 2000. Thus, if poor departments had greater growth rates than wealthy ones over time and the gap between them decreased. Our interest relies upon closing the debate on the existence of convergence across departments in Colombia by analyzing methodological issues and data sources that may have had affected results up to now. One important motivation of this study is the policy implication that can result as a consequence of wrongly assuming that departments converge automatically over time.

In order to explain the importance of the data used and the possible combinations of time series, we explain in the next subsection the available data sources and the relevance of two variables, gross departmental product and gross personal disposable income, arguing that the second one is more appropriate for measuring convergence for well-being.

3.2.2 Data Issues Affecting Convergence Results in Colombia

There are two different data sources of departmental accounts in Colombia: Department of Statistics (DANE) and Centro de Estudios Ganaderos (CEGA).

DANE provides per capita GDP by department for three different periods: one for 1980 through 1996 in constant prices as of 1975, one for 1990 through 2005 in constant prices as of 1994, and a final one for 2000 through 2005 in constant prices as of 2000. The first period was calculated applying concepts of the System of National Accounts of 1986 (SNA-86) and used an indirect method for collecting information. The second period was calculated using the System of National Accounts of 1993 (SNA-93) and combined direct and indirect methods for collecting information.[6] The third period did not include illicit crops in its estimation and is also based upon SNA-93. The classification of sectors, transactions, concepts, and methodology changed considerably in the SNA-93 and allowed for the inclusion of illegal activities as part of the GDP (DANE, 2008).[7]

It must be noted that statistical offices use different techniques to produce consistent time series of national accounts, particularly when international guidelines change.[8] For instancc, most (OECD) countries make regular revisions for short time periods (usually of about twenty years) to incorporate new available information and benchmark revisions, in order to provide users with consistent time series. In Latin America, only Chile and Perú offer consistent large time series of regional per capita GDP using statistical or interpolation methods (Serra et al., 2006).

In Colombia, DANE collected information for some overlapping years using both methodologies, but did not construct a consistent time series based only upon one. Although users do not have enough information to consistently recompute long time series, they tend to rebase series and connect them using growth rates, which can be problematic.[9]

Comparison of the series for the overlapping years shows different departmental growth rates and a different evolution of the logarithm of the standard deviation, explaining why convergence results change depending on how and when the researcher linked the different

[6]Direct methods take departmental information by product whenever data sources are available. Indirect ones use national aggregates and assign each department a percentage of those aggregates.

[7]The main changes concern the measurement of value-added taxes, the reclassification of transactions in the government sector, changes to the capital account, and productivity levels for the banking, energy, and insurance sectors.

[8]Techniques can be broadly classified into four groups: detailed reworking, proportion methods, interpolation between benchmarks, and indicator methods.

[9]For instance, the Canadian statistical office explicitly prohibits users from simply rebasing series using growth rates due to the large methodological differences derived from changing to SNA-93, and argues that only the statistics office in charge may comply series using detailed accounting and recomputing information according to the new procedures (Lal, 1999).

data series. Note in Figure 3.6 that the annual standard deviation of the logarithm of GDP of the three series of DANE yields different patterns. In the series of 1980 to 1996, the standard deviation increases sharply starting in 1990, while in the series from 1990 to 2005, it remains close to 0.36 until 1997 and falls thereafter. Concerning the third time series (2000 to 2005), the trend is similar to the series for 1990 through 2005, but the level of the standard deviation is higher.

The CEGA project compiled information at the departmental level in Colombia from 1975 to 2000 using SNA-93 and presented a simplified system of national accounts. The project used mixed methods for collecting information, classified some particular products differently than DANE, and did not include illicit crops in the agriculture category. Departmental results coincide between CEGA and DANE from 1990 onwards because both use SNA-93 (there are, however, important differences before 1990). CEGA produced consistent time series of two key variables relevant for convergence analysis, gross departmental product, which we will call henceforth PDB, and gross departmental income, which we will refer to as IDB. The first variable reflects production by residents in each department, while the second reflects the primary income received by those residents. The difference between these variables is the net external income of residents. CEGA also provided time series of gross household disposable income by department, which we will call IDBH, and which is the result of households' income after subtracting taxes on property and rental income and net payments to the social security, and adding other net current transfers. This variable is a more accurate measure of a population's welfare than per-capita PDB, as it reflects household income after paying taxes and having received transfers from public and private social projects.[10]

Due to the advantages provided by the CEGA database, and as this database is the only consistent time series covering a long time span, we present results and discussion on convergence for per capita PDB and IDBH.[11] Our final data set covers the period of 1975 to 2000 for 23 departments, the capital district of Bogotá, and the nine "New Departments" grouped into one observation, for a total of 25 units and 25 years. [12]

To calculate per capita figures of both PDB and IDBH, we use the latest available population data, computed after reconciliation of the census of 2005 with previous censuses.

[10]The abbreviations used refer to the original names in Spanish are Producto Departamental Bruto (PDB), Ingreso Departamental Bruto (IDB) and Ingreso Departamental Bruto (disponible) de los Hogares (IDBH).

[11]As will be explained in the next section, it would be best to work with data expressed as per unit of effective worker, but due to data availability, researchers often use per capita figures.

[12]The New Departments have existed formally since the 1991 constitutional reform when nine former intendancies and commissariats were acknowledged as departments (Amazonas, Arauca, Casanare, Guainía, Guaviare, Putumayo, San Andrés y Providencia, Vaupés, and Vichada).

According to the census of 2005, population is less than what had been forecasted using the 1993 census due to a lower birth rate and increased external migration (DANE, 2007). Although in most of the departments population was overestimated, there are some particular cases in which the contrary situation applies. We use yearly population data at the departmental level from DANE (2007) for the years 1985 to 2000, and for the years 1975 to 1985, we interpolated departmental population using the annual growth rate from 1973 to 1985 based on the 1973 census. The obtained values show a consistent evolution of population by department once connected to the official estimates from 1985 onwards.

Box plots of per capita PDB and IDBH in logs are shown in Figures 3.2 and 3.3. Box plots of relative PDB and relative IDBH in logs are shown in Figures 3.4 and 3.5. By relative we mean that the variables are expressed as ratios to the national average of the corresponding year. We can see that the ordering of departments is similar in both types of graphs, in levels and relatively, particularly in the upper and lower ends. The five departments with the lowest per capita PDB are Chocó, Sucre, Córdoba, Nariño, and Cauca, four of these being located on the Pacific Coast. Bogotá, Valle, Antioquia, Nuevos Departamentos, and Cundinamarca have the five highest PDBs. Concerning per capita IDBH, departments with the lowest values are almost the same, excepting Santander instead of Nuevos. The box plots show large variability in per capita figures of Guajira in both PDB and IDBH and low variability for Bogotá. This pattern is accentuated in figures relative to the average, as well as for the group of Nuevos and observing PDB. On the contrary, the log of per capita IDBH shows less variation and dispersion of values, but a higher difference between the richest and the poorest departments. Note also that the group of Nuevos Departamentos has large variability in PDB. That variability is not visible in IDBH. In the following two sections, we present two well-known approaches for testing for convergence-the classical approach to convergence analysis and the distributional approach.

3.3 The Solow Model and Its Estimation

3.3.1 The Solow Model

Empirical testing of convergence across economies is based upon the neoclassical growth model developed by Solow (1956)[13] in which economies have a transition dynamic towards the *steady state*, defined as a situation in which all variables per unit of effective worker remain unchanged over time. In the steady state, the ratio of capital to labor is constant given that the capital stock expands at the same rate as the labor force, and the capital expansion is sufficient to compensate for it.

[13]The neoclassical model was also developed in the original works of Ramsey (1928) and Cass (1965).

The neoclassical growth model assumes diminishing returns to factors and constant returns to scale. Due to this assumption, real returns of factors adjust to bring about full employment of labor and capital. Technology is exogenous and is the only force that explains changes in output and capital per worker. Any capital-to-labor ratio different than the one needed in the steady state readjusts as time passes so that economies tend towards the steady state. The speed at which this happens is known as the convergence rate and is inversely related to the distance from the steady state (Durlauf, 1996).

Robert Barro and Xavier Sala-i-Martin underline that smaller initial values of the capital-to-labor ratio k, under the framework of the neoclassical growth model, are associated with greater growth rates of the ratio production per worker (Barro and Sala-i-Martin, 1991, 1992a,b, 2004; Sala-i-Martin, 1996). They tested whether economies with lower capital per worker at a certain initial point in time grew more quickly in per-worker terms, using the following equation:

$$\log[\hat{Y}(t)] = (1-\exp^{-\beta^{*}t})\log(\hat{Y}^{*}) + \exp^{-\beta^{*}t}\, log[\hat{Y}(0)]), \tag{3.1}$$

where t represents time, β^* indicates how rapidly an economy's output per effective worker $\hat{Y}$ approaches its steady-state value $\hat{Y}^*$ in the neighborhood of the steady state. The corresponding definition of β^* with a constant saving rate s is $\beta^* = (1-\alpha)(x+n+\delta)$, where α is a constant representing the share of capital in production, n is the rate of population growth, x is the rate of exogenous growth, and δ is the depreciation rate. The speed of convergence is measured by how much the growth rate decreases as the capital stock increases in a proportional manner.[14] Equation 3.1 implies that the average growth rate of per-capita output Y over an interval from an initial time 0 to any future time T (higher than 0) is

$$\frac{\log[Y(T)/Y(0)]}{T} = x + \frac{(1-\exp^{-\beta T})}{T}\log[\hat{Y}^{*})/\hat{Y}(0)], \tag{3.2}$$

where x is the rate of technological progress or the steady-state growth rate.[15] Equation 3.2 also shows that the effect of the initial position $\hat{Y}(0)$ is conditioned on the steady-state position $\hat{Y}^*$ (conditional convergence) (Barro and Sala-i-Martin, 2004). The approach suggested by Barro and Sala-i-Martin (2004) is known as the regression approach or as the classical approach to convergence analysis (Sala-i-Martin, 1996; Magrini, 2004). There are two alternatives for applying this concept-testing for absolute convergence or for conditional convergence.

---

[14]Note that β^* is not the same as $\hat{\beta}$. It is the convergence rate in the proximity of the steady state and is determined by $(1-\alpha)$ for given values of x, n, and δ.

[15]Equation 3.2 indicates that the coefficient $(1-\exp^{-\beta T})/T$ declines, the higher T is for a given β, and as long as β is positive. Therefore, the average growth rate of Y decreases as $T \to \infty$ (and thus x) dominates the average growth rate. In contrast, for a given T, a higher β implies a higher coefficient $(1-\exp^{-\beta T})/T$.

3.3.2 Absolute Beta-Convergence

The concept of absolute beta-convergence (also known as unconditional convergence) is relevant for a group of closed economies that are structurally similar; they have the same values of the parameters x, s, n, and δ, and thus they have the same production function steady-state values k^* and Y^*. The only difference is the initial quantity of capital per person $k(0)$, which reflects past disturbances (wars, transitory shocks to production, etc.). Hence, economies with lower values of $k(0)$ and $Y(0)$ have unambiguously greater growth rates of k and Y. The estimation equation for absolute convergence is equation 3.2, omitting the $\hat{Y}^*$ term:

$$\frac{\log[Y_{i,t}/Y_{i,t-T}]}{T} = a - \frac{(1-\exp^{-\beta T})}{T}\log[Y_{i,t-T}] + w_{it,T}, \tag{3.3}$$

where $w_{it,T}$ represents the effect of the error terms w_t between dates t and T, i is the corresponding subscript for each region or country, and $a = x + (1-\exp^{-\beta T})\log(\hat{Y}^*)$. Absolute convergence arises when the term multiplying the initial income is negative, and implies that poor economies tend to grow more quickly than wealthy ones. One can estimate a regression with non-linear least squares (NLLS) to obtain the speed of convergence β directly.

3.3.3 Conditional Convergence

Conditional beta-convergence arises by allowing for heterogeneity across economies, particularly by dropping the assumption that all economies have the same parameters and the same steady state.[16] The main idea is that the further an economy is from its own steady-state value, the more quickly it grows:

$$\frac{\log[Y_{i,t}/Y_{i,t-T}]}{T} = a - \frac{(1-\exp^{-\beta T})}{T}\log[Y_{i,t-T}] + \gamma X_i + w_{it,T}, \tag{3.4}$$

where X_i is a set of variables that proxy for the steady-state level of income ($\hat{Y}_i^*$). Empirical studies show little evidence of unconditional convergence for large and heterogeneous samples of countries. Instead, they tend to find unconditional convergence in economies with similar structural characteristics (Barro and Sala-i-Martin, 1991) with speeds of convergence usually around 2 percent. However, there is no agreement on which variables to include as proxies for the steady state, and their selection depends mostly upon the researcher interest. An extensive review made by Durlauf et al. (2005) shows a list of about 145 different regressors used in convergence literature and points out that most of them have been found to be statistically significant. These regressors are classified by Durlauf et al. (2005) into 43 distinct growth theories or growth determinants, raising doubts about their usefulness.

[16]Under the assumption of different parameters, Equation 3.3 would provide biased estimates because the steady-state level of income $\hat{Y}_i^*$ would be correlated with the explanatory variable $\log[Y_{i,t-T}]$. To solve this problem, Barro and Sala-i-Martin (1992a) suggest incorporating into the regression a set of variables X_i as proxies for the steady-state level of income ($\hat{Y}_i^*$) and testing for conditional convergence.

3.3.4 Parameter Heterogeneity: Are There Different Steady States?

An alternative way to estimate conditional beta-convergence is to remove the assumption of parameter homogeneity, as suggested by Canova and Marcet (1995) and Maddala and Wu (2000), using time-series cross-sectional (TSCS) data.[17] Advocates of this approach argue that the Barro-type growth regressions create biases in the estimated coefficients by pooling data whenever there is heterogeneity in the parameters. Moreover, cross-sectional regressions lead to a waste of information, since they ignore unit-specific time variations in growth rates and prevent the estimation of a steady state for each region or country separately (e.g. Lee et al., 1997; Temple, 1999; Pritchett, 2000; Durlauf, 2001; Brock and Durlauf, 2001; Masanjala and Papageorgiou, 2004).[18]

Canova and Marcet (1995) propose a way to model heterogeneity and calculate steady states for each unit without proxying for the steady state of income with additional variables. The model allows calculation of the speed of adjustment for each unit to its own steady state. A weakness of the approach is the need for the time dimension t to be large; otherwise, estimates will have large standard errors and their small sample distribution may strongly deviate from the asymptotic one. Using cross-country data, they find an average speed of adjustment to be close to 11 percent, but reject the hypothesis of equal steady states for all cross-sectional units.[19] Using an iterative Bayesian approach with a similar cross-country data set, Maddala and Wu (2000) find average annual convergence rates of around 5 percent and further argue in favor of different steady states for each country.

The estimation relies upon transforming equation 3.2 in discrete time as follows:

$$\log(y_{i,T}) = \alpha + \rho_T \log(y_{i,0}) + \gamma X_i + u_i, \tag{3.5}$$

where $y_{i,t}$ is *relative* output per worker, which will be defined below, $\rho_T = \exp^{-\beta T}$, $t = 0, 1, 2, ..., T$, and the variables X_i are introduced to allow for shifts in the limit of the steady state means of y_i. The key to allow for parameter heterogeneity relies in dropping the assumptions that $\beta_i = \beta$ and $\alpha_i = \alpha\ \forall_i$. The first assumption is expressed by $\rho_i \neq \rho$; that is to

[17] For a description of time-series cross-sectional data, see, for example, Beck (2001) and Beck and Katz (2007).

[18] As indicated by Masanjala and Papageorgiou (2004), parameter heterogeneity in growth regressions has at least three interpretations: there are(i) multiple steady states, i.e., the parameters of a linear growth regression are not constant across countries (e.g. Durlauf, 1996), (ii) omitted growth determinants (e.g. Durlauf and Quah, 1999), and (iii) nonlinearities of the production function, i.e., the identical Cobb-Douglas aggregate production function may be unsuitable. After investigating the third interpretation, Masanjala and Papageorgiou (2004) conclude that using more general constant elasticity of substitution aggregate production functions does not explain away heterogeneity across countries, and they consequently suggest shifting attention to the other two interpretations.

[19] According to Shioji (1997) their convergence rates are high due to the type of Bayesian approach and the short period used (10 years).

say, the convergence rates among all economies are allowed to be different. After grouping $\alpha_i = \alpha + \gamma X_i$, the final estimation is

$$\log(y_{i,t}) = \alpha_i + \rho_i \log(y_{i,t-1}) + u_{i,t}. \tag{3.6}$$

Note that both Canova and Marcet (1995) and Maddala and Wu (2000) use relative per worker (capita) output $y_{i,t}$ for the estimation, defined as $Y_{i,t}$, i.e., per capita output of region i in period t, divided by the national average of output per capita in year t. A value higher (or lower) than 1 means that the region has a higher (or lower) per-capita output than the national average. Using $y_{i,t}$ instead of $Y_{i,t}$ has the advantage that the linear trend term disappears, as it is assumed that in steady state all $y_{i,t}$ should grow at the same rate of technological progress, although the levels may vary. It also corrects for problems of serial and residual cross-unit correlation and avoids specifying a process for growth, that is, whether it is trend or unit-root with drift (Maddala and Wu, 2000).

For each region, Equation 3.6 is an AR(1) process of $log(y_{i,t})$. If $|\rho| < 1$, the time series is stationary and given that $E(log(y_{i,t})) = E(log(y_{i,t-1}))$, the mean of $log(y_{i,t})$ converges in a mathematical sense to $\frac{\alpha_i}{1-\rho_i}$ as $t \to \infty$. If $|\hat{\rho}| < 1$, one could estimate the expected value as

$$\hat{E}(log(y_{i,t})) = \frac{\hat{\alpha}_i}{1-\hat{\rho}_i}, \tag{3.7}$$

where $\hat{\alpha}_i$ and $\hat{\rho}_i$ are obtained from regressions based on Equation 3.6.

According to Maddala and Wu (2000), the condition $|\rho| < 1$ ensures that region i converges towards its own steady state and is equivalent to the definition of beta-convergence in Barro and Sala-i-Martin (1992a). As long as $|\rho| < 1$, the speed of adjustment of each unit to its own steady state is given by $1 - \rho_i$.

Concerning the empirical estimation, and as discussed by Maddala and Wu (2000), equation 3.6 can be estimated by (i) pooling the data and assuming that $\forall_i\ \alpha_i = \alpha$ and $\rho_i = \rho$, (ii) running 25 separate regressions, one for each department, allowing for 25 α_i and ρ_i, or (iii) through shrinkage estimators that assume that α_i and ρ_i have two components, one fixed and one random. Additionally, one could estimate Equation 3.7, assuming that there is a fixed number of groups, allowing, for example, for three values of α and ρ, in other words, α_1, α_2, α_3 and ρ_1, and ρ_2 and ρ_3. The departments that belong to each group should be identified with the appropriate method. We will estimate equation 3.6 following all the alternatives presented.

3.3.5 Sigma-Convergence

An alternative to evaluating beta-convergence is to focus on whether there is a reduction over time in the dispersion of real per-capita income across entities, indicating a more equitable distribution of income. This is called sigma-convergence and arises when for $T > 0$

$$\sigma_{t+T} < \sigma_t, \tag{3.8}$$

where σ_t is the standard deviation of real per-capita income in period t (Sala-i-Martin, 1996). The existence of beta-convergence tends to generate sigma-convergence. However, there are cases in which shocks affecting each entity differently lead to the existence of beta-convergence but the lack of sigma-convergence. The example given by Sala-i-Martin (1996) in this regard is clear. Assume two economies, one rich and one poor. The initial poor economy grows so quickly that in the final period its distance from the rich one is the same as before, except that now the poor economy is the wealthier. In such a case, the resulting standard deviation would be the same in the initial and final period. One would observe beta-convergence, given that the poor economy is growing more quickly than the rich one, but no sigma-convergence. Hence, sigma-convergence is an indicator of dispersion of the overall entities, but does not tell much about mobility of each one. Beta-convergence is thus a necessary, but not sufficient, condition for observing sigma-convergence.

3.4 Distributional Approach: Quah's Critique

One important critique to the standard regression approach was raised by Danny Quah (Quah, 1993a,b, 1996, 1997), who argues that neither beta nor sigma-convergence can deliver useful answers to the question of whether poor countries or regions are catching up to wealthier ones. Quah argues that the classical approach does not give any information about mobility, stratification, or polarization, and suggests that the typically obtained 2-percent speed of convergence is a statistical artifact that arises in moderate size samples for reasons other than convergence (Durlauf et al., 2005). In his analysis using cross-country data, Quah finds some evidence of convergence clubs, but also evidence of poor countries becoming progressively poorer and wealthy countries, even wealthier.

Quah initially suggested working with a sequence of income distributions and, after discretizing the space of income values, counting the observed transitions into and out of the distinct cell values to construct a transition probability matrix (Quah, 1993a,b). Later, Quah (1997) argued that the discretization could distort dynamics if the underlying observations are indeed continuous variables. He proposed thinking of the distinct cells as tending towards infinity and towards the continuum, with the transition probability matrix tending to a matrix with a continuum of rows and columns, that is, becoming a stochastic kernel.[20]

The methodology is based upon tracking the evolution over time of the entire cross-sectional distributions across regions through the estimation of kernel densities for "relative" variables, which means that the variables of interest are expressed as being relative to the national average, allowing abstraction from changes in the mean when one evaluates how the distribution changes.

Before we define how we proceed to test for convergence using the distributional approach, we briefly present some concepts needed for our estimation.[21]

For the distributional approach, all variables are expressed relative to the Colombian value. Additionally, we take the logarithm of the relative variable, as it facilitates the comparison to the national level. Expressed in logs, a relative value equal to 0 indicates that the department has the same value as the country, while a value that is, for example, equal to -0.05 means that the value of the department is 5 percent lower than the national value.

A univariate kernel density estimate may be regarded as a generalization of a histogram:

$$\hat{f}_h(q) = \frac{1}{mh}\sum_{i=1}^{n} \kappa\left(\frac{q-Q_i}{h}\right), \tag{3.9}$$

where κ is a kernel, m is the number of observations, and $h > 0$ is the bandwidth, also called the smoothing parameter.[22] In the context of growth convergence, we are interested in checking whether we find unimodality or multimodality in the estimated densities of the logarithm of relative income, and in what way the estimated densities change between the starting and the final period.

Bivariate kernel density estimation requires two-dimensional data and a two-dimensional kernel. Here, $Q = (Q_1, Q_2)^T$ and the kernel K maps $\mathbb{R}^2$ into $\mathbb{R}_+$. The estimate is

$$\hat{f}_H(q) = \frac{1}{m}\sum_{i=1}^{m} \frac{1}{det(H)} K\{H^{-1}(q-Q_i)\}, \tag{3.10}$$

where K is a bivariate kernel function, m is the number of observations, and H is a symmetrical bandwidth matrix.

For the analysis of convergence, we estimate the bivariate kernel density for the relative variable in two periods and check whether or not a large portion of the probability mass

[20] For a technical derivation of a stochastic kernel see Quah (1997, section 4).

[21] A review of the statistical principles of univariate and multivariate kernel density estimations can be found, for example, in Härdle et al. (2004).

[22] Kernel refers to any smooth function satisfying the conditions $\kappa(q) > 0$, $\int \kappa(q)dq = 1$, $\int q\kappa(q)dq = 0$, and $\sigma_\kappa^2 \equiv \int q^2\kappa(q)dq > 0$ (Wasserman, 2006).

remains clustered around the 45-degree diagonal, which would indicate persistence in the distribution. We present the 3D representation of the estimated bivariate density and a contour plot showing the highest density regions.

3.5 Empirical Estimation and Results

We empirically test for convergence in PDB and IDBH, using both the classical and distributional approaches to convergence, as we are interested in checking if, in the Colombian case, there is a contradiction of the results obtained when employing both approaches, as suggested by the existing literature on Colombia. We do not use population weights in our calculations, as we are interested in investigating whether or not departments that were lagging behind have been able to catch up, and consider this to be a pertinent question in the Colombian case where departments are important political entities, with elected local governments and separate department assemblies.

Our empirical analysis begins with the classical approach, testing for sigma and beta-convergence. In the case of beta-convergence, we test absolute and conditional convergence. Conditional convergence is tested with cross-sectional regressions with control variables and also with AR(1) regressions using time-series cross-sectional data for relative income, starting with a pooled model that assumes homogeneity in the parameters and then allows for heterogeneity.

We then follow the distributional approach and compute univariate and bivariate kernel density estimators for relative income in 1975 and 2000.

3.5.1 Sigma-Convergence

Results of sigma convergence are presented in Figure 3.7. As may be observed, there exists evidence of sigma-convergence in IDBH but not in PDB. From 1975 to 1984, the standard deviation of the log of both variables remains close to 0.40. From 1985 onwards, IDBH decreases and has a value close to 0.32 in 2000. On the contrary, PDB remains around 0.40. Thus, the distribution of IDBH has become more equitable, while the distribution of PDB has not.

3.5.2 Absolute Beta-Convergence

Figure 3.8 shows a weak inverse relationship between the growth rate of per-capita PDB between 1975 and 2000 and its value in 1975. Cross-sectional regression results based upon Equation 3.3 and using NLLS are shown in Table 3.2. We use HC3 robust standard errors as proposed by Davidson and MacKinnon (1993) to account for possible heteroscedasticity, considering that the number of observations is small (Long and Ervin, 2000). The estimated speed of convergence is 0.7 percent, but it is not significantly different from 0 at the 5 percent level. The adjusted R-squared of the regression is extremely low (0.01) suggesting that this model does not explain departmental PDB growth rates. These results do not change if one excludes Chocó, Nuevos, and Guajira, which have a large influence on results, as suggested by Cook's distance computed after the first regression (Figure 3.9).

In the case of IDBH, Figure 3.10 shows a stronger negative relationship between the growth rate of per-capita IDBH between 1975 and 2000 and its value in 1975. This is confirmed with the regression presented in Table 3.3, where the estimated speed of convergence is 1.2 percent and statistically significant. The adjusted R-squared is 0.35. Excluding Guajira, as suggested by Cook's distance, and then rerunning the regression yields similar results.

Hence, we find evidence of absolute beta-convergence using IDBH, but not using PDB.

3.5.3 Conditional Beta-Convergence Using Control Variables

As explained in Subsection 3.3.3, one may drop the assumption that all economies have the same parameters, and hence the same steady state, and try to proxy for the steady-state level of income with a set of variables X_i, running regressions based upon Equation 3.4.

There is no agreement as to which variables to include as proxies for the steady state with cross-sectional data (Durlauf et al., 2005). We use variables that are based upon theoretical arguments and our choice is limited by data availability at the departmental level. We use the logarithm of population growth and a variable based upon saving rates.[23] Additionally, we use three variables proxying for human capital: log of life expectancy in 1975, log of literacy in 1973, and log of net enrolment rate in 1985. Several specifications for the average growth rate of per-capita PDB are shown in Table 3.4 and for per-capita IDBH in Table 3.5.[24]

Results for PDB show that the speed of convergence remains statistically insignificant in all the specifications, including the variables proxying for the steady state, as was the case with absolute convergence. We find no evidence of conditional convergence using PDB data.

In the case of IDBH, where we find evidence of absolute convergence, once we include variables X_i proxying for the steady-state level of income, the speed of convergence turns insignificant. We find no evidence of conditional convergence using IDBH data.

3.5.4 Beta-Convergence Using Time-Series Cross-Sectional Data

Recall that with TSCS data, the regression is based upon Equation 3.6, defined in subsection 3.3.4 as

$$\log(y_{i,t}) = \alpha_i + \rho_i \log(y_{i,t-1}) + u_{i,t},$$

[23]As the saving rates that are available from CEGA (2006b,a) include values that are negative, we add a constant to all values, so that the transformed data are all positive and we can compute the logs.

[24]The number of departments included depends upon data availability

which uses the measure of relative income $y_{i,t}$, that is, income of each department expressed as the ratio to the national average. One may estimate the equation in several ways. First, we begin by pooling the data, assuming homogeneity in the parameters. Second, we use linear mixed models where the parameters are assumed to have a fixed component, common to all departments, and a random part. Third, we estimate 25 separate ordinary least squares(OLS) regressions for each entity. Finally, we assume that there are several groups of departments which share the same α and ρ, and explore this issue with finite mixture models.

In all cases, the key issue is whether the estimated value for ρ is lower than 1, which would suggest that there is economic convergence.

Pooled Data and OLS

The assumption of $\alpha_i = \alpha$ and $\rho_i = \rho \ \forall_i$ in Equation 3.6 is equivalent to assuming that there is a common steady state to all departments. Hence, the results are comparable to those obtained using cross-sectional data when we tested for absolute beta-convergence in subsection 3.5.2.

Tables 3.6 and 3.7 present the results for PDB and IDBH using TSCS pooled data and estimating with OLS. In both cases, the estimated ρ is less than 1 (0.989 for PDB and 0.986 for IDBH). However, it must be noted that while the value 1 is not included in the 95 percent confidence interval of ρ for IDBH, it is included for PDB, confirming the evidence of absolute convergence in IDBH, but not in PDB.

For IDBH the implied estimated speed of convergence β, computed with the estimated ρ value, is 1.4 percent, slightly higher than the one observed using cross-sectional data in Section 3.5.2.

Mixed Models

We follow here a frequentist approach for the estimation of Equation 3.6. Following Maddala et al. (1997) and using matrix notation, we define

$$Z_i = \begin{pmatrix} \log(y_{i,1}) \\ \vdots \\ \log(y_{i,T}) \end{pmatrix}, \quad X_i = \begin{pmatrix} 1 & \log(y_{i,0}) \\ \vdots & \vdots \\ 1 & \log(y_{i,T-1}) \end{pmatrix}, \quad b_i = \begin{pmatrix} \alpha_i \\ \rho_i \end{pmatrix}, \text{ and } \ U_i = \begin{pmatrix} u_{i,1} \\ \vdots \\ u_{i,T} \end{pmatrix},$$

with $i = 1, ..., N$, where N is the number of regions in the data.

We consider the autoregressive regression model

$$Z_i = X_i b_i + U_i, \qquad i = 1, ..., N, \tag{3.11}$$

with the assumptions $U_i \sim N(0, \sigma_i^2 I)$, and $b_i \sim N(\mu, \Sigma)$, where I is the identity matrix and Σ is a nonzero covariance matrix. [25] We further assume that the U_i are independent across the N equations, and that b_i and U_i are independent for different regions.

[25]The results of the estimation assume no special structure of the matrix Σ.

We work with a linear mixed model (McCulloch and Searle, 2001). If we write b_i as $b_i = \mu + \eta_i$, with $\eta_i \sim N(0, \Sigma)$, we can rewrite $Z_i, (i = 1, ..., N)$ as

$$\begin{aligned} Z_i &= X_i(\mu + \eta_i) + U_i \\ &= X_i\mu + X_i\eta_i + U_i \qquad (3.12) \\ &= X_i\mu + w_i, \qquad (3.13) \end{aligned}$$

with $w_i \sim N(0, \Omega_i)$, Ω_i being the variance covariance matrix defined as

$$\Omega_i = X_i \Sigma X_i^{'} + \sigma_i^2 I. \qquad (3.14)$$

In Equation 3.12, the vector μ represents the fixed effects and η_i represent the random effects. In linear mixed models, fixed effects are used for modeling the mean of the response variable and the random effects are used to model the variance-covariance structure of it (McCulloch and Searle, 2001). The parameters in our linear mixed model are then μ, Σ, and σ_i^2. The last two parameters are in fact variance components, as presented in Equation 3.14.

One can obtain an estimator for μ and best-linear unbiased predictors for the random effects η_i with maximum likelihood or restricted maximum likelihood (REML). [26] Here, we prefer REML for three reasons: (i) the estimators are based upon taking into account the degrees of freedom for the fixed effects in the model, (ii) because of its unbiasedness in the case of balanced panels, and (iii) as REML estimators seem to be less sensitive to outliers in the data.[27] With the obtained values for μ and η_i, one could compute the estimated values for the N differently from α_i and ρ_i.

We are interested in the estimation of the fixed effects. As was mentioned before, the literature suggests that in some cases, the estimated β can be substantially higher than the one obtained by assuming there are no random effects. We also compare the results with those assuming homogeneity in the parameters using likelihood ratio tests and the Akaike information criterion (AIC) in order to investigate if a more flexible model allowing for heterogeneity in the parameters should be preferred.

Results for PDB are presented in Table 3.8. The estimated coefficients for the fixed effects are similar to the coefficients estimated when assuming homogeneity in the parameters (Table 3.6). In the case of ρ, the estimated value for the linear mixed model is 0.984, close to the value 0.989 obtained with OLS and assuming no random effects. It must be noted that the standard error of the fixed effect of ρ is higher than for the coefficient estimated in the model

[26] For the algorithms used for obtaining maximum likelihood and restricted maximum likelihood estimates in the case of a linear mixed model, see Pinheiro and Bates (2000).

[27] For a review of linear mixed models and a discussion of the estimation with maximum likelihood and REML, see McCulloch and Searle (2001).

assuming homogeneity in the parameters. The estimated standard deviations of both random effects are quite low, especially the one for α, with a value close to 0, suggesting there is no evidence of different steady states. The value for the Akaike information criterion for the linear mixed model is larger than for the simpler model, assuming parameter homogeneity, and hence the simpler model is preferred. This is also corroborated by a likehood ratio test.

Table 3.9 shows the results for IDBH. Once again, the coefficients for the fixed effects are close to the ones obtained with the model in the previous section, in which we assumed parameter homogeneity (Table 3.7), with ρ equal to 0.986 in both cases. The estimated standard deviations of both random effects are low, in particular the one for α, which is close to 0, giving no support for the existence of different steady states. The AIC suggest that the simpler model is better, which is confirmed with a likelihood ratio test.[28]

Separate Regressions for Each Department

We also treat all departments as separate entities and run an AR(1) regression for each one. These separate regressions shed light upon the effect of past values on current values, but due to the low amount of observations for each department (25 years), estimations are not reliable. In Table 3.12, we present results for PDB. The slope coefficient ρ is lower than 1 for all departments but has large standard errors and is not significant at the 5-percent level for Cauca and Boyacá.[29] The resulting speeds of convergence are implausibly high with values ranging from 10 to 60 percent in the case of PDB, a result influenced by the fact that the period only covers 25 years. Results for IDBH are similar (Table 3.13).

The graphical analysis of each time series is more informative. In Figure 3.12, we plot the individual time series for relative PDB in logs for all departments. We observe that in almost all departments, the values change little over time and the series seem stationary. They remain either above or below the national average with the exception of Guajira and Nuevos. The time series do not become closer to the national value over time, except for Guajira, indicating a lack of economic convergence among departments.

Results for IDBH (Table 3.12) show that most of the time series seem stationary. Interestingly, the wealthiest department, Bogotá, moves slightly closer to the national average, as does as the poorest department, Chocó. Guajira, although becoming closer to the national average, still remains below it.

---

[28]Although it is possible to calculate the implied speed of convergence for each department, the interpretation is difficult. For illustrative purposes, we present them in Tables 3.10 for PDB and 3.11 for IDBH. The associated speeds of convergence have a larger variability for PDB than for IDBH. The average speed of convergence is 1.6 percent for PDB and 1.4 percent for IDBH).

[29]The expected value can be calculated when $|\rho| < 1$ and is relevant if $t \to \infty$, so that $E(log(y_{i,t}))$ approaches $\frac{\alpha_i}{1-\rho_i}$.

Mixture Models

In the previous sections, we estimated a model assuming that α and ρ are the same for all departments. We then allowed these parameters to be different for each department, in the context of a linear mixed model, where the parameters are assumed to have a fixed component, common to all departments, and a random part. Then, we estimated 25 separate AR(1) regressions, one for each department.

Another possibility is that there are several groups of departments which share the same α and ρ. We explore this possibility with a finite mixture model, as described in Leisch (2004) and Grün and Leisch (2008). These types of models can be applied, assuming that observations originate from various groups, where the group affiliations are unknown. Finite mixture models with a fixed number of components are estimated with the expectation-maximization (EM) algorithm within a maximum likelihood framework.

We assume three groups and fit the model with the statistical software R (R Development Core Team, 2008) and the package *flexmix* (Leisch and Grün, 2008). Results for PDB and IDBH are presented in Tables 3.14 and 3.15. We show estimated α and ρ for each group of departments, as well as the departments composing each group.

Results for PDB (Table 3.14) show that Group 1 includes many of the poorest departments (e.g., Chocó, Sucre, Nariño, and Córdoba), Group 2 is composed of Nuevos Departamentos and La Guajira, and Group 3 includes the richest departments (e.g., Bogotá, Valle, and Antioquia).[30] Estimated values for α and ρ are similar for Groups 1 and 3, with α being negative and close to 0 and ρ being close to 0.99, a result that is similar to the estimated value obtained in subsection 3.5.4, assuming homogeneity in the parameters. The implied speed of convergence for these two groups is close to 1 percent. If one believes in the validity of the estimated expected value of the time series, one would expect that departments belonging to Group 1 would remain well below the national average over time, while those from Group 3 would remain below, as well, but would be closer to it. As was discussed before, Nuevos Departamentos and La Guajira experienced high growth rates between 1975 and 2000, associated with the production of oil and coal. The model captures this, suggesting that both departments are far from their steady states, showing a large implied speed of convergence (10 percent), and predicting that both would remain above the national average.

Concerning IDBH (Table 3.15), the grouping of departments is similar as above, with Group 1 including many of the poorest departments and Group 3 including the richest ones. Group 2 now includes Nuevos Departamentos, La Guajira, and Sucre. Groups 1 and 3 have

[30] Mixture models are only identifiable up to a permutation of the component labels (Leisch, 2004). The names, Group 1, Group 2, etc., have no special meaning here, and the order of the groups is irrelevant.

values for the estimated α that are quite similar to one another, and close to 0. Values for the estimated ρ are also similar with 0.98 for Group 1 and 0.99 for Group 3, both being close to the estimated value obtained, assuming homogeneity in the parameters (Subsection 3.5.4). Nuevos Departamentos, La Guajira, and Sucre have values for α and ρ that are different than those from the other two groups (-0.01 for α and 0.96 for ρ). Once again, the model suggests that these departments are far from the steady state, with an implied speed of convergence of 4 percent, which speed is greater than that for Groups 1 (2 percent) and 3 (1 percent). Once again, with an analyzed time period of only 25 years, it is questionable whether one should rely upon the estimated expected values.

3.5.5 Kernel Density Estimators

All the results for kernel density estimations were computed with the statistical software R (R Development Core Team, 2008) and the package *ks*.[31] For both univariate and bivariate kernel density estimations, we use Gaussian kernels and smoothed cross validation bandwidth selectors[32] (Jones et al., 1991; Duong and Hazelton, 2005). In the bivariate case, the smoothed cross validation is unconstrained, meaning that we do not impose that the (nonsingular) bandwidth matrix H has to be diagonal in Equation 3.10. Hence, we are able to handle correlation between components, as we allow kernels to have an arbitrary orientation (Wand and Jones, 1995). As we are especially interested in checking whether a large portion of the probability mass remains clustered around the 45-degree diagonal, this flexibility is relevant for us. If we were to impose a diagonal matrix H, only kernels which are oriented to the coordinate axes would be allowed.

Univariate kernel density estimations of the logarithm of relative departmental PDB for the years 1975 and 2000 are shown in Figure 3.14. Both densities seem unimodal and are very similar. Thus, according to this figure, there were almost no changes in the distribution. Bivariate kernel-density estimators are presented in Figures 3.15 and 3.16. Both figures make clear that most of the mass is concentrated along the 45-degree diagonal and hence support persistence in the distribution. Departments with a relative GDP that was above (or below) average in the year 1975 tend to remain above (or below) average in 2000. Two interesting cases are La Guajira and Nuevos Departamentos, as they show some mobility. Nuevos Departamentos was close to the national average in 1975 and is clearly above the average in 2000, while La Guajira was clearly below the national average in 1975 and is quite close to it in 2000.

---

[31] *ks* is currently the most comprehensive kernel density estimation package in R (Duong, 2008). All the estimations were done with the function *kde*.

[32] We have also tried direct plug-in methods as suggested by Sheather and Jones (1991) and obtained results that are not very dissimilar.

Turning to results using the logarithm of relative departmental IDBH, Figure 3.17 presents the univariate kernel estimators for the years 1975 and 2000, showing a slight shift of the distribution to the right in 2000. The distribution narrowed between 1975 and 2000 and the two modes observed in 1975 in the left and right tails of the distribution almost disappeared in 2000. Bivariate kernel density estimators in Figures 3.18 and 3.19 show some mobility, as well. In the contour plot (Figure 3.19), the mass of the distribution rotates slightly clockwise, suggesting mild convergence in the distribution.

3.6 Conclusions

Returning to the questions raised at the beginning of the study, we do not find absolute or conditional convergence in PDB using the regression approach. The distributional approach shows persistence in the distribution, i.e., relative to the average, each department remains in the position where it was located in 1975. Results of both methods point in the same direction-there is no convergence but persistence in PDB does exist.

Analysis of IDBH shows absolute convergence using the regression approach. After testing different models allowing for parameter heterogeneity, we found that there is no evidence of the existence of different steady states. The pooled model using TSCS provides our preferred estimators. Bivariate kernel density estimators show some improvements in the distribution. However, the changes are small and consistent with the low speed of convergence of around 1.4 percent.

Different factors explain our results. Differences in geography, infrastructure, and population density among departments are relevant factors to explain lack of convergence in PDB, as are differences in production structures and value added by department. Excepting for the mining departments, the different production structures remained almost unchanged between 1975 and 2000 (Table 3.16).[33]

However, mineral exploitation in Colombia is relatively recent, going back only to the mid eighties, and this fact explains why the group of Nuevos and the department of La Guajira are the only initial poor departments that grew more quickly than the wealthier departments, according to PDB data. Previous literature had already pointed to the fact that once the mining departments are excluded, any hint of convergence disappears (Birchenall and Murcia, 1997) and that departments with a high share of agricultural production had the lowest growth rates (Bonet, 1999). Three departments concentrated at least 50 percent of PDB in both evaluated years: Antioquia, Bogotá, and Valle del Cauca. These three departments combined produced 65 percent of the manufacturing output in 1975 and 60 percent in 2000. The stability of

[33]Nuevos Departamentos increased their participation in the mining sector from 11 percent in 1975 to 55 percent in 2000.

the shares in other sectors is also remarkable, indicating departmental concentration and low mobility of production factors across the country.

At least two of the assumptions of the Solow model, which is the usual theoretical framework for studying convergence, seem problematic for application to the Colombian case. First, the neoclassical model assumes mobility of factors, which is in this case constrained by geographic, climatic, and infrastructural issues, as well as by the internal conflict issue. For instance, several productive sectors periodically suffer from attacks by violent groups, not only on physical capital, but also human capital through kidnapping and extortion. Second, the assumption of constant returns to scale is an oversimplification that does not hold for all sectors in the economy. As has been argued by World Bank (2009), while returns to scale in agriculture tend to be constant, those in manufacturing and services are increasing.

The slow convergence observed in IDBH can be explained by recent redistributive policies, particularly higher public spending in social sectors and infrastructure. Literature dealing with the direct link between convergence and public spending is scarce, but suggests that it affected the relative position of some departments, although not the distribution as a whole (Ardila Rueda, 2004), and that efficiency of public spending has been decreasing over time, mainly due to political interests and corruption.

Increased social spending has also benefited from mining sector revenues which are distributed across all departments through the fiscal system. Oil revenues are divided between direct and indirect revenues and correspond to about eight to 25 percent of total extracted crude oil income. Direct revenues are those given to producing departments, municipalities, and ports of exports basically to finance investment in social sectors, and account for about 76 percent of oil revenues. Indirect revenues are those distributed among non-producing departments (Hernández, 2004). IDBH of mining departments is still very low and did not exhibit the high growth rates observed in PDB.[34] One reason for this is that fiscal decentralization began in the late eighties and the reforms are thus still too recent to be fully evaluated. A second reason is that financial resources from mining sectors are not efficiently spent because of corruption and are not sufficient to compensate for the low starting point in income of these departments.

Recall that in 1975, La Guajira was the second poorest department in Colombia and that a large part of its population is indigenous and poorly linked to the departmental economy. Previous research suggests that even if revenues of coal exports in La Guajira were distributed

[34]Producing departments are obliged to spend at least 50 percent of the received mining revenues on social investment until having achieved certain minimum thresholds for infant mortality, health care, education, water, and sanitation. Indirect revenues are distributed according to projects presented through territorial entities (Law 141 of 1994).

efficiently and without any corruption-related loss (corruption levels seem to be particularly high in mining departments), IDB of that department would still be about 60 percent of national IDB in 2000(Meisel, 2007a).

Although overall public spending has increased, the transfer system bears some disadvantages for poor departments. Evidence shows that after totaling all public revenue (not only that directed to social sectors), there is no fiscal equalization in Colombia and the system is regressive; wealthy municipalities have the highest shares of public funds.

Two other issues have to be taken into consideration for interpreting the results of both PDB and IDBH. One is that in 2000, our last year of analysis, the country was experiencing a large economic crisis which affected public and private finances. Transfers from the central government were thus also affected by the crisis. A second issue is related to the domestic conflict. Between 1998 and 2002, violence escalated dramatically when the groups involved in the war were fighting one other for control of strategic areas. Sánchez and Palau (2006), who deal directly with this last issue, argue that decentralization policies, political and fiscal, affected the interests of armed groups and even strengthened them through the sharp increase in local resources. The higher political autonomy at the local level increased the ability of armed groups to intimidate politicians and to extract rents from public funds. Guerrillas relocated in strategic zones with greater levels of prosperity, the facility for processing illicit drugs, and an intimidated local population (Sánchez and Palau, 2006).

One of the policy implications of this study is the necessity of monitoring the efficiency of social spending and enforcing decentralization policies so that a faster convergence in IDBH can be achieved. Concerning convergence in PDB, reallocation of productive sector resources is not easy to achieve and could yield to efficiency losses, but the state can, for example, encourage the accumulation of human capital and improve infrastructure in lagging departments, which would help attract investments in the long run. Additionally, it is crucial to find a way out of the internal conflict to foster factor mobility in Colombia, particularly in those areas without significant state presence. We consider it vital to have an explicit regional policy in Colombia to foster growth in departments lagging behind national averages, after conducting case studies to assess which policies could be most effective in each case.

Finally, for monitoring convergence across departments in the future, it is essential to have consistent time series constructed under a single methodology. Unfortunately, the work done by CEGA for the period 1975 to 2000 did not continued for the years after 2000. Such a project is of high policy relevance for the country.

Summary of Results

	Per capita income measure used	
	PDB	IDBH
Classical Approach: Convergence?		
Sigma	No	Yes
Absolute Beta	No	Yes
Conditional Beta Cross Sections	No	No
Conditional Beta Pooled TSCS assuming homogeneity of parameters	No	Yes
Distributional Approach		
Univariate Kernel Estimators	Distribution Unchanged	Dispersion Decreases
Bivariate Kernel Estimators	Persistence in the Distribution	Suggests slow Convergence

Note: Results for conditional beta convergence with TSCS data and for the distributional approach based on relative values, i.e., ratios to the national level

3.7 Tables

Table 3.1: Colombia. Gross Domestic Product (Constant Million Pesos of 1994), Per Capita GDP and Population. 1980-2006.

Year	GDP (million)	Per capita GDP	Growth rate	Population	Growth rate
1980	40822304	1503335		27154504	
1981	41846404	1503069	-0.02	27840636	2.53
1982	42160220	1476873	-1.74	28546950	2.54
1983	42820420	1462737	-0.96	29274176	2.55
1984	44217404	1472781	0.69	30023068	2.56
1985	45475604	1476748	0.27	30794424	2.57
1986	48189708	1533078	3.81	31433316	2.07
1987	50775504	1582200	3.20	32091720	2.09
1988	52808848	1611804	1.87	32763808	2.09
1989	54544940	1630958	1.19	33443488	2.07
1990	56873928	1666658	2.19	34124536	2.04
1991	58222936	1671462	0.29	34833548	2.08
1992	60757528	1710026	2.31	35530176	2.00
1993	64226880	1773819	3.73	36208244	1.91
1994	67532864	1832015	3.28	36862624	1.81
1995	71046216	1895088	3.44	37489664	1.70
1996	72506824	1904234	0.48	38076640	1.57
1997	74994024	1940536	1.91	38646044	1.50
1998	75421328	1923949	-0.85	39201320	1.44
1999	72250600	1817821	-5.52	39745712	1.39
2000	74363832	1846071	1.55	40282216	1.35
2001	75458112	1849177	0.17	40806312	1.30
2002	76917224	1861165	0.65	41327460	1.28
2003	79884488	1908947	2.57	41847420	1.26
2004	83772432	1977279	3.58	42367528	1.24
2005	87727928	2045484	3.45	42888592	1.23
2006	93881688	2162904	5.74	43405388	1.20

Source: Own calculations based on National Accounts and Census 2005, DANE

Table 3.2: Beta Convergence Using Cross-sections and Non Linear Least Squares. Dependent Variable: Average Growth Rate of pc PDB 1975-2000.

Variable	Coefficient	Robust HC3 Std. Err.	95% conf. interval	
Intercept	0.1055481	0.1258539	-0.1548005	0.3658967
β	0.0067474	0.0107561	-0.0155033	0.028998
β (%)	0.67			
Number of observations	25			
Adj.R-squared	0.0112			

Source: Own calculations based on data from CEGA. Constant prices of 1994.
Source: HC3 standard errors calculated according to Davidson and MacKinnon (1993).

Table 3.3: Beta Convergence Using Cross-sections and Non Linear Least Squares. Dependent Variable: Average Growth Rate of pc IDBH 1975-2000.

Variable	Coefficient	Robust HC3 Std. Err.	95% conf. interval	
Intercept	0.1533007	0.0392428	0.0721207	0.2344807
β	0.0119014	0.0039056	0.003822	0.0199809
β (%)	1.19			
Number of observations	25			
Adj.R-squared	0.3514			

Source: Own calculations based on data from CEGA. Constant prices of 1994.
Source: HC3 standard errors calculated according to Davidson and MacKinnon (1993).

Table 3.4: NLLS Regressions. Dependent Variable Average Growth Rate of pc PDB. 1975-2000.

Regressors	(1) b/se	(2) b/se	(3) b/se	(4) b/se	(5) b/se
constant	0.1157	0.1534	0.3533	0.2753	0.2271
	(0.1306)	(0.4804)	(0.3071)	(0.2533)	(0.3062)
speed of convergence β	0.0076	0.0401	0.0186	0.0226	0.0375
	(0.0114)	(0.0809)	(0.0250)	(0.0278)	(0.0622)
log (life expectancy 1975)		0.0402	-0.0092		
		(0.1344)	(0.0785)		
log (literacy 1973)		0.0355		0.015	
		(0.0645)		(0.0367)	
log (transformed saving rate)		0.0017	0.0047	0.0036	0.0043
		(0.0059)	(0.0064)	(0.0086)	(0.0128)
log (population growth + 0.05)		0.0378	0.032	0.0293	-0.0009
		(0.0443)	(0.0373)	(0.0371)	(0.0313)
log (net enrollment rate 1985)					0.0342
					(0.0414)
Number of observations	24	24	24	25	24
R-square	0.06	0.31	0.28	0.24	0.31
Adjusted R-square	0.02	0.12	0.13	0.09	0.16

* $p < 0.05$, ** $p < 0.01$, *** $p < 0.001$

Note: HC3 robust standard errors (Davidson and MacKinnon, 1993) in brackets.

Table 3.5: NLLS Regressions. Dependent Variable Average Growth Rate of pc IDBH. 1975-2000.

Regressors	(1) b/se	(2) b/se	(3) b/se	(4) b/se	(5) b/se
constant	0.1574***	0.1272	0.335	0.1400	0.1233
	(0.0402)	(0.2917)	(0.1817)	(0.0962)	(0.1038)
speed of convergence β	0.0123**	0.0282	0.0135	0.0254	0.0262
	(0.0040)	(0.0280)	(0.0110)	(0.0126)	(0.0155)
log (life expectancy 1975)		0.0063	-0.0443		
		(0.0777)	(0.0485)		
log (literacy 1973)		0.031		0.0279	
		(0.0309)		(0.0161)	
log (transformed saving rate)		0.0007	0.0036	0.0009	0.0019
		(0.0033)	(0.0046)	(0.0021)	(0.0055)
log (population growth + 0.05)		-0.001	-0.0079	-0.0037	-0.0227
		(0.0224)	(0.0181)	(0.0183)	(0.0127)
log (net enrollment rate 1985)					0.0241
					(0.0171)
Number of observations	24	24	24	25	24
R-square	0.40	0.58	0.53	0.56	0.64
Adjusted R-square	0.37	0.47	0.43	0.48	0.56

* $p < 0.05$, ** $p < 0.01$, *** $p < 0.001$

Note: HC3 robust standard errors (Davidson and MacKinnon, 1993) in brackets.

Table 3.6: OLS Linear Regression. TSCS Data. Dependent Variable $log(y_{i,t})$. Relative Per capita PDB. 1975-2000.

Variable	**Coefficient**	**Std. Err.**	**95% conf. interval**	
Intercept	-0.0022949	0.0032097	-0.008598	0.0040083
$log(y_{i.t-1})$	0.9890855	0.0069185	0.975499	1.002672
Implied β	1.09%			
Number of observations	625			
R-squared	0.9730			
AIC	-1632			

Source: Own calculations based on data from CEGA. Constant prices of 1994.

Table 3.7: OLS Linear Regression. TSCS Data. Dependent Variable $log(y_{i,t})$. Relative Per Capita IDBH. 1975-2000.

Variable	**Coefficient**	**Std. Err.**	**95% conf. interval**	
Intercept	-0.0013856	0.0017381	-0.0047989	.0020276
$log(y_{i.t-1})$	0.9861798	0.0046479	0.9770525	0.9953072
Implied β	1.38%			
Number of observations	625			
R-squared	0.9867			
AIC	-2183			

Source: Own calculations based on data from CEGA. Constant prices of 1994.

Table 3.8: Linear Mixed Model (REML). TSCS Data. Dependent Variable: $log(y_{i,t})$. Relative Per Capita PDB. 1975-2000.

Fixed effects		
Variable	**Coefficient**	**Std. Err.**
Intercept	-0.002679	0.003366
$log(y_{i,t-1})$	0.983587	0.008332
Random effects		
Standard deviation	**Estimate**	
Intercept	6.0571e-09	
$log(y_{i,t-1})$	0.016325	
Number of observations	625	
Number of groups	25	
AIC	-1606	

Source: Own calculations based on data from CEGA. Constant prices of 1994.

Table 3.9: Linear mixed model (REML). TSCS Data. Dependent Variable: $log(y_{i.t})$. Relative Per Capita IDBH. 1975-2000.

Fixed effects		
Variable	**Coefficient**	**Std. Err.**
Intercept	-0.001425	0.002192
$log(y_{i,t-1})$	0.985925	0.004710
Random effects		
Standard deviation	**Estimate**	
sd(Intercept)	0.0000000	
$log(y_{i,t-1})$	0.0026213	
Number of observations	625	
Number of groups	25	
AIC	-2155	

Source: Own calculations based on data from CEGA. Constant prices of 1994.

Table 3.10: Implied Convergence Rates Using TSCS Data and Linear Mixed Models (REML). Per capita PDB. 1975-2000

Department	Intercept α	Slope ρ	Implied β (%)	Expected Value
Nuevos Departamentos	-0.003	0.976	2.4	-0.111
Antioquia	-0.003	0.984	1.6	-0.168
Atlántico	-0.003	0.983	1.7	-0.156
Bogotá D. C.	-0.003	0.986	1.4	-0.197
Bolívar	-0.003	0.982	1.8	-0.149
Boyacá	-0.003	0.981	1.9	-0.140
Caldas	-0.003	0.981	1.9	-0.137
Caquetá	-0.003	0.990	1.0	-0.265
Cauca	-0.003	0.986	1.4	-0.193
Cesar	-0.003	0.986	1.4	-0.187
Córdoba	-0.003	0.989	1.1	-0.242
Cundinamarca	-0.003	0.983	1.7	-0.161
Chocó	-0.003	0.994	0.6	-0.483
Huila	-0.003	0.983	1.7	-0.162
La Guajira	-0.003	0.957	4.3	-0.063
Magdalena	-0.003	0.986	1.4	-0.194
Meta	-0.003	0.981	1.9	-0.143
Nariño	-0.003	0.988	1.2	-0.220
Norte Santander	-0.003	0.986	1.4	-0.192
Quindío	-0.003	0.977	2.3	-0.119
Risaralda	-0.003	0.982	1.8	-0.148
Santander	-0.003	0.982	1.8	-0.152
Sucre	-0.003	0.998	0.2	-1.095
Tolima	-0.003	0.983	1.7	-0.158
Valle	-0.003	0.985	1.5	-0.174
Mean			1.6	
Median			1.7	

Source: Own calculations based on data from CEGA. Constant prices of 1994.

Table 3.11: Implied Convergence Rates Using TSCS Data and Linear Mixed Models (REML). Per capita IDBH. 1975-2000

Department	Intercept α	Slope ρ	Implied β (%)	Expected Value
Nuevos Departamentos	-0.001	0.986	0.0	-0.10
Antioquia	-0.001	0.986	1.4	-0.10
Atlántico	-0.001	0.986	1.4	-0.10
Bogotá D. C.	-0.001	0.986	1.4	-0.10
Bolívar	-0.001	0.986	1.4	-0.10
Boyacá	-0.001	0.986	1.4	-0.10
Caldas	-0.001	0.986	1.4	-0.10
Caquetá	-0.001	0.986	1.4	-0.10
Cauca	-0.001	0.986	1.4	-0.10
Cesar	-0.001	0.986	1.4	-0.10
Córdoba	-0.001	0.986	1.4	-0.10
Cundinamarca	-0.001	0.986	1.4	-0.10
Chocó	-0.001	0.987	1.3	-0.11
Huila	-0.001	0.986	1.4	-0.10
La Guajira	-0.001	0.985	1.5	-0.09
Magdalena	-0.001	0.986	1.4	-0.10
Meta	-0.001	0.986	1.4	-0.10
Nariño	-0.001	0.986	1.4	-0.10
Norte Santander	-0.001	0.986	1.4	-0.10
Quindío	-0.001	0.986	1.4	-0.10
Risaralda	-0.001	0.986	1.4	-0.10
Santander	-0.001	0.986	1.4	-0.10
Sucre	-0.001	0.987	1.3	-0.11
Tolima	-0.001	0.986	1.4	-0.10
Valle	-0.001	0.986	1.4	-0.10
Mean			1.4	
Median			1.4	

Source: Own calculations based on data from CEGA. Constant prices of 1994.

Table 3.12: Autoregressive Processes of Order 1. Dependent Variable: $log(y_{i.t})$. Per Capita PDB. 1975-2000.

Department	Intercept (α)		Slope (ρ)		Regression	Expected	Implied
	Coefficient	Sdt.Error	Coefficient.	Std.Error	Adjusted R^2	Value	β (%)
Nuevos Departamentos	0.03	0.03	0.85	0.14	0.62	0.21	14.75
Antioquia	0.06	0.03	0.65	0.16	0.41	0.16	35.48
Atlántico	-0.02	0.01	0.85	0.06	0.88	-0.15	14.99
Bogotá D. C.	0.08	0.09	0.84	0.17	0.52	0.48	16.10
Bolívar	-0.05	0.02	0.69	0.15	0.48	-0.14	31.16
Boyacá	-0.09	0.03	0.29	0.21	0.08		
Caldas	-0.11	0.03	0.39	0.18	0.17	-0.17	61.42
Caquetá	-0.16	0.08	0.76	0.13	0.58	-0.64	24.10
Cauca	-0.26	0.13	0.62	0.18	0.33	-0.68	38.31
Cesar	-0.07	0.04	0.85	0.10	0.77	-0.45	15.34
Córdoba	-0.18	0.09	0.77	0.12	0.66	-0.78	22.95
Cundinamarca	0.01	0.00	0.87	0.13	0.68	0.06	12.51
Chocóó	-0.37	0.17	0.67	0.16	0.45	-1.11	33.14
Huila	-0.11	0.05	0.66	0.16	0.43	-0.31	34.25
La Guajira	0.01	0.03	0.90	0.06	0.92	0.06	10.36
Magdalena	-0.29	0.11	0.52	0.18	0.27	-0.59	48.31
Meta	-0.04	0.02	0.67	0.15	0.48	-0.11	32.80
Nariño	-0.30	0.14	0.63	0.16	0.40	-0.83	36.65
Norte Santander	-0.47	0.11	0.09	0.21	0.01		
Quindío	-0.04	0.03	0.64	0.16	0.41	-0.12	36.26
Risaralda	-0.02	0.01	0.74	0.15	0.52	-0.07	25.89
Santander	0.00	0.01	0.86	0.11	0.71	0.01	13.89
Sucre	-0.24	0.09	0.75	0.10	0.72	-0.96	25.32
Tolima	-0.09	0.05	0.71	0.15	0.51	-0.30	29.06
Valle	0.05	0.05	0.80	0.20	0.41	0.23	19.61
Mean	-0.11		0.68				
Median	-0.07		0.71				

Source: Own calculations based on data from CEGA. Constant prices of 1994.

Note: Expected values $(\alpha/(1-\rho))$ calculated only for ρ significant at 5% level and lower than 1.

Table 3.13: Autoregressive Processes of Order 1. Dependent Variable: $log(y_{i.t})$. Per capita IDBH. 1975-2000.

Department	Intercept (α)		Slope (ρ)		Regression	Expected	Implied
	Coefficient	Sdt.Error	Coefficient.	Std.Error	Adjusted R^2	Value	β (%)
Nuevos Departamentos	-0.02	0.02	0.71	0.17	0.44	-0.08	29.39
Antioquia	0.02	0.01	0.86	0.11	0.74	0.11	14.22
Atlántico	-0.01	0.01	0.84	0.09	0.78	-0.07	15.57
Bogotá D. C.	-0.04	0.03	1.04	0.04	0.96		
Bolívar	-0.06	0.03	0.83	0.10	0.76	-0.35	16.92
Boyacá	-0.04	0.03	0.60	0.23	0.23	-0.11	39.76
Caldas	0.00	0.02	0.93	0.06	0.91	-0.01	6.81
Caquetá	-0.14	0.08	0.76	0.13	0.59	-0.58	23.54
Cauca	-0.02	0.06	0.95	0.12	0.75	-0.32	5.03
Cesar	-0.01	0.03	0.95	0.10	0.79	-0.19	5.30
Córdoba	-0.13	0.07	0.79	0.11	0.68	-0.60	20.87
Cundinamarca	-0.01	0.01	0.90	0.07	0.88	-0.07	9.80
Chocó	-0.08	0.12	0.92	0.10	0.78	-1.07	7.87
Huila	-0.09	0.04	0.68	0.13	0.52	-0.27	32.45
La Guajira	-0.07	0.05	0.86	0.07	0.86	-0.50	13.79
Magdalena	-0.03	0.07	0.95	0.12	0.73	-0.49	5.46
Meta	-0.05	0.02	0.71	0.10	0.67	-0.17	28.72
Nariño	-0.23	0.13	0.71	0.16	0.46	-0.82	28.68
Norte Santander	-0.05	0.05	0.87	0.10	0.75	-0.40	12.91
Quindío	-0.04	0.02	0.74	0.12	0.61	-0.15	25.57
Risaralda	-0.04	0.02	0.63	0.14	0.47	-0.11	36.51
Santander	-0.02	0.01	0.65	0.18	0.35	-0.05	35.48
Sucre	-0.19	0.09	0.74	0.13	0.60	-0.71	26.37
Tolima	-0.01	0.03	0.96	0.09	0.82	-0.27	3.53
Valle	0.03	0.02	0.79	0.16	0.51	0.14	20.62
Mean	-0.05		0.82				
Median	-0.04		0.83				

Source: Own calculations based on data from CEGA. Constant prices of 1994.

Note: Expected values ($\alpha/(1-\rho)$) calculated only for ρ significant at 5% level and lower than 1.

Table 3.14: Mixture Model with 3 Components. Fitted with ML. Dependent Variable: $log(y_{i,t})$. Relative Per capita PDB. 1975-2000.

Department	Group	Intercept α	Slope ρ	Implied β (%)	Expected value
Bolívar	1	-0.007	0.988	1.168	-0.618
Boyacá	1				
Caldas	1				
Caquetá	1				
Cauca	1				
Cesar	1				
Córdoba	1				
Chocó	1				
Magdalena	1				
Meta	1				
Nariño	1				
Quindío	1				
Risaralda	1				
Sucre	1				
Tolima	1				
Nuevos Departamentos	2	0.015	0.900	9.986	0.153
La Guajira	2				
Antioquia	3	-0.001	0.990	1.045	-0.139
Atlántico	3				
Bogotá D.C	3				
Cundinamarca	3				
Huila	3				
Norte Santander	3				
Santander	3				
Valle	3				

Source: Own calculations based on data from CEGA. Constant prices of 1994.

Table 3.15: Mixture Model with 3 Components. Fitted with ML. Dependent Variable: $log(y_{i,t})$. Relative Per Capita IDBH. 1975-2000.

Department	Group	Intercept α	Slope ρ	Implied β (%)	Expected value
Bolívar	1	0.000	0.982	1.757	-0.004
Caquetá	1				
Cauca	1				
Cesar	1				
Córdoba	1				
Chocó	1				
Magdalena	1				
Nariño	1				
Quindío	1				
Nuevos Departamentos	2	-0.013	0.961	3.893	-0.325
La Guajira	2				
Sucre	2				
Antioquia	3	-0.003	0.988	1.174	-0.239
Atlántico	3				
Bogotá D.C	3				
Boyacá	3				
Caldas	3				
Cundinamarca	3				
Huila	3				
Meta	3				
Norte Santander	3				
Risaralda	3				
Santander	3				
Tolima	3				
Valle	3				

Source: Own calculations based on data from CEGA. Constant prices of 1994.

Table 3.16: Share of Total PDB and Share of selected PDB Sectors by Department. Years 1975 and 2000.

	Percentage of total PDB		Agriculture		Mining		Manufacturing		Financing		Government		Commerce	
Department	1975	2000	1975	2000	1975	2000	1975	2000	1975	2000	1975	2000	1975	2000
Antioquia	15.3	14.4	12.2	13.9	21.3	4.0	21.0	18.0	14.1	15.7	15.5	10.9	18.4	16.9
Atlántico	5.3	4.3	0.8	0.7	0.0	0.0	7.5	6.1	4.8	4.0	2.7	3.4	6.4	5.1
Bogotá D.C	22.4	23.6	0.7	0.0	0.5	0.0	25.4	22.6	40.1	45.6	27.8	24.8	21.2	18.3
Bolívar	4.0	4.1	3.3	2.9	2.3	0.9	4.8	5.6	2.0	1.8	3.4	2.9	4.1	6.3
Boyacá	3.8	2.9	7.2	7.1	13.1	2.8	2.5	1.8	1.9	1.2	3.7	4.6	3.2	2.1
Caldas	2.5	2.0	3.7	2.6	0.7	0.1	2.2	2.0	2.3	1.8	2.4	2.9	2.0	1.9
Caquetá	0.5	0.5	1.2	1.6	0.0	0.0	0.1	0.0	0.1	0.2	0.7	0.9	0.2	0.2
Cauca	1.8	1.9	4.0	3.3	0.5	0.2	1.0	2.2	0.9	0.7	2.3	3.0	1.5	2.3
Cesar	1.6	1.5	3.7	3.0	0.0	5.5	0.6	0.4	1.3	0.5	1.2	1.8	1.5	0.9
Chocó	0.4	0.3	0.5	1.0	6.0	0.3	0.0	0.0	0.2	0.1	1.2	0.7	0.2	0.2
Córdoba	2.0	1.9	6.2	3.7	1.5	2.8	0.1	1.9	1.0	0.7	2.1	2.2	1.2	1.6
Cundinamarca	4.8	5.7	8.4	12.7	7.5	1.2	4.2	8.2	1.6	1.4	4.7	7.1	5.2	8.6
Guajira	0.4	1.3	0.6	0.6	3.6	12.3	0.1	0.0	0.4	0.3	0.6	0.8	0.3	0.1
Huila	1.6	1.7	3.1	2.5	1.5	5.4	0.4	0.6	1.2	1.0	2.0	2.3	1.1	1.1
Magdalena	1.8	1.5	3.6	3.4	1.9	0.0	0.4	0.3	1.1	0.7	1.8	1.9	1.0	0.8
Meta	1.2	1.5	2.4	2.8	0.3	5.1	0.4	0.7	1.2	0.9	1.0	1.3	0.9	1.4
Nariño	1.6	1.6	2.9	3.8	1.0	0.1	0.4	0.4	1.3	1.0	1.7	2.5	1.2	1.1
Norte de Santander	2.0	1.8	3.1	3.3	5.3	0.6	0.9	0.7	1.7	1.4	2.9	2.7	1.3	1.0
Nuevos	1.3	4.7	2.4	3.9	10.7	55.0	0.1	0.1	1.2	1.0	2.0	2.9	0.5	0.8
Quindío	1.2	1.1	2.2	2.3	0.0	0.0	0.6	0.3	1.1	1.1	1.4	1.2	1.2	0.6
Risaralda	2.0	1.9	2.1	1.5	0.1	0.0	2.2	2.3	2.0	1.6	1.6	1.7	2.0	2.0
Santander	5.2	5.0	6.2	6.9	18.9	2.1	5.2	6.5	3.8	3.5	4.0	5.3	5.0	7.7
Sucre	1.0	0.7	3.0	1.6	0.3	0.1	0.2	0.2	0.6	0.3	1.0	0.9	0.6	0.4
Tolima	3.2	2.6	7.0	6.0	0.9	1.3	1.1	1.9	2.3	1.6	4.1	3.1	2.7	2.7
Valle	13.2	11.4	9.3	8.8	2.0	0.3	18.5	17.2	12.0	11.8	7.8	8.3	17.1	16.1

Source: Own calculations based on data from CEGA. Constant prices of 1994.

Figure 3.4: Box Plot: Log of Relative Per Capita PDB. 1975-2000.

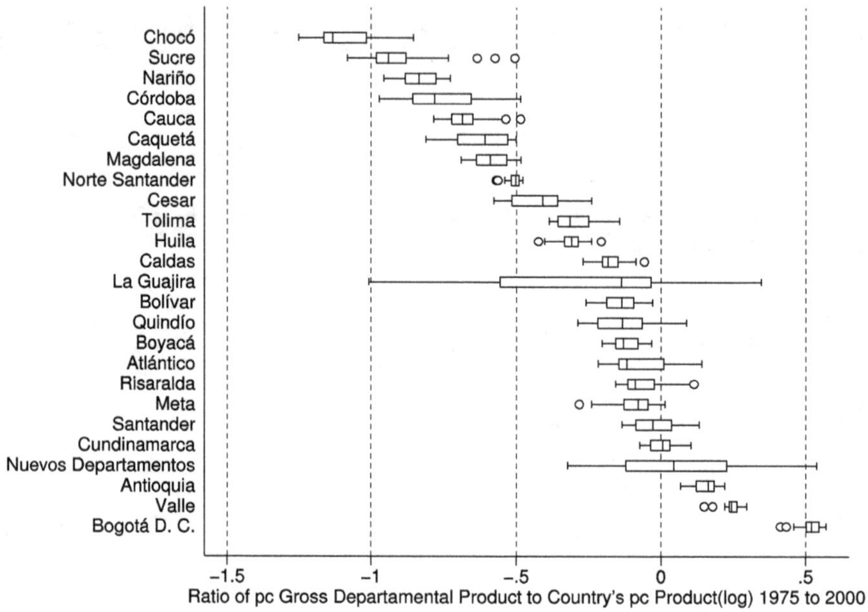

Source: Own calculations based on data from CEGA. Constant prices of 1994.

Figure 3.5: Box Plot: Log of Relative Per Capita IDBH. 1975-2000.

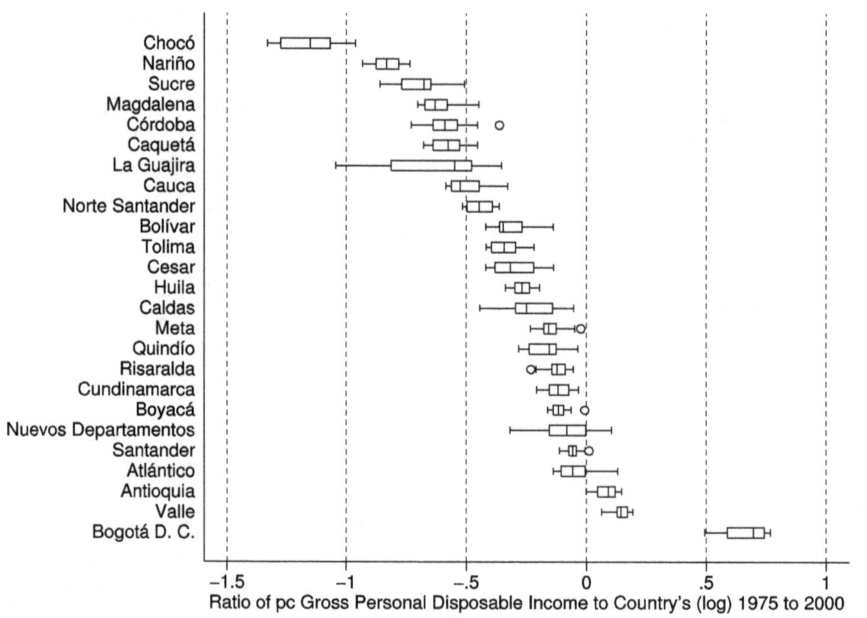

Source: Own calculations based on data from CEGA. Constant prices of 1994.

Figure 3.6: Sigma Convergence. GDP by Department.

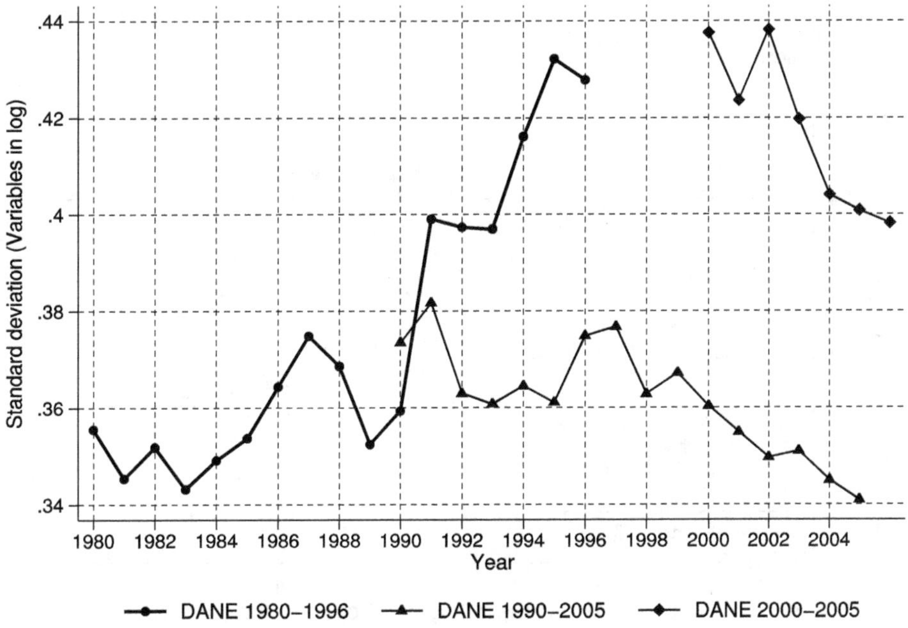

Figure 3.7: Sigma Convergence. Per Capita Gross Departmental Product (PDB) and Gross Personal Disposable Income (IDBH). 1975-2000.

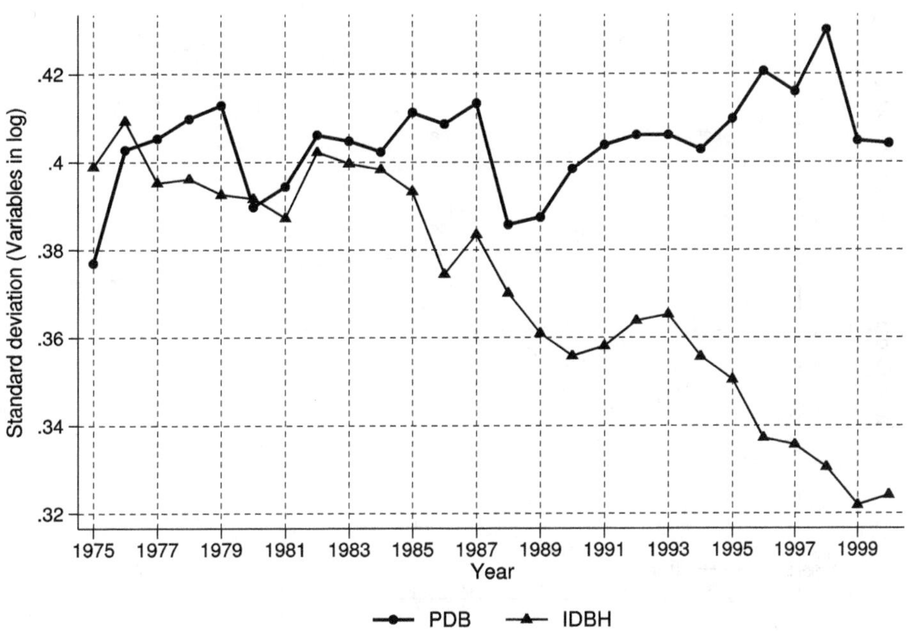

Source: Own calculations based on data from CEGA. Constant prices of 1994.

Figure 3.8: Beta Convergence. Per Capita PDB. 1975-2000.

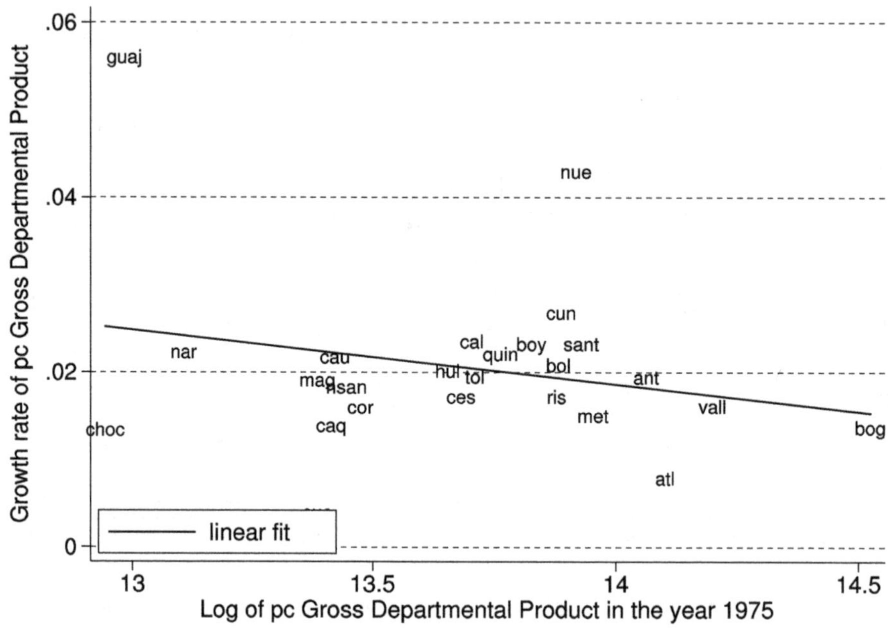

Source: Own calculations based on data from CEGA. Constant prices of 1994.

Figure 3.9: Beta Convergence without Nuevos, Chocó and Guajira. Per Capita PDB. 1975-2000.

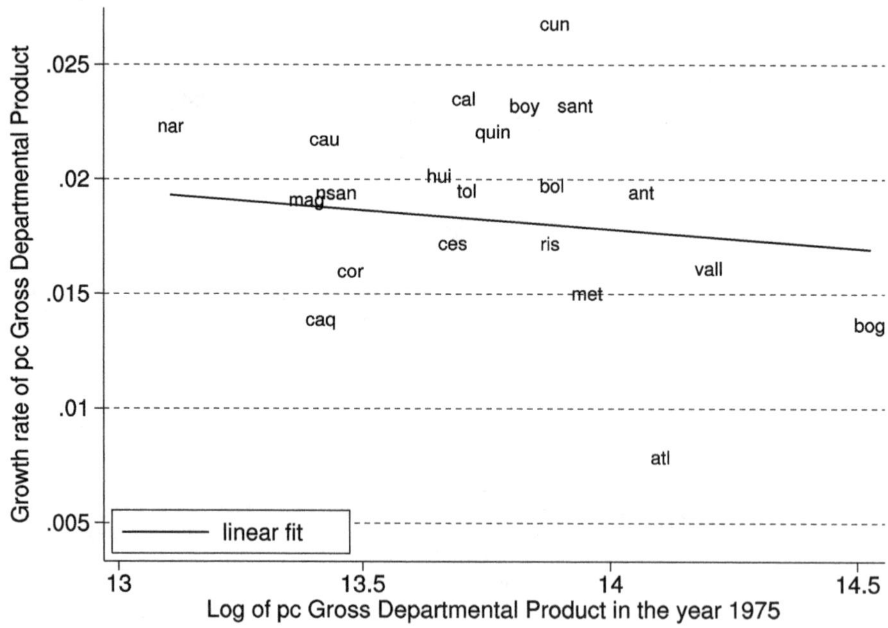

Source: Own calculations based on data from CEGA. Constant prices of 1994.

Figure 3.10: Beta Convergence. Per Capita IDBH. 1975-2000.

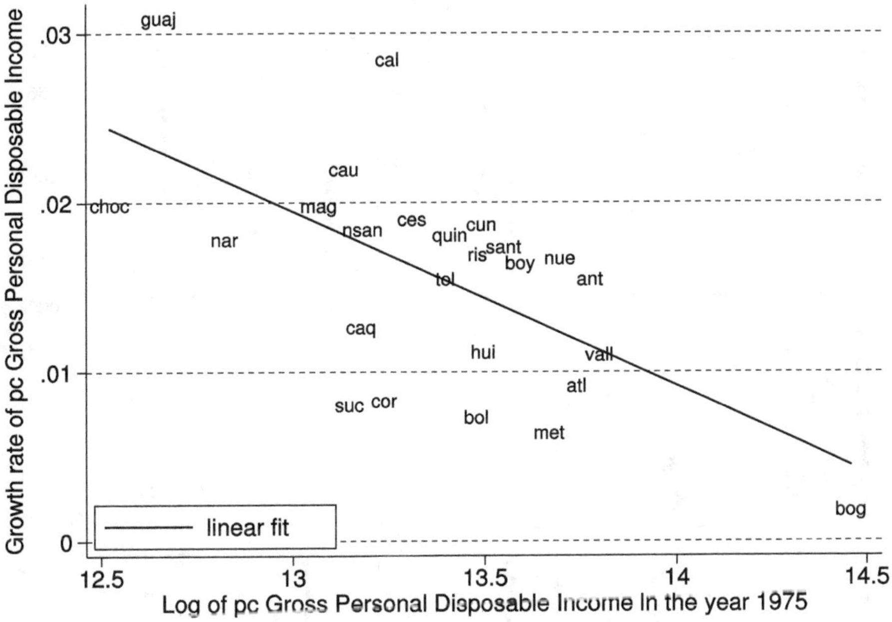

Source: Own calculations based on data from CEGA. Constant prices of 1994.

Figure 3.11: Beta Convergence without Guajira. Per Capita IDBH. 1975-2000.

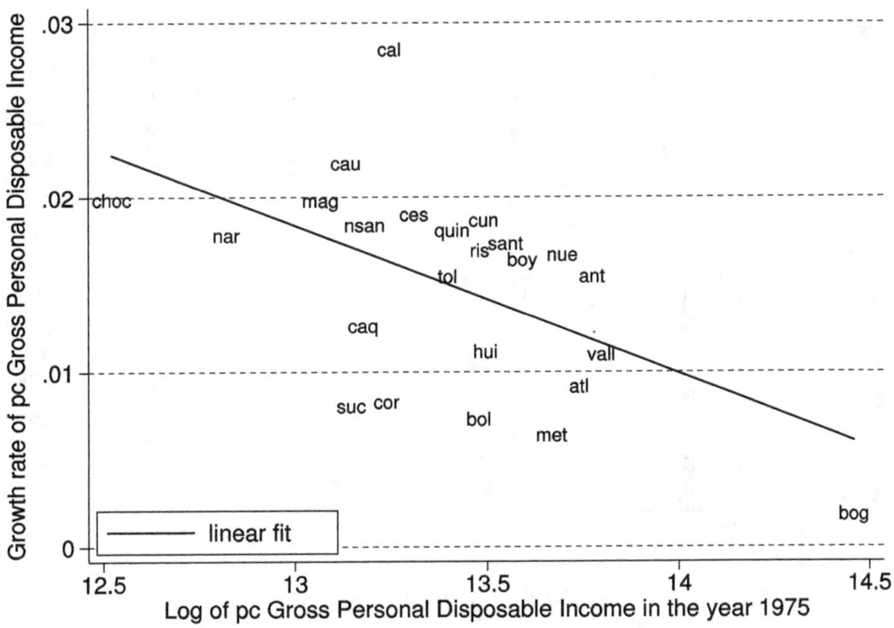

Source: Own calculations based on data from CEGA. Constant prices of 1994.

Figure 3.12: Log of Relative PDB by Department. 1975-2000.

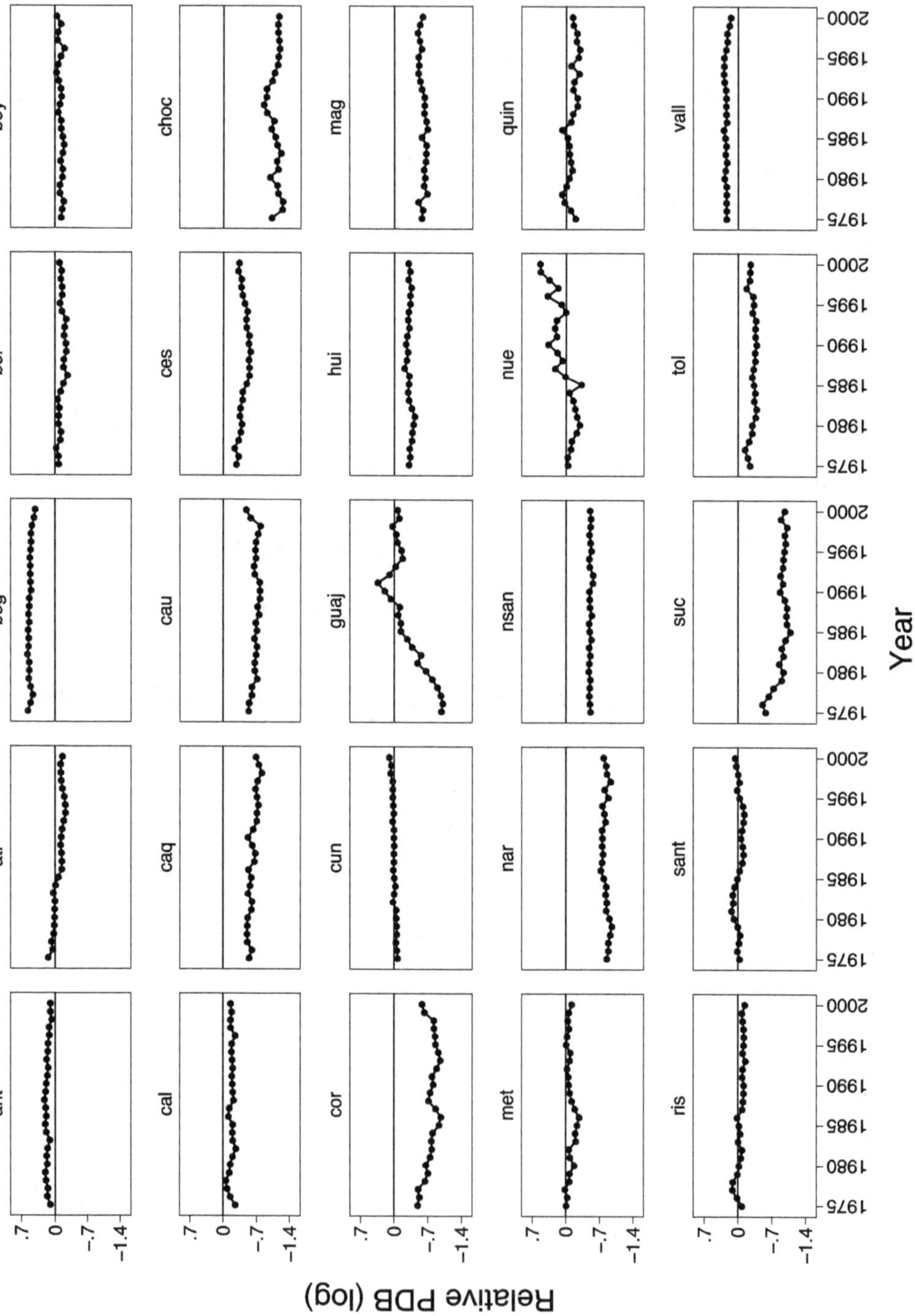

Source: Own calculations based on data from CEGA. Constant prices of 1994.

Figure 3.13: Log of relative IDBH by department. 1975-2000.

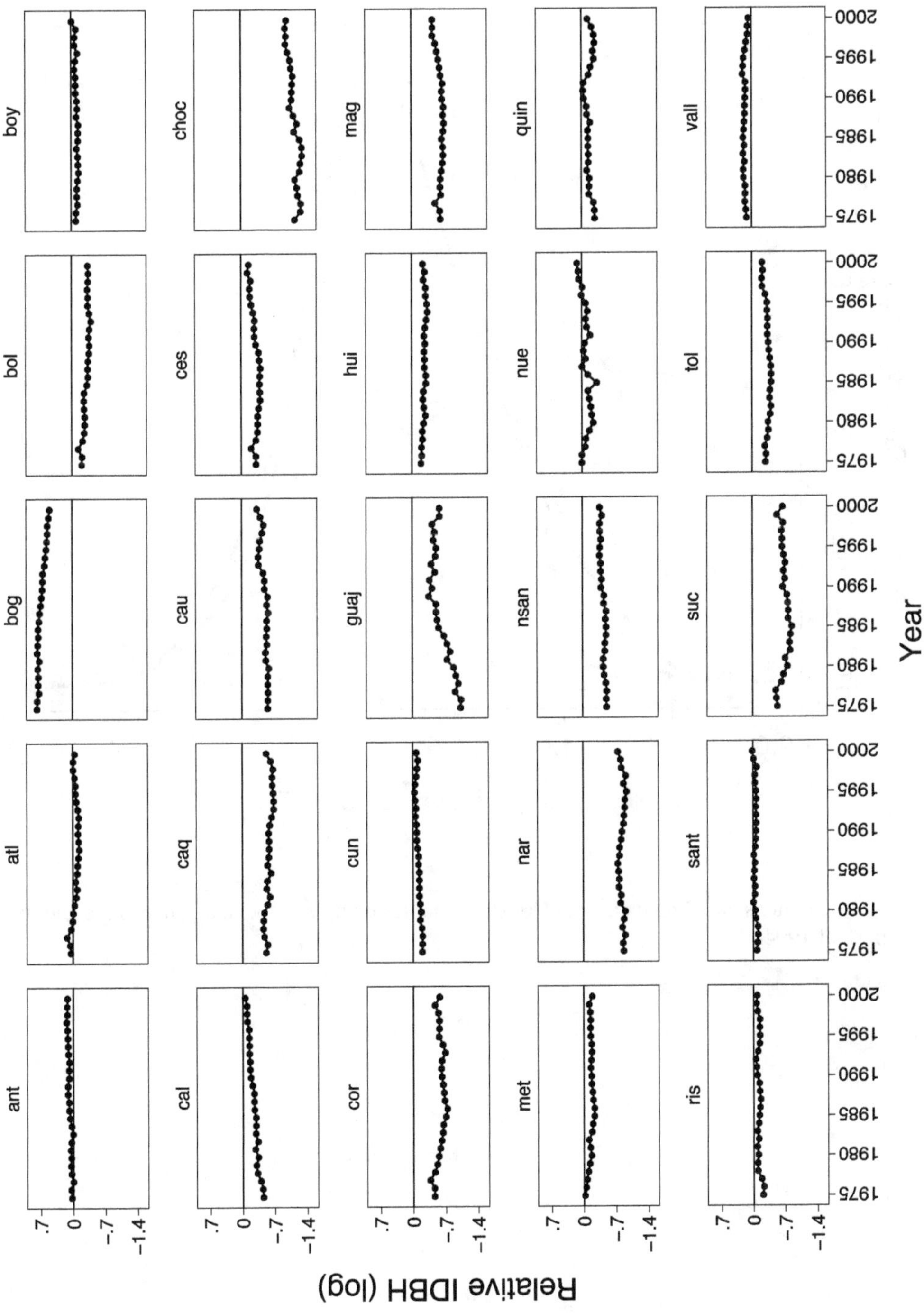

Source: Own calculations based on data from CEGA. Constant prices of 1994.

Figure 3.14: Univariate Kernel Density Estimators. Relative Per Capita PDB. 1975 and 2000.

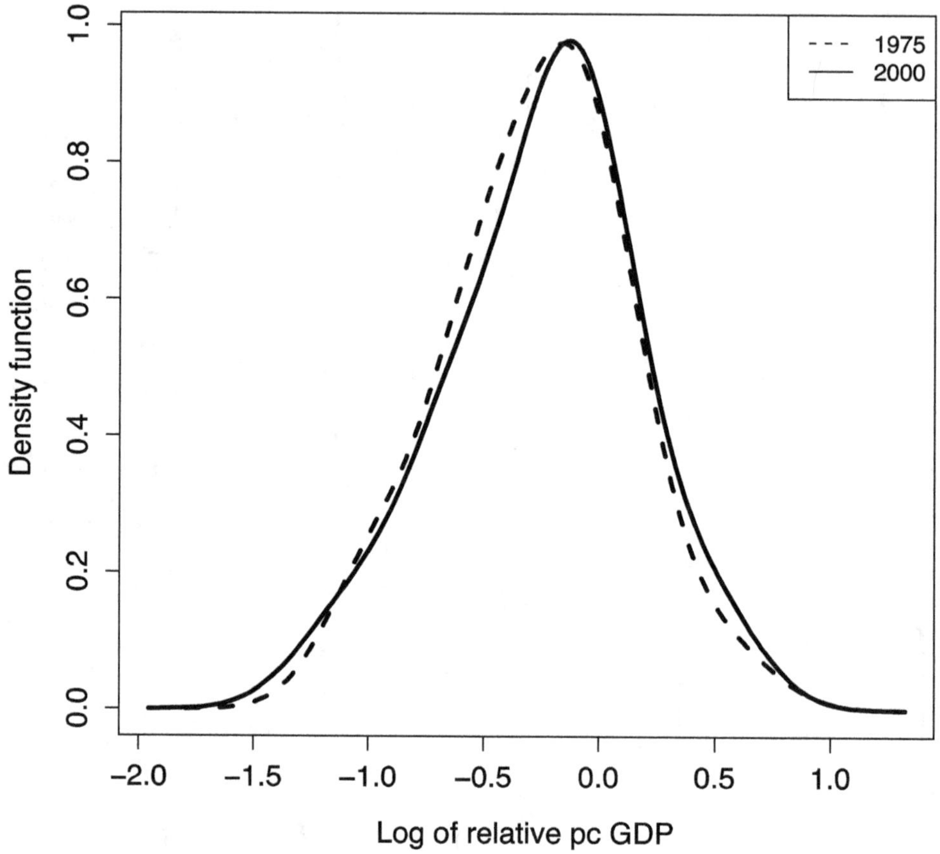

Source: Own calculations based on data from CEGA. Variables relative to the national average and in logs. Constant prices of 1994

Figure 3.15: Relative Per Capita PDB Dynamics.1975 and 2000.

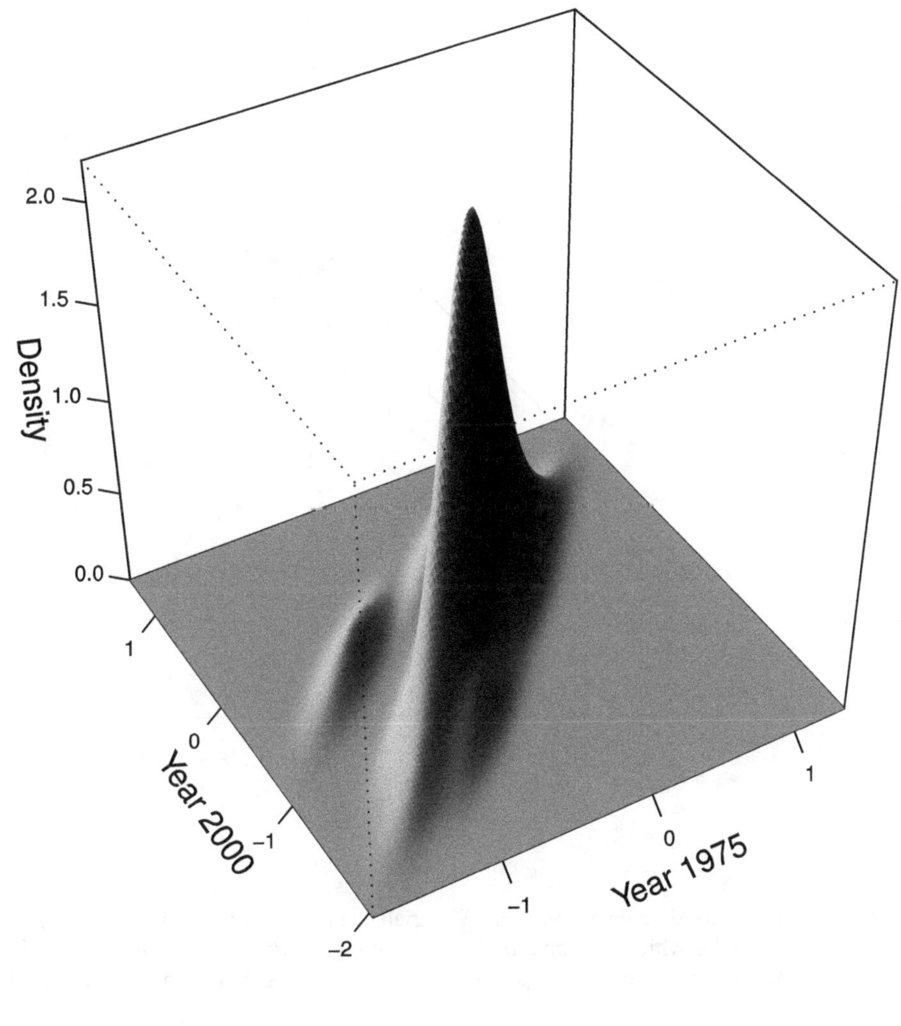

Source: Own calculations based on data from CEGA. Variables in logs. Constant Prices of 1994.

Figure 3.16: Relative per capita PDB Dynamics: Contour Plot. 1975 and 2000.

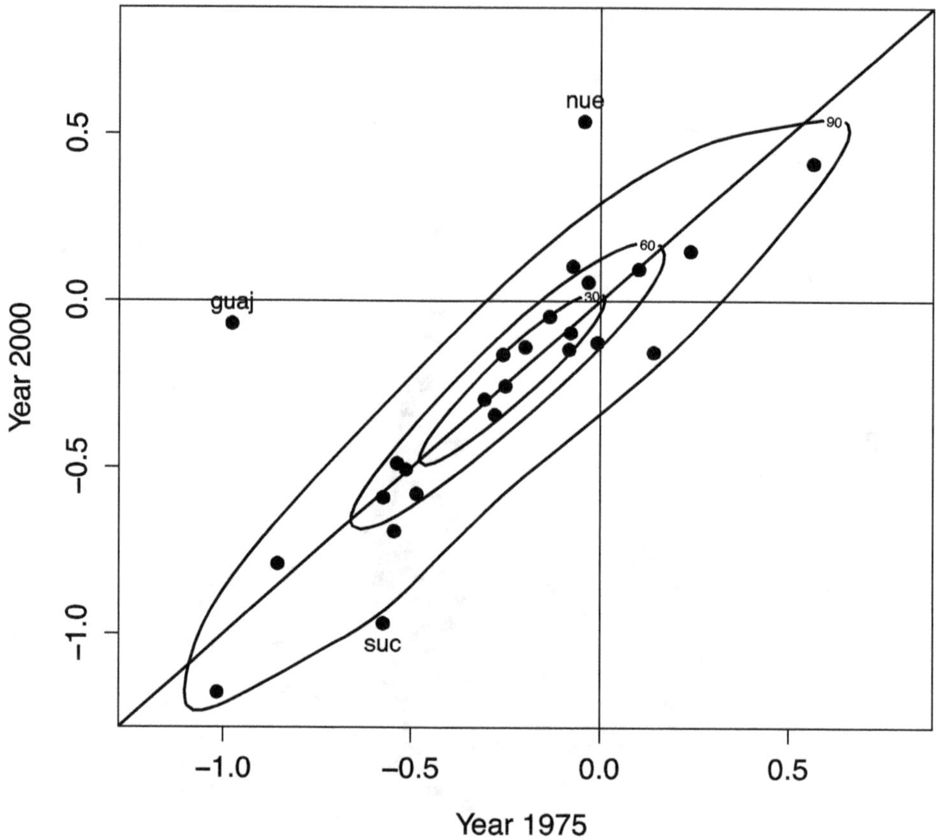

Source: Own calculations based on data from CEGA. Variables in logs. Constant Prices of 1994. Contours are drawn at 30%. 60%. and 90% which are upper percentages of highest density regions. The points represent the 25 observations. Points outside the 90% contour are identified. A 45 degree line is added to the plot.

Figure 3.17: Univariate Kernel Density Estim. Relative per Capita IDBH. 1975 and 2000.

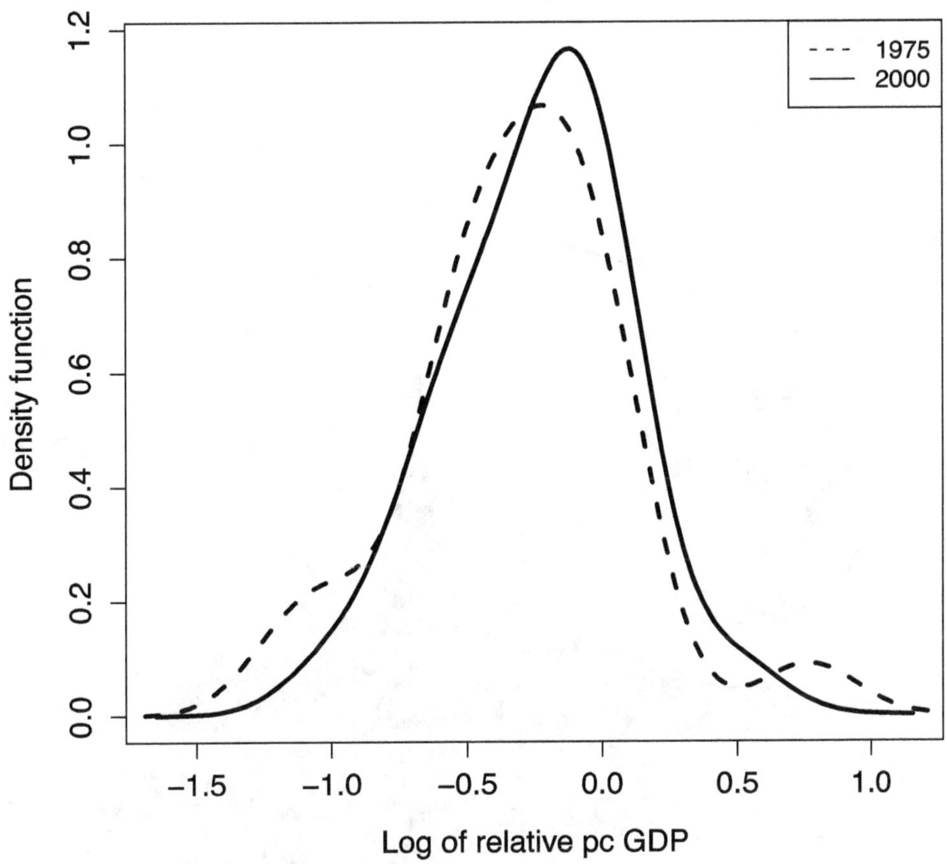

Source: Own calculations based on data from CEGA. Variables in logs. Constant Prices of 1994.

Figure 3.18: Relative Per Capita IDBH Dynamics. 1975 and 2000.

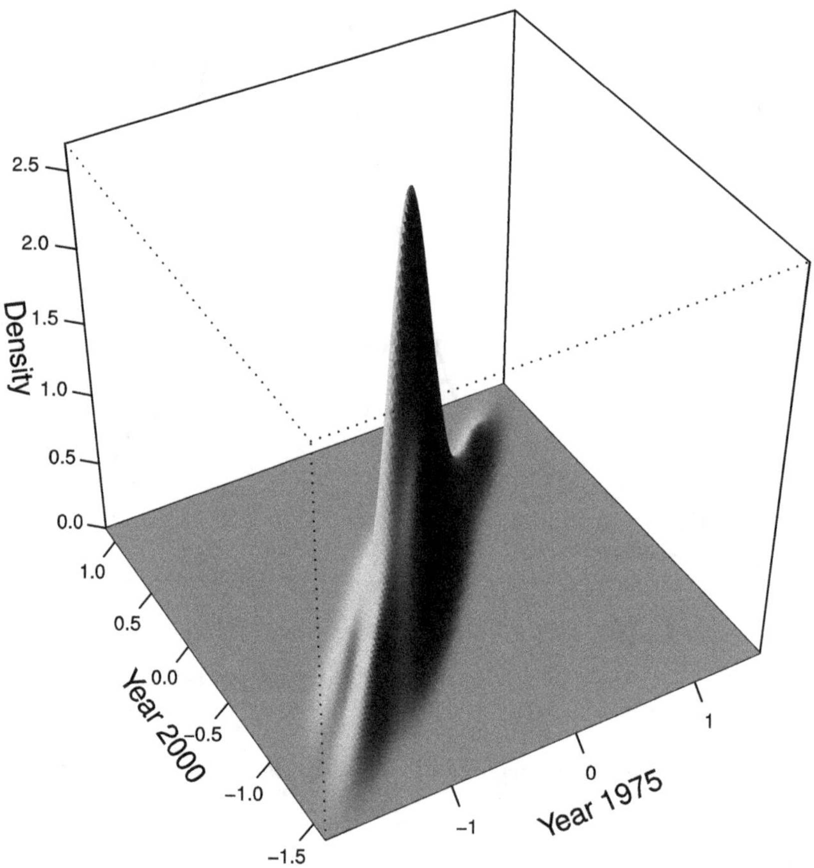

Source: Own calculations based on data from CEGA. Variables in logs. Constant Prices of 1994.

Figure 3.19: Relative per Capita IDBH Dynamics: Contour Plot. 1975 and 2000.

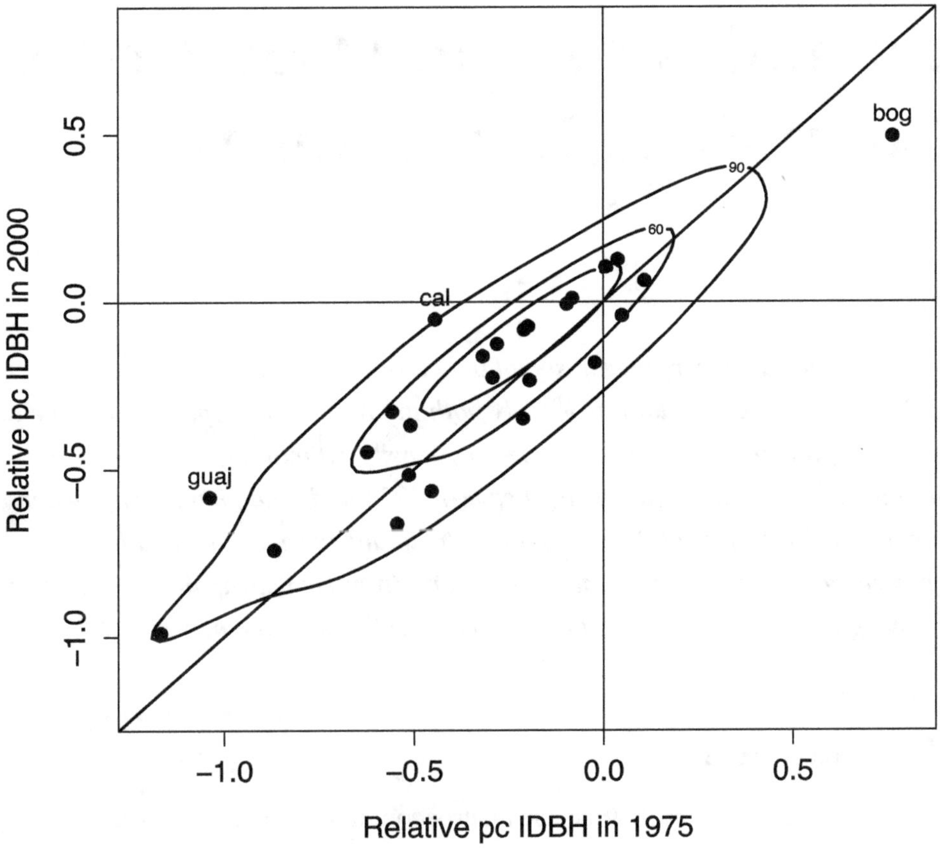

Source: Own calculations based on data from CEGA. Variables in logs. Constant Prices of 1994. Contours are drawn at 30%. 60%. and 90% which are upper percentages of highest density regions. The points represent the 25 observations. Points outside the 90% contour are identified. A 45 degree line is added to the plot.

4

Social Indicators and Convergence in Columbian Departments

Abstract

*This paper investigates convergence in social indicators among Colombian departments from 1973 to 2005. We use census data and apply both the regression approach and the distributional approach (univariate and bivariate kernel density estimators). Using literacy rate as a proxy for education, we find convergence between 1973 and 2005, but persistence in the distribution between 1975 and 2000, when we use the infant survival rate and life expectancy at birth as proxies for health. Additionally, using data from Demographic and Health Surveys, we find convergence in the rate of children that are well-nourished between 1995 and 2005.**

4.1 Introduction

The majority of studies on convergence use macroeconomic aggregates to study whether poor countries are catching up with wealthier countries, and are particularly interested in the speed at which this process occurs, when it does occur. A large part of the empirical analysis of convergence is based on the neoclassical model developed by Solow (1956) and the estimation procedure suggested by Barro and Sala-i-Martin (1992a). Most of these studies use cross-sectional regressions based on per capita gross domestic product (GDP) to investigate if poor regions have higher rates of growth as they develop than wealthier areas.

In recent years, some authors have also tested if there is convergence in living standards, given that it is well-being that really matters, and arguing that per capita GDP is not the appropriate indicator for it.[1] For example, Neumayer (2003) and Kenny (2004) conclude that

---

*Based on joint work with Boris Branisa Caballero

[1]In this paper, we will refer indistinctly to non-income indicators, social indicators, quality-of-life variables, and living standards.

even in the absence of convergence in per capita GDP, there is convergence in living standards among poor and rich countries, a phenomenon praised by Neumayer as one of the greatest success stories of development in the last century.

This argument seems to be valid for cross-country analysis, but few studies exist investigating regional convergence in living standards in developing countries. Within a particular country, convergence analysis is important, not only to focus development assistance towards regions lagging behind in economic growth, but also to evaluate the efficiency and scope of public policies. Lack of convergence and the persistence of inequalities inside a country can lead to political instability, social unrest, and violence, given that people are concerned not only with their own improvements, but also with meeting the living standards of the wealthiest regions (Kenny, 2004). In Colombia, high regional inequality in living standards is one of the possible underlying causes of the ongoing domestic conflict, which is fueled by drug trafficking and corruption, particularly in isolated regions with a low level of governmental presence and a high incidence of poverty.

Over the past 30 years, Colombia has witnessed important reforms in social areas, particularly in health care and education. These reforms were marked by increased governmental intervention during the mid seventies, such as the creation of a national health care system and vaccination campaigns to eradicate tropical diseases like malaria, and, in the early eighties, policy formulations to reduce mortality and increase primary education. At the beginning of the nineties, decentralization accelerated in order to reduce the fiscal burden on the central government, making municipalities more responsible for generating and administrating their own resources, and partially moving the provision of health services to the private sector (Hernández and Obregón, 2002).

The link between decentralization policies and the improvement in living standards in Colombia is a topic of extensive debate. While some researchers argue that the health policies have categorically failed, others conclude that they have been successful, although recognizing that there is still a large margin for improvement, particularly given that the system in place is still too recent to make a general judgement (Homedes and Ugalde, 2005; Barrera and Domínguez, 2006). Evidence shows that even though social spending increased considerably and reforms were designed to compensate municipalities with weak fiscal capacities, fiscal equalization has not been achieved.

Although Colombia has experienced improvements in living standard indicators at the national level, particularly those related to health, education, and access to public services, there is evidence of a heterogeneous distribution of improvements. Thus, investigating regional convergence in social indicators is relevant, as it is a relatively under-researched topic. Out of 20 research documents about regional convergence in Colombia produced in the last 15 years (Aguirre, 2008), only two published articles that deal with convergence in non-income indicators (Aguirre, 2005; Meisel and Vega, 2007).

The objective of this study is to analyze whether departments that were lagging behind in social indicators in the 1970s were able to catch up by the year 2000. We use both the regression approach suggested by Barro and Sala-i-Martin (1991), among others, and the distributional approach pioneered by Quah (1997) to test for convergence in three variables, based on census data. Using literacy rate as a proxy for education, we find regional convergence between 1973 and 2005, but persistence in the distribution between 1975 and 2000 when we use the infant survival rate and life expectancy at birth as proxies for health. Additionally, using data from Demographic and Health Surveys (DHS), we find convergence between 1995 and 2005 in the percentage of children that are well-nourished.

This paper is divided into six sections. After this introduction, we argue in section 4.2 that it is fundamental to focus upon indicators other than income and that the analysis of convergence at the department level is relevant for Colombia. We present two methods to empirically test for convergence in section 4.3. Section 4.4 describes the data used and the details of our empirical estimation. Results are presented in section 4.5 and discussed in section 4.6.

4.2 Motivation

The importance of analyzing social indicators, instead of focusing only upon income, has been extensively discussed in the work of Amartya Sen, who argues that *social opportunities* are one of the five types of instrumental freedoms that contribute to the overall freedom people have to live as they choose (Sen, 1999). Social opportunities are understood to be the arrangements that a society makes which influence the individual's substantive freedom to live better, such as providing education and health care, which are important, not only for the the citizens in the conduct of their private lives, but also for more effective participation in societal economic and political activities.

Public policies have a crucial influence on social opportunities (e.g., they can influence longevity through epidemiological policies and education through the provision of the corresponding facilities). Thus, it is important to shift attention to elements that affect individual well-being and freedom but which are not captured by income statistics (Sen and Foster, 1997).

Particular attention shall be given herein to health status when analyzing social inequalities. Sen (1998) argues that mortality is a key economic indicator, given that it mirrors the success or failure of a society. Indicators like the infant survival rate, which responds very rapidly to public health polices, are central to that kind of analysis (Mazumdar, 2003). Along the same lines, indicators referring to the level of nutrition reflect one of the most basic needs for survival, namely access to adequate food (Sen, 2002).

In Colombia, awareness of the influence and scope of the government on health and education gradually increased in the second half of the 20th century, and has translated into programs, as well as legislation, aimed at achieving universal access to health care and primary education. Policies for both sectors experienced important changes in the last quarter of the century, reflecting the transition from a centralist system to a locally managed one.

In the seventies, polices on education focused upon reducing illiteracy and increasing the coverage of primary education, particularly in rural areas, where public schools and teachers were almost nonexistent.[2] However, rural areas continued to lag behind. Adult education and literacy campaigns continued through the eighties, together with the expansion of secondary and preschool education.

Due to macroeconomic imbalances at the end of the eighties, the government initiated a decentralization program to reduce the financial burden on the central government, and transferred substantial revenues and responsibilities to local administrations. The country has been praised as a leading example of fiscal decentralization, which policy had the objective of increasing social expenditures and efficiency in social sectors, as well as financially compensating territories with weak fiscal capacities. This process accelerated with the new constitution in 1991 (Rojas, 2003; Barrera and Domínguez, 2006). As a result, social spending increased from 7 to 15 % of GDP between 1991 and 2001. Concerning education, evidence shows that reforms were beneficial for the urban sector, but less so for the rural sector, which lags behind the former on the issues of quality of education and net enrolment rates, particularly for secondary education (Velez et al., 2003).

Concerning health policies, by the mid seventies, the government had increased its role as a provider of health care and had implemented programs to improve neonatal care and nutrition, eliminate tropical diseases through mass vaccinations, and promote reproductive health. At the same time, coverage of public services in the country expanded. An important result of these campaigns was the reduction in infant mortality, due in part to better access to drinking water. This reduction led to higher life expectancy at birth (Profamilia, 2005).

In the nineties, the policy orientation shifted; the government increased the role of the private sector as health provider and tried to strengthen the national health care system through the decentralization of services at the local level. Implementation of a dual system, combining the contribution of formal sector employees with subsidies for the population outside the

[2] With society facing limited resources, secondary and tertiary education was left largely to the private sector under the argument that spending in public universities would favor middle and upper income groups.

system, yielded an increase in health coverage, which attained 58% in 2000 (Hernández and Obregón, 2002).

Statistics on health and education at the national level show significant improvements in the last quarter of the 20th century, and indicate that the country is a successful case within Latin America. Colombia ranks well within the Latin American average in many social indicators, or even slightly above. As an example, in 1970, the average adult literacy rate was 78% and increased to 93% in 2005, which is higher than the Latin American average of 90% (World Bank, 2008).[3] However, these gains do not seem to have been homogeneously distributed across society. Inequality is anchored within different levels - between departments (the main administrative units), between urban and rural areas, and also inside urban areas.[4] Given that Colombia is a land of contrasts, where one can find well-developed modern metropolitan areas with reasonable infrastructure and large underdeveloped low density areas, lacking even basic infrastructure, looking at variables at the national level clearly masks differences.

Colombia is divided into 32 departments and the capital district of Bogotá, a division that has existed formally since the 1991 constitutional reform, when nine former intendancies and commissariats, sparsely populated areas, were acknowledged as departments (Amazonas, Arauca, Casanare, Guainía, Guaviare, Putumayo, San Andrés y Providencia, Vaupés, and Vichada).[5] Departments are important political entities in Colombia, with elected local governments and separate department assemblies. Hence, it is relevant to analyze the performance in social indicators by department, investigating whether those that were lagging behind in the early seventies have been able to catch up in the year 2000.

In this paper, we test the hypothesis that among Colombian departments, there was convergence in social indicators in the period from 1973 through 2005. This hypothesis is based on the following facts. First, starting in the mid seventies, national policies aimed at reducing illiteracy and improving neonatal care were put into place. Second, decentralization reforms were conducted, starting in the late eighties, to increase the efficiency of spending on education and health care. Third, after decentralization, social spending, as a share of total gross domestic product, doubled. Fourth, as will be discussed later, social indicators are naturally bounded, which fact facilitates convergence if better-off departments are close to the

---

[3]Similarly, in 1980, live expectancy at birth was 66 years, and in 2005, it reached 73 years, which is the average for the region. Infant mortality for each 1,000 live births fell from 68 deaths in 1970 to 17 in 2005, compared to a regional average of 23 (World Bank, 2008).

[4]As an example of inequality, the income Gini coefficient, which had modest decreases in the eighties, reached 0.56 in 2004, almost as high as the value for Brazil for the same year.

[5]As it is often done in studies with Colombian data at the department level due to lack of data, we group them as one unit under the name Nuevos departamentos.

upper bound in the initial year. Finally, empirical results obtained by Branisa and Cardozo (2009b), using per capita gross disposable income [6] as a proxy for well-being, suggest slow convergence among Colombian departments between 1975 and 2000.

We explain in the next two sections the methods used to test for convergence and the variables included in the analysis.

4.3 Methods for Measuring Convergence

We will consider two alternatives to empirically test for convergence. The first one is the *regression approach* (Magrini, 2004), also called the *classical approach to convergence analysis* (Sala-i-Martin, 1996), which is the most frequently used analysis in the literature. Robert Barro and Xavier Sala-i-Martin are among the best known authors associated with it (Barro and Sala-i-Martin, 1991, 1992a,b, 2004; Sala-i-Martin, 1996). The second alternative is the *distributional approach to convergence*, pioneered by, among others, Danny Quah (Quah, 1993a,b, 1996, 1997). Both approaches are presented briefly in this section.

Within the classical approach to convergence analysis, the concepts of beta-convergence and sigma-convergence are relevant. Beta-convergence is related to the mean-reversion of the variable of interest. This is typically done by regressing the average growth rate of the variable of interest at the initial level.[7] If the regression coefficient is negative and statistically significant, this means that the variable tends to grow more quickly in regions that lagged behind at the beginning of the period considered.

A reduction over time in the dispersion of the variable of interest across entities (in our case, departments) indicates a more equitable distribution and is known as sigma-convergence. Testing for sigma-convergence is performed by checking the evolution of the standard deviation over time, or the coefficient of variation if the mean of the variable changes. The existence of beta-convergence tends to generate sigma-convergence. Beta-convergence is a necessary, but not a sufficient condition for observing sigma-convergence. Sigma-convergence is an indicator of dispersion of departments, but does not tell much about the mobility of each one.

Quah (1997) criticizes the classical approach to convergence analysis, arguing that neither beta-convergence nor sigma-convergence can deliver useful answers to the question of whether poor countries or regions are catching up to wealthy ones. Quah argues that the classical approach does not provide any information about mobility, stratification, or polarization, and suggests analyzing the distribution dynamics directly. One alternative proposed

[6] IDBH is the abbreviation, based on the Spanish denomination Ingreso Departamental Bruto disponible de los Hogares (CEGA, 2006b).

[7] To be precise, we are discussing here *absolute* or unconditional beta-convergence, which assumes that regions are structurally similar.

by him is to work with a sequence of distributions and, after discretizing the space of values, to count the observed transitions into and out of the distinct cell values and construct a transition probability matrix (Quah, 1993a,b).

Quah (1997) warns, however, that a discretization could distort dynamics if the underlying observations are indeed continuous variables. He therefore suggests not to discretize at all, and rather to think of the distinct cells as tending to infinity and to the continuum, with the transition probability matrix tending to a matrix with a continuum of rows and columns, i.e., becoming a stochastic kernel.[8] In particular, the proposed methodology is based upon tracking the evolution of the entire cross-section distributions across regions over time through the estimation of kernel densities for '*relative*' variables. By relative variables, we mean that the variables of interest are expressed as relative to the national average, which allows abstraction from changes in the mean when we look at how the distribution changes.

Empirically, in a graph showing how the cross-sectional distribution of the relative variable of interest changes between two periods, if most of the mass of the estimated bivariate kernel density is concentrated along the 45-degree diagonal, then regions basically remain where they started. We will refer to this situation as *persistence* in the distribution of the relative variable of interest.

4.4 Data and Empirical Estimation

The convergence analysis in our paper is done at the department level. Using two cross-sections per variable, we treat each department as an observation and do not use population weights. We are interested in investigating whether departments that were lagging behind were able to catch up, and consider this to be a pertinent question in the Colombian case where, as mentioned in section 4.2, departments are important political entities.

In this section, we deal briefly with the selection of variables, the transformation of the variables needed in some cases, and the particular choices we apply for the empirical estimation.

4.4.1 Data

As discussed by Micklewright and Stewart (1999), many quality-of-life variables have a complement (e.g., the infant survival rate is 1,000 minus the infant mortality rate). They warn that sigma-convergence results may depend upon whether one uses a variable or its complement. Kenny (2004) argues for measuring convergence towards a maximum and not towards zero, claiming that the latter approach favors small absolute changes, close to zero, above large absolute changes, further from zero. Additionally, he claims that convergence towards the

[8]For a technical derivation of a stochastic kernel, see Quah (1997, section 4).

maximum (i.e., a positive value) is what the majority of the literature on global trends does. We follow these arguments and use in this study '*positive*' variables. By this we mean that we transform the variables so that they are, in theory, positively correlated with living standards.

We have tried to obtain data at the department level for years close to 1975 and 2000, as we additionally want to compare our regional convergence results with those found for two income measures in Branisa and Cardozo (2009b) for the period from 1975 to 2000. Evaluating a period of 25 years to investigate convergence seems reasonable as the time span roughly represents a generation. Our main source of data at the department level is DANE.[9] It kindly provided illiteracy rate data that were computed from information obtained in censuses for the years 1973 and 2005. For health data, we obtained infant mortality rates and life expectancy at birth. Data for the year 1975 are from DANE (1990) and for 2000, from DANE (2007). As explained before, we transform two of the variables so that they are 'positive' - we work with literacy rates instead of illiteracy rates, and with infant survival rates instead of infant mortality rates.

The literacy rate (LIT) is the percentage of literate population above age 5. Being illiterate can be considered a deprivation of a very basic capability. As argued by Sen (1999), basic education can additionally be considered a semi-public good, as it is not only the literate person who benefits from it, but society in general, for example through the reduction in fertility and mortality.

The infant survival rate (ISR) is the number of babies that survive until their first birthday out of every 1,000 live-born babies during a particular year. It is a measure of nutrition and hygiene in the first months of life, and also reflects the degree of the existence of contagious diseases (Mazumdar, 2003). There are many empirical studies that show that women's education and literacy tend to increase the survival rates of children (Sen, 1999).

Life expectancy at birth (LEX) is the average number of years that a newborn is expected to live if current mortality rates continue to apply. This variable reflects the level of health care, nutrition, and income. However, at least at the cross-country level, some studies show that the connection between income and life expectancy works mainly through two channels, public expenditure on health care and the success of poverty eradication efforts (Sen, 1999).

In addition to the data provided by DANE, we use data from Demographic and Health Surveys for Colombia for the years 1995 and 2005 containing information about child nutrition at the department level. As this variable covers a shorter time period than the other three variables and is based upon data that are not always representative at the department level, we will treat the results based on the 'positive' variable, well-nourished rate, carefully.

---

[9]Departamento Administrativo Nacional de Estadística. DANE is the official statistical agency in Colombia (http://www.dane.gov.co/).

Our well-nourished rate (WR) is defined as 100 minus the percentage of children which are underweight. Underweight means insufficient weight for age and is commonly used as a summary indicator of undernutrition (UNICEF, 1998). Undernutrition depends upon both food intake and the ability to make nutritive use of it, which ability is influenced by general health conditions that depend on health care and public health provisions (Drèze and Sen, 1989; Sen, 1999).

4.4.2 Empirical estimation

As the mean of the variables of interest has changed in the period considered, to test for sigma-convergence, we use the coefficient of variation, defined here as 100 times the ratio of the standard deviation to the mean.

For testing for beta-convergence, we follow one of the estimations used by Bloom and Canning (2007). We run regressions as

$$y_i = \alpha + \beta x_i + \varepsilon_i, \tag{4.1}$$

where x_i is the initial value of the variable of interest for department i, and y_i is the change in the variable of interest in the period considered. [10] We assume that $\varepsilon_i \sim N(0, \sigma^2)$ and estimate the regressions with ordinary least squares (OLS). We use HC3 robust standard errors, as proposed by Davidson and MacKinnon (1993), to account for possible heteroscedasticity, considering that the number of observations is relatively small (Long and Ervin, 2000). We are interested in checking whether the estimated coefficient β is negative and statistically different from 0 at the 5% level, meaning that lower initial levels of the variable of interest are associated with larger improvements in the periods considered. To check whether the results are robust, after the regression, we compute Cook's distance to detect observations that have an unusual influence or leverage, and re-run the regressions on the restricted sample, excluding those observations.

For the distributional approach, all variables are expressed relative to the Colombian value, as was explained in section 4.3. We additionally take the logarithm of the relative variable, as it facilitates the comparison to the national level. Expressed in logs, a relative value that is equal to 0 means that the department has the same value as the country, while a value that is, for example, equal to -0.05 means that the value of that department is 5% lower than the national value.

[10] We have also tried a specification proposed by Barro and Sala-i-Martin (1992a) that uses the average growth rate as the dependent variable and a function of the logarithm of the initial value as a regressor, obtaining similar results.

Before we define how we proceed to test for convergence using the distributional approach, we briefly present some concepts needed for our estimation.[11]

A univariate kernel density estimate can be regarded as a generalization of a histogram. It has the form

$$\hat{f}_h(q) = \frac{1}{nh}\sum_{i=1}^{n} \kappa\left(\frac{q-Q_i}{h}\right), \tag{4.2}$$

where κ is a kernel[12], $h > 0$ is the bandwidth, also called the smoothing parameter, and n is the number of observations.

In the context of convergence, we are interested in checking whether we find unimodality or multimodality in the estimated univariate densities of the relative variable of interest in both periods, and in determining how the estimated densities changed.

Bivariate kernel density estimation requires two-dimensional data and a two-dimensional kernel. Here, $Q = (Q_1, Q_2)^T$, and the kernel K maps $\mathbb{R}^2$ into $\mathbb{R}_+$. The estimate has the form

$$\hat{f}_H(q) = \frac{1}{n}\sum_{i=1}^{n} \frac{1}{det(H)} K\{H^{-1}(q-Q_i)\}, \tag{4.3}$$

where K is a bivariate kernel function, H is a symmetric bandwidth matrix, and n is the number of observations.

For the analysis of convergence, we estimate the bivariate kernel density for the relative variable in two periods and check whether a large portion of the probability mass remains clustered around the 45-degree diagonal, which would indicate persistence in the distribution. We present the 3D representation of the estimated bivariate density and a contour plot showing the highest density regions.

All the results for kernel density estimation presented in section 4.5 were computed with the statistical software R (R Development Core Team, 2008) and the package *ks*.[13] For both univariate and bivariate kernel density estimation, we use gaussian kernels and smoothed cross validation (SCV) bandwidth selectors[14] (Jones et al., 1991; Duong and Hazelton, 2005). In the bivariate case, the smoothed cross validation in unconstrained, i.e., we do not impose the requirement that the (nonsingular) bandwidth matrix H has to be diagonal. Hence, we

[11] A review of the statistical principles of univariate and multivariate kernel density estimation can be found in Härdle et al. (2004), for example.

[12] Kernel refers to any smooth function satisfying the conditions $\kappa(q) > 0$, $\int \kappa(q)dq = 1$, $\int q\kappa(q)dq = 0$, and $\sigma_\kappa^2 \equiv \int q^2\kappa(q)dq > 0$ (Wasserman, 2006). In kernel density estimation, the choice of the kernel does not have a large impact on the estimation, but the choice of the bandwidth does.

[13] *ks* is currently the most comprehensive kernel density estimation package in R (Duong, 2008). All the estimations were done with the function *kde*.

[14] We also tried direct plug-in methods for bandwidth selection suggested by Sheather and Jones (1991) and obtained results that are not very different.

are able to handle correlation between components, as we allow kernels to have an arbitrary orientation (Wand and Jones, 1995). As we are especially interested in checking whether a large portion of the probability mass remains clustered around the 45-degree diagonal, this flexibility is relevant for us. If we were to impose a diagonal matrix H, only kernels which are oriented to the coordinate axes would be allowed.

4.5 Results

We address in this paper the question of regional "positive convergence" in Colombia (Micklewright and Stewart, 1999); that is, we investigate whether departments which were lagging behind at the beginning of the period in certain variables of interest proxying for health care and education have been able to catch up in a period that has been one of improvement in average.[15] As can be observed in the descriptive statistics of the variables (Table 4.1), there has been a general improvement in all the variables chosen as proxies for living standards.

4.5.1 Literacy Rate

We find strong evidence of convergence in literacy rates. Both sigma-convergence (Table 4.2) and beta-convergence are observed (Tables 4.3 and 4.4). In the OLS regression with all available observations, Bogotá and La Guajira are identified as having an unusual influence on regression results; the coefficient of the initial level remains negative and statistically significant, however, if one excludes these two departments. In Bogotá literacy rates were already high in 1974 (90%), making it more difficult to achieve further improvements. La Guajira is in the opposite position, a department with very low literacy rates in 1973 and with a minor improvement in the 32 years of analysis. As suggested by Meisel (2007a) in a study of this department, illiteracy is widespread in the indigenous population, consisting of the Wayúu group, which predominantly lives in rural areas. Estimations of this author suggest that around 80% of the Wayúu's had not even finished primary school in 2005.

The univariate kernel in Figure 4.2 shows that the distribution has narrowed between 1973 and 2005. In 1973 one can observe three modes that are no longer visible in 2005. However, one small group lags behind in 2005. In Figure 4.4, one can observe a clear pattern of convergence, as most of the mass of the estimated bivariate density is concentrated in an axis that is flatter than the 45-degree line. Nevertheless, the case of La Guajira raises attention; it was among the worst relative performers in 1973, and in 2005, it was the worst relative performer. La Guajira had literacy rates that were 28% lower than the national average in 1973 and 33% in 2005.

[15]"Negative convergence," (European Commission, 1996) a situation of general deterioration towards the standard of the worst, is not relevant for Colombia in the period considered.

Although one can praise improvements for the other departments that were lagging behind in 1973, it is important to note that the literacy rate only indicates the existence of a basic education level, which is definitely important, but probably not adequate. [16] Even considering this very basic indicator, it is worrisome that in many departments (La Guajira, Chocó, Sucre, Córdoba, Magdalena, Caquetá, Cesar, Nariño, and Bolívar), more than 15% of the population is still illiterate. Unfortunately, we have not been able to access data at the department level that proxies higher levels of education.

4.5.2 Infant Survival Rate

Between 1975 and 2000, the average departmental infant survival rate per thousand live births improved, increasing from 936 to 962 (Table 4.1). Results show that the coefficient of variation of this indicator decreased slightly, suggesting mild sigma-convergence (Table 4.2). However, this result tells us little about how exactly the distribution of departments changed.

When looking at beta-convergence, we find a negative coefficient for infant survival rate in 1975, but it is not statistically significant unless we exclude the department of Chocó from the regression (Tables 4.5 and 4.6). This exclusion is based on unusual influence or leverage and indicates that this department has an important influence on the lack of convergence. Chocó had the lowest performance in 1975 and even though infant survival rate improved there, by 2000, it was the furthest from the departmental average. Notice that the infant survival rate in Chocó in 2000 was lower than the departmental average in 1975 (Table 4.1).

Figure 4.5 shows that after Chocó, departments with the lowest starting infant survival rates were Nariño, Caldas, Risaralda, and Quindío. Of these, Caldas, Risaralda, and Quindío achieved the largest improvements during the period of analysis. Changes in departments that were close to the average in 1975 vary considerably. Antioquia, Norte de Santander, and Valle experienced important improvements, while Cauca, Córdoba, Guajira, and Bolívar stagnated.

Kernel density estimators allow a closer look at changes in the distribution in relative terms. In Figure 4.6 we observe that the density was slightly narrower in 2000 than in 1975. Both years had a bimodal distribution. The bivariate kernel in Figure 4.7 and the corresponding contour plot in Figure 4.8 suggest persistence in the infant survival rate, as most of the estimated density is concentrated along the 45-degree diagonal. Thus, in relative terms, departments basically remained where they were in 1975. The departments of Chocó, Nariño, and Cauca are outside of the 90% contour.

[16] Additionally, as discussed in Velez et al. (2003), there is some evidence that despite large and increasing public expenditures on public education, particularly after decentralization, the quality of education is decreasing.

To summarize, coastal regions have the lowest infant survival rates, although the rates have improved over time. The infant survival rate is particularly low in 2000 in the Pacific region (e.g., 912 children per 1,000 births in Chocó) where population density is low and a large share of the population lives in rural areas with precarious sanitation infrastructure. This department is also prone to a higher prevalence of tropical diseases, given that it is one of the rainiest and humid regions in the world. Transport between small rural villages along the river shores, which are prone to floods, is possible only within the extensive network of rivers. This also explains why the the scope and reach of health programs are limited.[17]

In contrast, an important increase in infant survival rates has been observed in central regions located along the main transport corridors of the country. Increased vaccination was achieved in large cities and in departments where agglomeration around urban centers allows easier access to the population.

4.5.3 Life Expectancy at Birth

In Colombia, the average departmental life expectancy at birth was 62 years in 1975 and increased to 70 years in 2000 (Table 4.1). The coefficient of variation decreased from 5.7 to 3.7, suggesting sigma-convergence (Table 4.2). Beta-convergence analysis shows a negative relationship between the starting value in 1975 and its change up to 2000 (4.9). The regression coefficient is negative and statistically significant when including all observations, but it is insignificant once we exclude influential observations, in this case Chocó and Nariño, which experienced large improvements. In Nariño, people born in 2000 were expected to live 14 years longer than those born in 1975, and in Chocó the gain was 13 years. Once again the coffee-growing region (Caldas, Quindío, and Risaralda) had outstanding improvements. Sucre, located in the Atlantic coast, had the longest life expectancy at birth by 2000, even exceeding that of the capital district of Bogotà, which ranks frequently in first place for economic and well-being indicators. On the contrary, the set of departments that we group as Nuevos Departamentos in the eastern and southern parts of the country experienced modest improvements, taking into account their low starting position.

The univariate kernel density estimators of life expectancy at birth for 1975 and 2000 show that the distribution has become narrower, as was expected from the sigma-convergence result. Even if both distributions seem bimodal, the mode on the left of the distributions is much closer to the main mode in 2000 than in 1975.

[17]According to the Demographic and Health Survey from 2005, 20% of women in La Guajira did not have any kind of prenatal care before delivery. These rates are also very high for Caquetá (20%), Cauca (15%), Chocó (15%), and CŮórdoba(14%). In Chocó, 40% of births were attended at home (usually by a midwife). The corresponding figures for Caquetá and Cauca are 32% and 31%, respectively (Profamilia, 2005).

In Figures 4.11 and 4.12, we observe the bivariate kernel density estimator, which is computed using life expectancy at birth relative to the national average for both years. Once again the results suggest persistence, rather than convergence, as most of mass of the estimated bivariate density is concentrated along the 45-degree diagonal. In relative terms, departments basically remained where they were in 1975. Chocó, Nariño, and Nuevos are the three departments outside of the 90% contour. As mentioned before, Chocó and Nariño improved dramatically in their relative positions, while Chocò remained the worst performer both years.

4.5.4 Nourishment

As was mentioned before, we must treat the results concerning nourishment with care, as we only have data for 1995 and 2005, a period which is shorter than that used for other variables, and as we are using data for 23 departments[18] from Demographic and Health Surveys which are not always representative at the department level. Nevertheless, we consider that some insight can be gained investigating convergence in the rate of well-nourished children.

Table 4.1 shows that between 1995 and 2005, the departmental average of the well-nourished rate (WR) improved from 93% to 95%. Both sigma-convergence (Table 4.2) and beta-convergence are observed. Figure 4.13 plots the value of WR in 1995 against the change in WR between 1995 and 2005. There is a clear negative relationship between them which is confirmed with the regressions presented in Tables 4.9 and 4.10.

Figure 4.14 shows the estimated univariate kernel density estimators of the log of relative WR and confirms that the distribution is less skewed in 2005, but the bimodality observed in 1995 remains in 2005. Bivariate kernel density estimators shown in Figures 4.15 and 4.16 suggest mild convergence in this indicator. Most of the mass of the estimated bivariate density is concentrated in an axis that is flatter than the 45-degree line.

4.6 Conclusions

Several points are important for the discussion. First, unlike in the case when one is dealing with income indicators, social indicators have natural upper bounds (Neumayer, 2003; Kenny, 2004). In the case of the three rates we use (infant survival rate, literacy rate, and well-nourished rate), the upper bound is evident and constant (e.g., no department can have a more than 100% literacy rate). In the case of life expectancy at birth, the upper bound can be thought of as variable, but a slow moving one.[19] As discussed by Neumayer (2003)

[18] No information is available for Caquetá and Nuevos Departamentos.

[19] There is no consensus among scientists concerning the upper bound of life expectancy at birth and values between 85 years (which is the value currently used in the Human Development Reports) and 100 years have been mentioned. Olshansky et al. (1990), for example, claim that it seems unlikely that life expectancy at birth

and Kenny (2004), among others, convergence is more likely to be observed in variables with an upper bound when some departments are close to that bound in the initial year. Our results show that this is the case for the classical approach to convergence, where sigma-convergence is found in all cases, and beta-convergence also in all, with the exception of the infant survival rate. Working with relative values and using the distributional approach, it is possible to make a more precise evaluation if one uses bivariate kernel estimators. For example, the distributional approach yields persistence in the distribution of life expectancy at birth, while the beta-convergence analysis shows convergence. Obviously, regression results can be driven by outliers, as is the case for this variable. If one excludes outliers, no evidence of beta-convergence is observed.

Second, it has been argued that at least at the cross-country level, one can observe convergence in social indicators even in the absence of convergence in income. Two reasons advanced for this are high returns to small marginal increases in income at low income levels and causal relationships between the social indicators, themselves (Kenny, 2004), for example between literacy and mortality. Additionally, the dispersion of best practices in health care can lead to improvement in health outcomes, even without income convergence. This is relevant for us, as results in Branisa and Cardozo (2009b) suggest that there has been persistence in the distribution of departmental per capita GDP between 1975 and 2000.[20]

Third, the role of urbanization should also be highlighted, as it is relevant in our case. The percentage of total population in Colombia that lived in urban areas increased from 59% in 1973 to 75% in 2005. Urbanization facilitates convergence in social indicators, as it is easier to provide social services to urban residents than to rural (Kenny, 2004). As shown by Bettencourt et al. (2007), cities make economies of scale in infrastructure possible. Nevertheless, we stress that living in an urban area does not guarantee access to services.

Fourth, departments in Colombia differ according to climatic and geographic conditions, which conditions have been historically determinant for agglomeration and the availability of infrastructure, particularly roads. Two important consequences are that some diseases only affect departments that are located in the tropics and that access to sanitation services is more limited in isolated areas.

will exceed the age of 85, while other studies, based on extrapolations from historical trends, predict that it could attain 100 years in developed countries by 2060 (Oeppen and Vaupel, 2002) or by 2300 (United Nations, 2004).

[20]PDB is the abbreviation used by Branisa and Cardozo (2009b) for departmental GDP, based on the Spanish denomination "Producto Departamental Bruto" (CEGA, 2006b).

Fifth, and related to the last point, the internal conflict in Colombia is not of the same intensity across all departments.[21] Although it is a widespread problem affecting the whole country, sparsely populated departments, with predominantly rural areas having limited access due to geographic conditions and in which state presence has been historically low or weak, are more prone to the presence of illegal groups.

With these issues in mind, we begin the discussion of the results concerning convergence in education. In the final quarter of the last century, we find clear evidence of regional convergence in literacy rates in Colombia. As discussed by Barrera and Domínguez (2006), since the seventies, there have been policies in place having the objective of reducing illiteracy and increasing the coverage of primary education, which policies are partially responsible for our result. Urbanization probably also played a role here. While some of the departments with the best indicators in 1973 had a population that was primarily urban, many of the worst performers in that year had a population that was mainly rural and urbanization increased relatively more in the worst performers.[22] Another possible reason for the convergence result is that our indicator considers the population above five years of age in both periods. The elder population in 1973, which was no longer alive in 2005, likely had relatively high illiteracy rates, particularly in the departments which were lagging behind in 1973. Thus, there is a generational effect; the older cohorts included in 1973 are no longer visible in the statistics in 2005, while younger cohorts, who benefited from improved educational resources and literacy campaigns, are included.

Even if regional convergence in literacy rates seems to be a robust result, one should keep in mind that it only reflects very basic education and we do not know whether convergence was observed in education at higher levels. The department of La Guajira deserves special attention as it still lags far behind in literacy rates.[23]

---

[21]The current internal conflict began almost 50 years ago with the emergence of leftist guerrilla groups, the root motivations of which were mainly ideological. Up until 1980, the military capacity of these groups was limited and Was concentrated in marginal areas of the country. Parallel to those, paramilitary groups developed slowly in the eighties to defend isolated areas from guerrilla attacks. During the coca bonanza ("bonanza coquera") and the consolidation of drug trafficking in the eighties, illegal armed groups found new ways of financing operations and expanding through the control of areas where illegal crops where grown, as well as in territories that are rich in natural resources, particularly oil (Díaz and Sánchez, 2004).

[22]As examples for well performing departments in terms of literacy rates in 1973, consider Antioquia, which had an urban percent of population of 62% in 1973 and 78% in 2005, and Valle, which had 76% in 1973 and 87% in 2005. Examples for poorly performing departments in 1973 are Chocó, which had an urban percentage of population of 26% in 1973 and 54% in 2005, and Sucre, which had an urban percentage of population of 47% in 1973 and 64% in 2005.

[23]As mentioned before, this department has a large indigenous population (44%) of which population 80% has not attained any educational degree (Meisel, 2007a).

Considering indicators of the health status of the population and using infant survival rates (ISR) as a proxy, we find no evidence of beta-convergence. Following the distributional approach and values expressed relative to the national levels, we find evidence of persistence in the distribution. In 2005 departments are basically where they were in 1973, in relative terms. These results can also be explained by a low prevalence of prenatal care in departments of the Pacific and Atlantic coasts (Profamilia, 2005).

Using life expectancy at birth as a proxy for health yields similar results (persistence) according to the distributional approach. In relative terms, in the year 2005, departments are basically where they started in 1973. However, the two departments that had the lowest values at the beginning of the period improved substantially in relative terms. Beta-convergence is driven by these two departments. Results regarding nourishment show regional convergence in the 10 years studied (1995 through 2005). (As previously mentioned, estimates have to be considered cautiously because the sample of 1995 is not representative for all departments.) Two interesting issues emerge. First, the well-nourished rate deteriorated slightly for some departments that were close to the upper bound in the initial year. Second, the three poorest departments in the Pacific coast improved considerably in relative terms, as pointed by Profamilia (2005). Interestingly, in the Atlantic coast, nourishment relative to the national average stagnated.

Our results differ from those in the scarce literature on convergence among departments in Colombia which used health and education indicators. Some of our results contradict those obtained by Aguirre (2005), who finds convergence in life expectancy at birth, but not in education. The difference concerning life expectancy can be explained as follows. We find that beta-convergence is driven by two influential observations, and once we use bivariate kernel estimators with the variable expressed as a ratio to the the national value, we find persistence in the distribution of life expectancy rather than convergence. The difference concerning education could be due to the fact that Aguirre uses *illiteracy* rate for the analysis, while we use literacy rates. Note that while Aguirre also computes univariate kernel density estimators for the variables in both periods, they are based on absolute values (i.e., not relative to the national average), making judgements as to distributional changes more difficult given that the means vary.

Finally, the study of Meisel and Vega (2007) considers a much longer period (1870 through 2003) for investigating regional convergence in Colombia, using the evolution of adult height over time as an alternative perspective on the standard of living. They find both sigma and beta-convergence among departments and highlight that nutritional improvements are among the main explanations of this result. Even if our results concerning nourishment cover a much shorter period (1995 through 2005), they point to the same conclusion. It could be interesting to test for convergence among departments with the distributional approach using the sample of Meisel and Vega (2007). Lack of convergence among Colombian departments in the two variables proxying for health raises some doubts as to the effectiveness of current policies, as convergence is what one would expect, for the reasons explained above. Understanding why some departments still lag behind is relevant, as it is not clear whether the reasons are due mainly to the differences in per capita income, climatic and geographic conditions, infrastructure, or behavior, or to still other factors. It is crucial to understand the main causes of infant and adult morbidity and mortality in the departments lagging behind to assess which specific policies could improve living conditions in each case.

Summary of Results

	Social indicator used			
	Literacy rate	Infant survival rate	Life expectancy at birth	Well-nourished rate
Classical Approach				
Sigma	Yes	Yes	Yes	Yes
Absolute Beta (all obs.)	Yes	No	Yes	Yes
Absolute Beta (excl. outliers)	Yes	Yes	No	Yes
Distributional Approach				
Univariate Kernel Estimators	Dispersion decreases	Dispersion decreases	Dispersion decreases	Dispersion decreases
Bivariate Kernel Estimators	Convergence	Persistence in the distribution	Persistence in the distribution	Suggests slow convergence

4.7 Tables

Table 4.1: Descriptive Statistics of the Variables Used

Variable	**Literacy rate**		**Infant survival rate**		**Life expectancy at birth**		**Well-nourished rate**	
Year	**1973**	**2005**	**1975**	**2000**	**1975**	**2000**	**1995**	**2005**
mean	70.3	85.8	935.9	962.3	61.7	69.9	93.0	95.3
median	69.0	87.4	940. 1	967.8	62.5	69.9	93.8	95.7
stand. deviation	9.38	6.8	16.6	14.4	3.6	2.6	4.2	2.3
skewness	-0.0	-1.8	-2.0	-2.0	-1.6	-1.0	-1.4	-0.9
kurtosis	2.5	6.5	7.8	7.6	6.6	4.4	4.8	3.9
range	37.3	30.2	81.3	64.8	17.6	11.5	17.8	9.8
minimum	52.2	63.1	876.7	911.5	49.7	62.4	80.9	88.9
maximum	89.6	93.4	958.1	976.3	67.3	73.8	98.7	98.7
Number of obs.	25	25	24	24	24	24	23	23

Source: Own calculations based on data at the department level from DANE and DHS.

Table 4.2: Evolution of Point Estimates and 95% Confidence Intervals of the Coefficients of Variation (CV)

Literacy rate		
Year	1973	2005
CV	13.3	7.9
95% conf. int. of CV	10.6 - 17.5	4.9 - 13.3
Infant survival rate		
Year	1975	2000
CV	1.8	1.5
95% conf. int. of CV	1.0 - 2.7	0.9 - 2.6
Life expectancy at birth		
Year	1975	2000
CV	5.8	3.7
95% conf. int. of CV	3.7 - 9.8	2.6 - 5.6
Well-nourished rate		
Year	1995	2005
CV	4.6	2.4
95% conf. int. of CV	2.8 - 6.8	1.8 - 3.6

Source: Own calculations based on data from DANE.
Note: The coefficient of variation is defined as 100 times the ratio of the standard deviation to the mean. The confidence intervals were calculated using the adjusted bootstrap percentile (BCa) method.
(Davison and Hinkley, 1997; R Development Core Team, 2008)

Table 4.3: Beta Convergence (OLS) using all available Observations. Dependent Variable: Change in Literacy Rate (LIT) between 1973 and 2005

Variable	Coefficient	Robust Std. error	p-value
Intercept	43.42	9.56	0.000
LIT in 1973	-0.40	0.13	0.005
Number of observations	25		
R-squared	0.50		

Source: Own calculations based on data from DANE.

Note: HC3 robust standard errors calculated following Davidson and MacKinnon (1993).

Table 4.4: Beta convergence (OLS) excluding Outliers. Dependent Variable: Change in Literacy Rate (LIT) between 1973 and 2005

Variable	Coefficient	Robust Std. error	p-value
Intercept	49.36	5.93	0.000
LIT in 1973	-0.47	0.08	0.000
Number of observations	23		
R-squared	0.81		

Source: Own calculations based on data from DANE.

Notes: Two departments (Bogotá and La Guajira) were excluded using Cook's distance to detect for unusual influence or leverage after the regression with all observations. HC3 robust standard errors calculated following Davidson and MacKinnon (1993).

Table 4.5: Beta Convergence (OLS) using all available Observations. Dependent Variable: Change in Infant Survival Rate (ISR) between 1975 and 2000

Variable	Coefficient	Robust Std. error	p-value
Intercept	370.75	297.25	0.257
ISR in 1975	-0.37	0.32	0.225
Number of observations	24		
R-squared	0.28		

Source: Own calculations based on data from DANE.

Note: HC3 robust standard errors calculated following Davidson and MacKinnon (1993).

Table 4.6: Beta Convergence (OLS) excluding Outliers. Dependent Variable: Change in Infant Survival Rate (ISR) between 1975 and 2000

Variable	Coefficient	Robust Std. error	p-value
Intercept	660.00	195.01	0.003
ISR in 1975	-0.68	0.21	0.004
Number of observations	23		
R-squared	0.41		

Source: Own calculations based on data from DANE.

Notes: One department (Chocó) was excluded using Cook's distance to detect for unusual influence or leverage after the regression with all observations. HC3 robust standard errors calculated following Davidson and MacKinnon (1993).

Table 4.7: Beta Convergence (OLS) using all available Observations. Dependent Variable: Change in Life Expectancy at Birth (LEX) between 1975 and 2000

Variable	Coefficient	Robust Std. error	p-value
Intercept	34.69	6.67	0.000
LEX in 1975	-0.43	0.11	0.001
Number of observations	24		
R-squared	0.48		

Source: Own calculations based on data from DANE.

Note: HC3 robust standard errors calculated following Davidson and MacKinnon (1993).

Table 4.8: Beta Convergence (OLS) excluding Outliers. Dependent Variable: Change in Life Expectancy at Birth (LEX) between 1975 and 2000

Variable	Coefficient	Robust Std. error	p-value
Intercept	27.48	10.46	0.016
LEX in 1975	-0.32	0.17	0.070
Number of observations	22		
R-squared	0.19		

Source: Own calculations based on data from DANE.

Notes: Two departments (Chocó and Nariño) were excluded using Cook's distance after the regression with all observations to detect for unusual influence or leverage.

HC3 robust standard errors calculated following Davidson and MacKinnon (1993).

Table 4.9: Beta Convergence (OLS) using all available Observations. Dependent Variable: Change in Well-nourished Rate (WR) between 1995 and 2005

Variable	Coefficient	Robust Std. error	p-value
Intercept	0.86	0.23	0.001
WR in 1995	-0.90	0.24	0.001
Number of observations	23		
R-squared	0.74		

Source: Own calculations based on data from DHS.

Note: HC3 robust standard errors calculated following Davidson and MacKinnon (1993).

Table 4.10: Beta Convergence (OLS) excluding Outliers. Dependent Variable: Change in Well-nourished Rate (WR) between 1995 and 2005

Variable	Coefficient	Robust Std. error	p-value
Intercept	0.99	0.16	0.000
WR in 1975	-1.04	0.17	0.000
Number of observations	21		
R-squared	0.68		

Source: Own calculations based on data from DHS.

Notes: Two departments (Chocó and La Guajira) were excluded using Cook's distance after the regression with all observations to detect for unusual influence or leverage.

HC3 robust standard errors calculated following Davidson and MacKinnon (1993).

Table 4.11: Poverty Headcount Index (% of Households below the Poverty Line) by Department. 1996 to 2005

Department	1996	1999	2002	2003	2004
Antioquia	54.1	57.8	58.9	55.6	54.1
Atlántico	49.5	57.9	53.2	52.1	48.2
Bogotá	37.8	46.3	36.1	34.2	29.5
Bolivar	60.3	59.9	67.8	51.5	54.6
Boyacá	65.0	62.6	72.3	70.3	71.5
Caldas	54.3	54.0	59.6	58.8	57.7
Caquetá	58.0	59.9	53.5	54.5	56.8
Cauca	61.4	73.3	64.5	69.0	63.0
Cesar	49.7	53.7	67.2	61.6	59.3
Chocó	70.9	78.0	62.6	70.3	71.6
Córdoba	74.3	72.6	68.5	66.5	70.8
Cundinamarca	44.5	50.9	58.4	51.9	53.6
Huila	62.9	62.7	74.4	69.7	66.3
Guajira	49.3	50.2	68.4	54.6	52.8
Magdalena	62.6	62.7	66.4	55.4	55.0
Meta	50.9	52.4	47.9	44.3	42.5
Nariño	68.1	71.7	70.7	71.2	67.3
N.Santander	61.3	58.2	57.3	57.3	57.9
Quindío	45.4	51.4	49.3	41.3	47.3
Risaralda	52.1	51.5	47.9	45.3	44.7
Santander	48.9	55.4	50.2	48.6	48.6
Sucre	47.9	64.0	69.4	56.5	65.7
Tolima	59.3	58.4	60.6	58.8	60.1
Valle	47.4	47.6	44.1	37.4	38.9

Source: Own calculations based on Household Surveys from DANE.

4.8 Figures

Figure 4.1: Evolution of Literacy Rate. 1973-2005

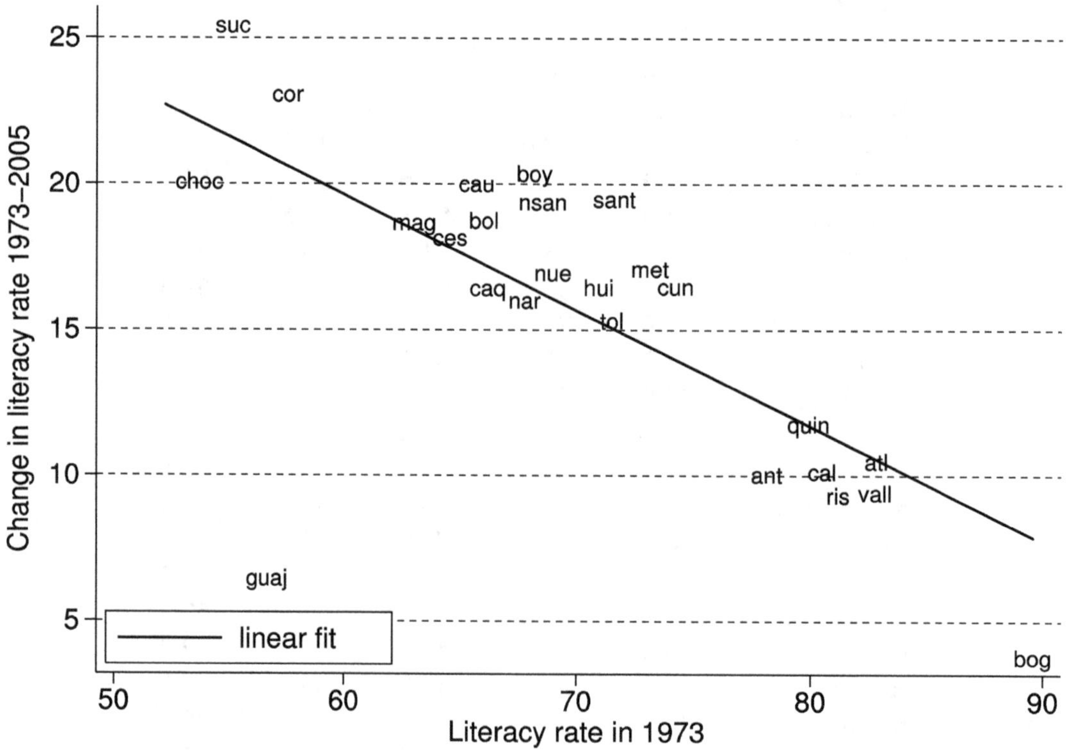

Source: Own calculations based on data from DANE.

Figure 4.2: Univariate Kernel Density Estimators of Relative Literacy Rate. 1973 and 2005.

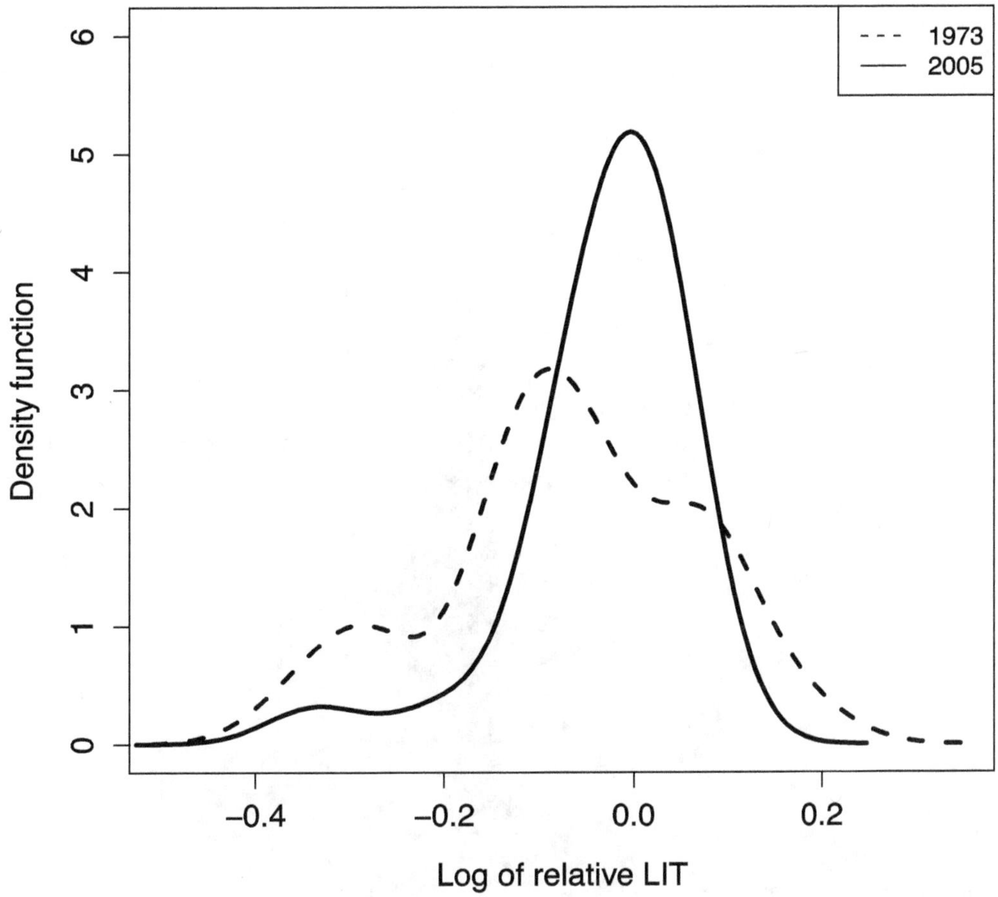

Source: Own calculations based on data from DANE. Variables relative to the national average and in logs.

Figure 4.3: Bivariate Kernel Density Estimators of Relative Literacy Rate. 3D Representation. 1973 and 2005.

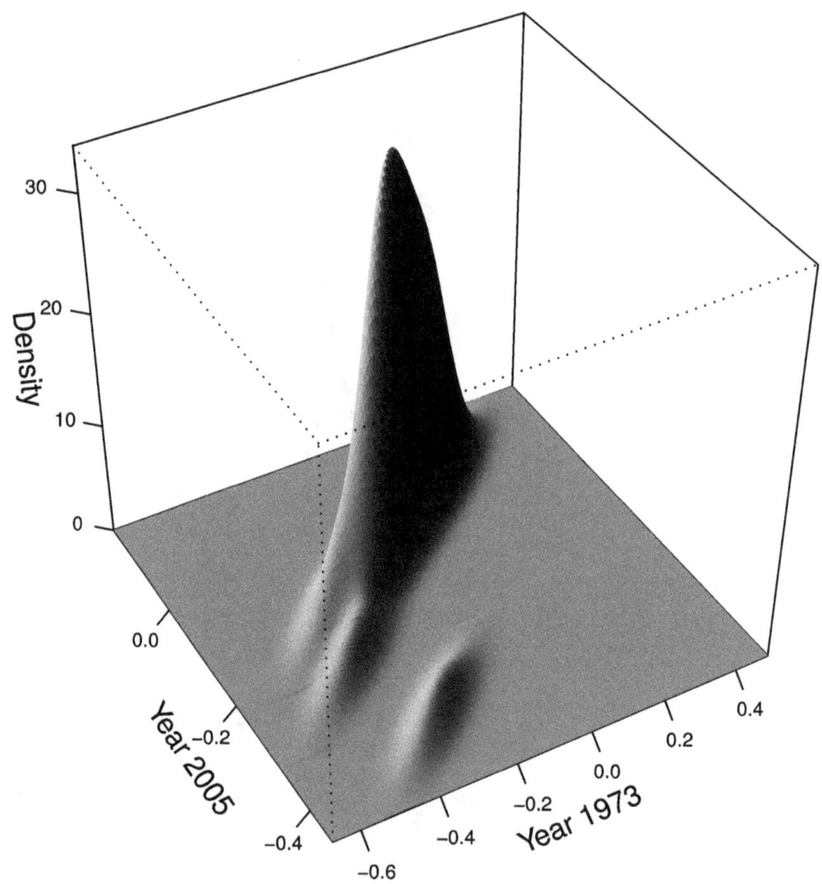

Source: Own calculations based on data from DANE. Variables relative to the national average and in logs.

Figure 4.4: Bivariate Kernel Density Estimators of Relative Literacy Rate. Contour Plot. 1973 and 2005.

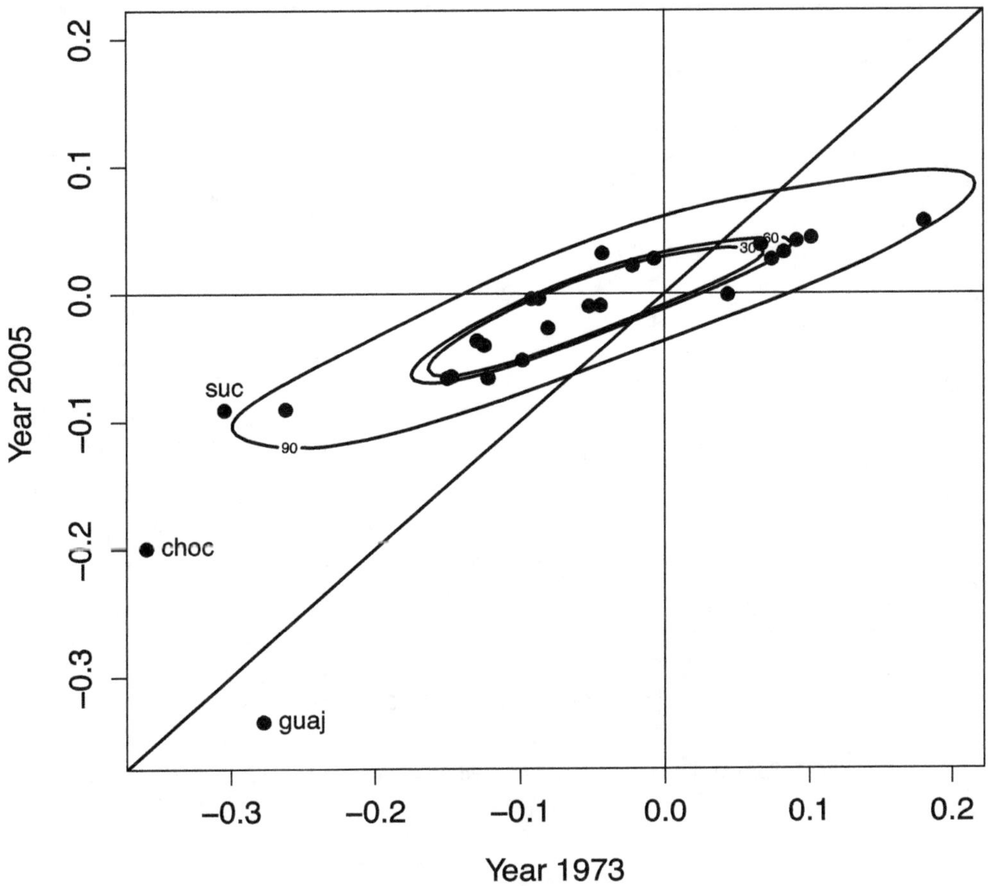

Source: Own calculations based on data from DANE. Variables in logs. Contours at drawn at the 30%, 60%, and 90% which are upper percentages of highest density regions. The points represent the 25 observations. Points outside the 90% contour are identified. A 45 degree line is added to the plot.

Figure 4.5: Evolution of Infant Survival Rate. 1975-2000

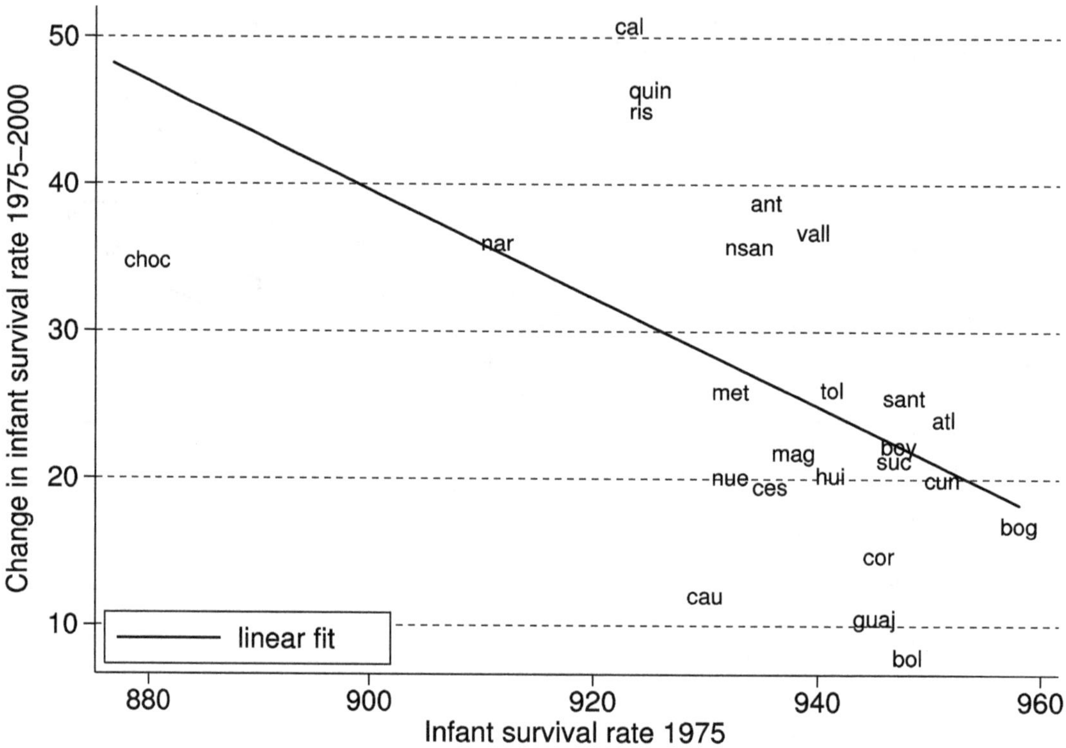

Source: Own calculations based on data from DANE.

Figure 4.6: Univariate Kernel Density Estimators of Relative Infant Survival Rate. 1975 and 2000.

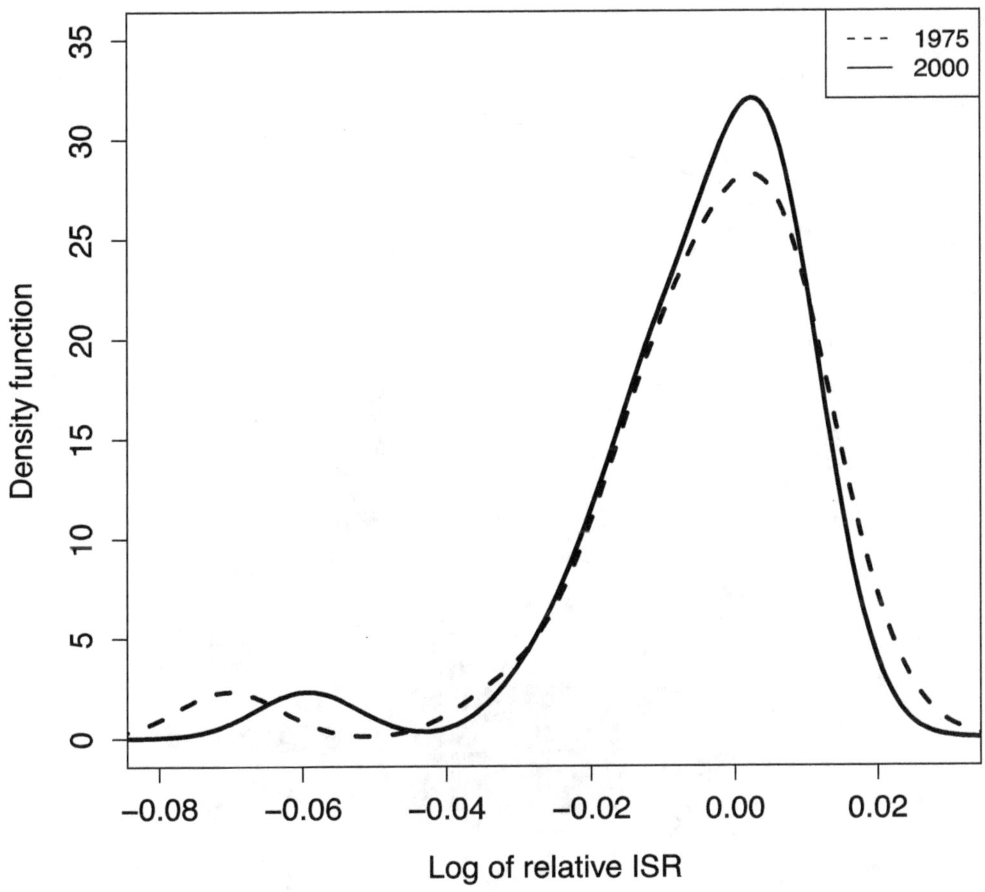

Source: Own calculations based on data from DANE. Variables relative to the national average and in logs.

Figure 4.7: Bivariate Kernel Density Estimators of Relative Infant Survival Rate. 3D Representation. 1975 and 2000.

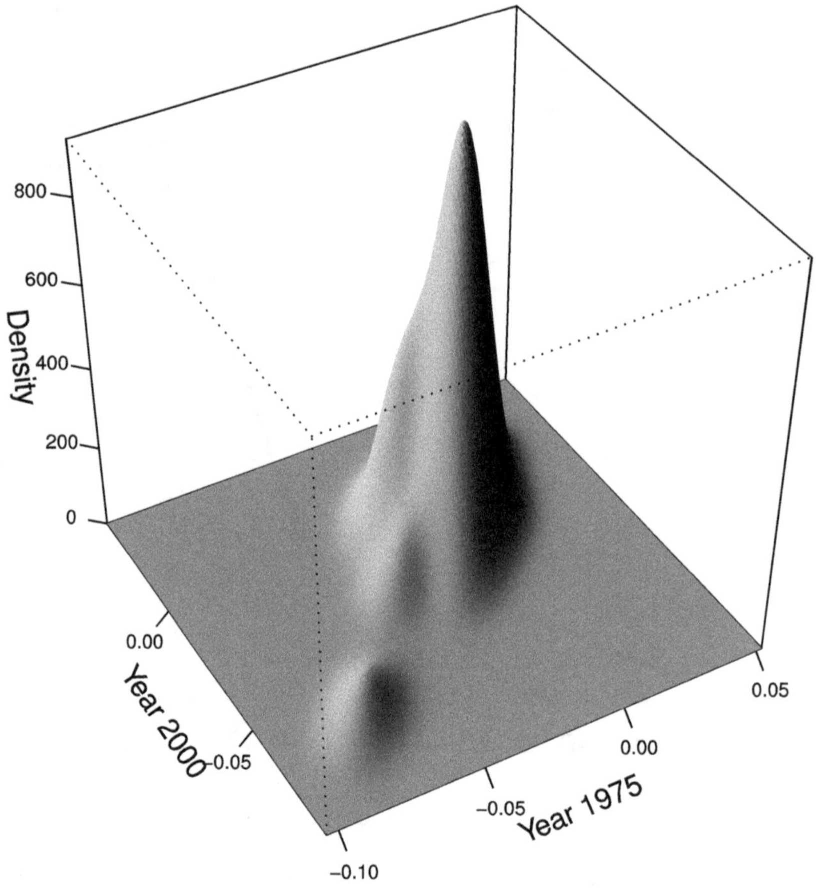

Source: Own calculations based on data from DANE. Variables relative to the national average and in logs.

Figure 4.8: Bivariate Kernel Density Estimators of Relative Infant Survival Rate. Contour Plot. 1975 and 2000.

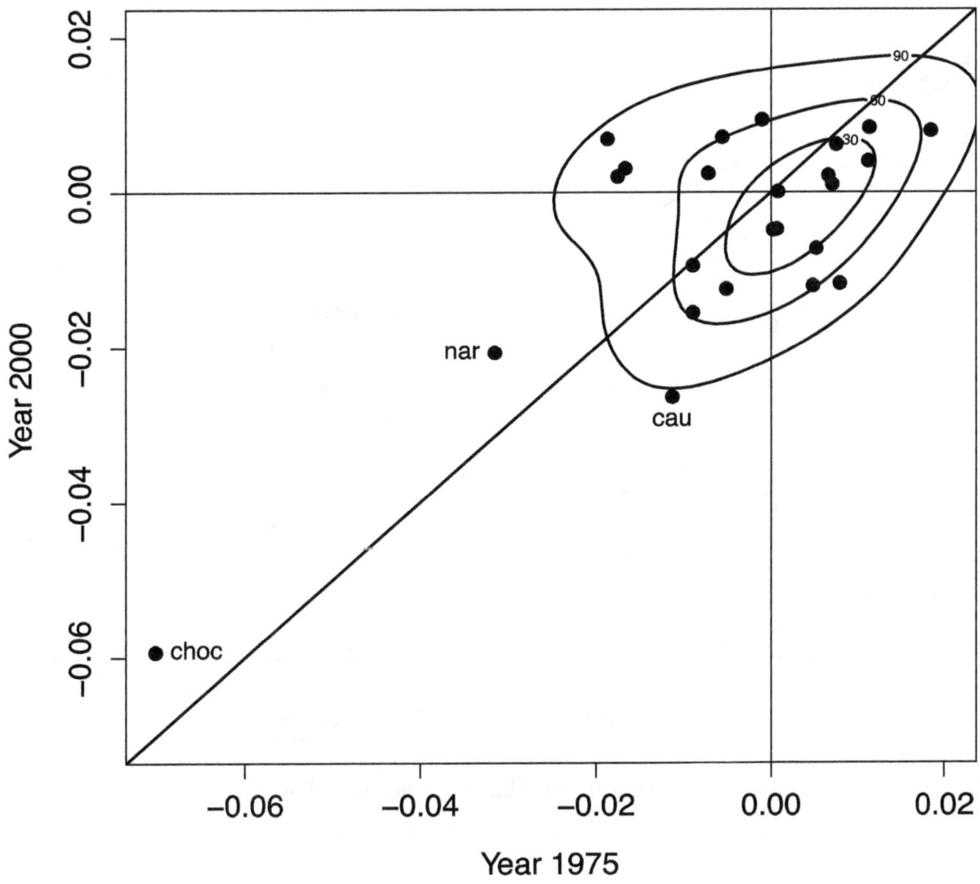

Source: Own calculations based on data from DANE. Variables in logs. Contours at drawn at the 30%, 60%, and 90% which are upper percentages of highest density regions. The points represent the 25 observations. Points outside the 90% contour are identified. A 45 degree line is added to the plot.

Figure 4.9: Evolution of Life Expectancy at Birth. 1975-2000

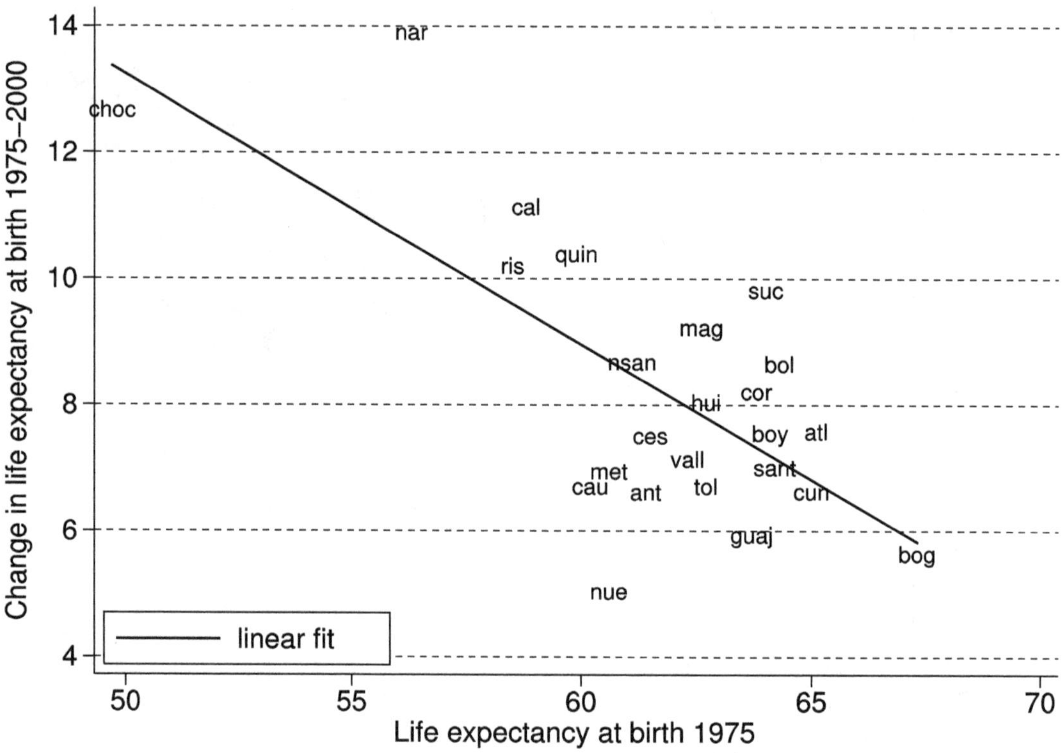

Source: Own calculations based on data from DANE.

Figure 4.10: Univariate Kernel Density Estimators of Relative Life Expectancy at Birth. 1975 and 2000.

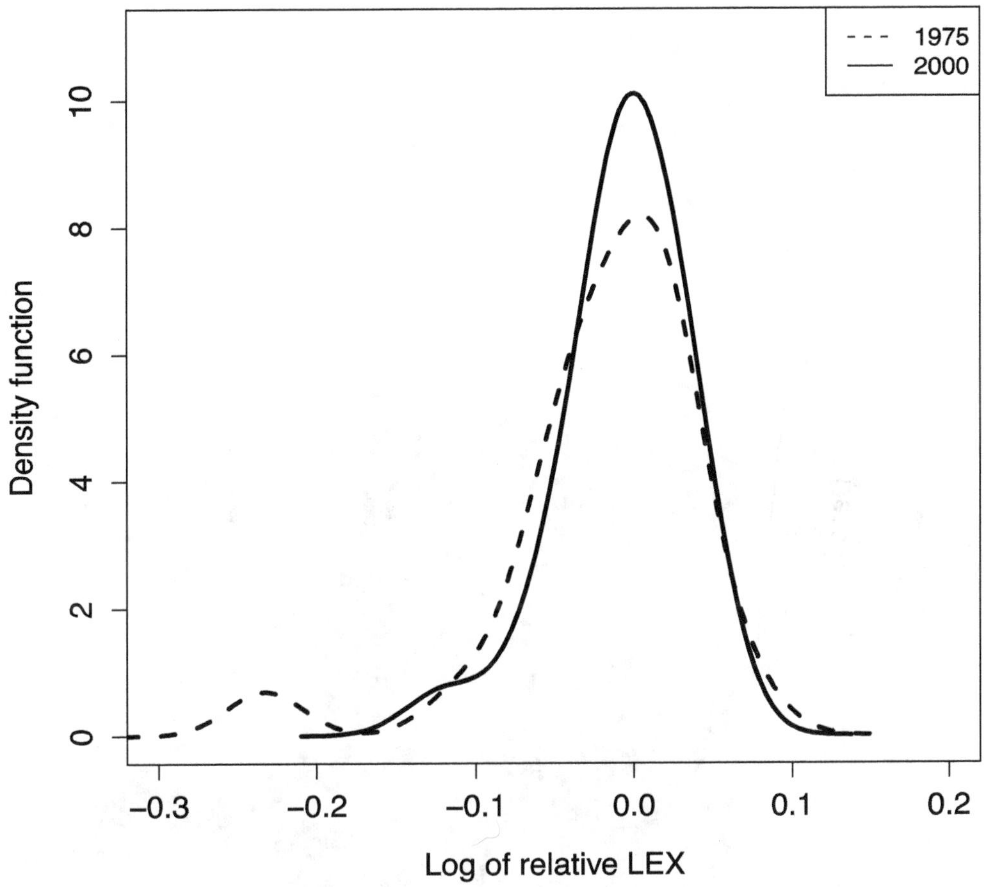

Source: Own calculations based on data from DANE. Variables relative to the national average and in logs.

Figure 4.11: Bivariate Kernel Density Estimators of Relative Life Expectancy at Birth. 3D Representation. 1975 and 2000.

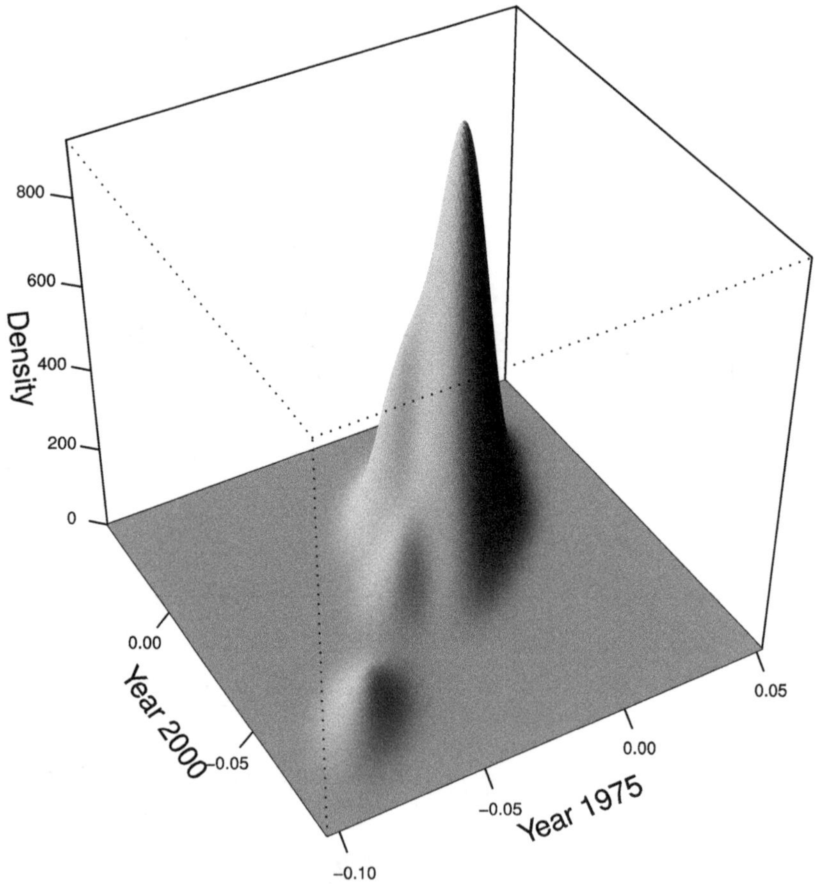

Source: Own calculations based on data from DANE. Variables relative to the national average and in logs.

Figure 4.12: Bivariate Kernel Density Estimators of Relative Life Expectancy at Birth. Contour Plot. 1975 and 2000.

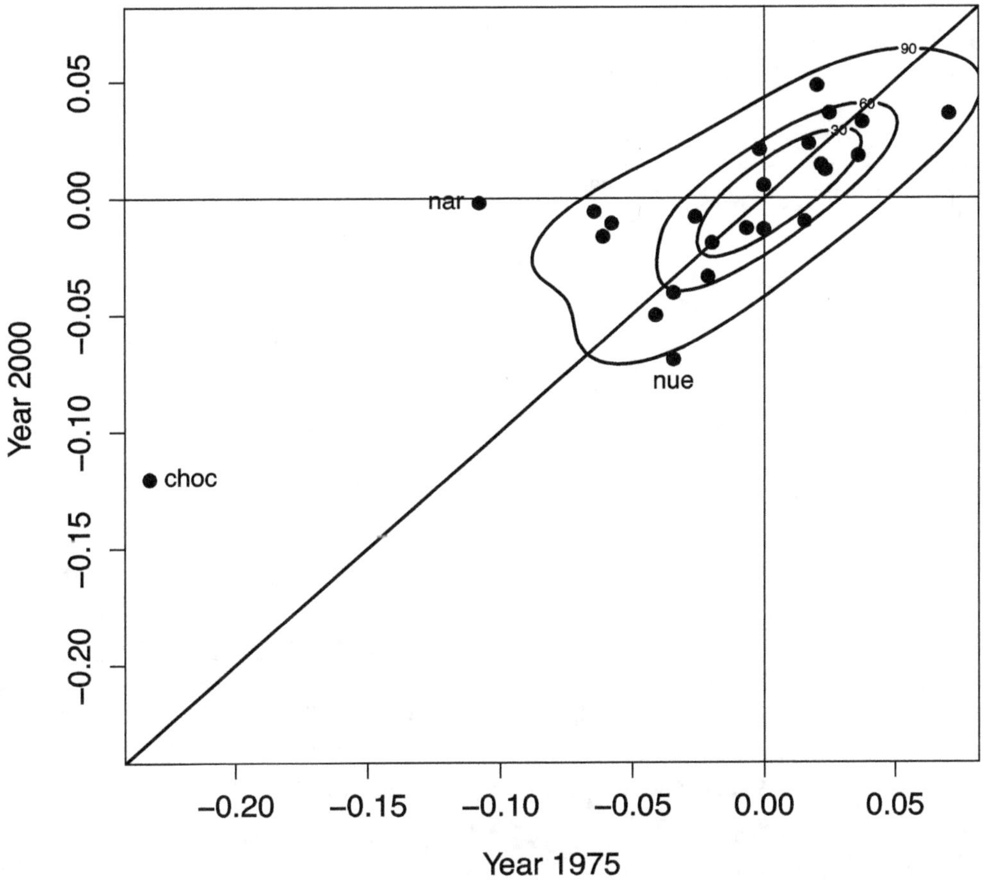

Source: Own calculations based on data from DANE. Variables in logs. Contours at drawn at the 30%, 60%, and 90% which are upper percentages of highest density regions. The points represent the 25 observations. Points outside the 90% contour are identified. A 45 degree line is added to the plot.

Figure 4.13: Evolution of Well-Nourished Rate. 1995-2005

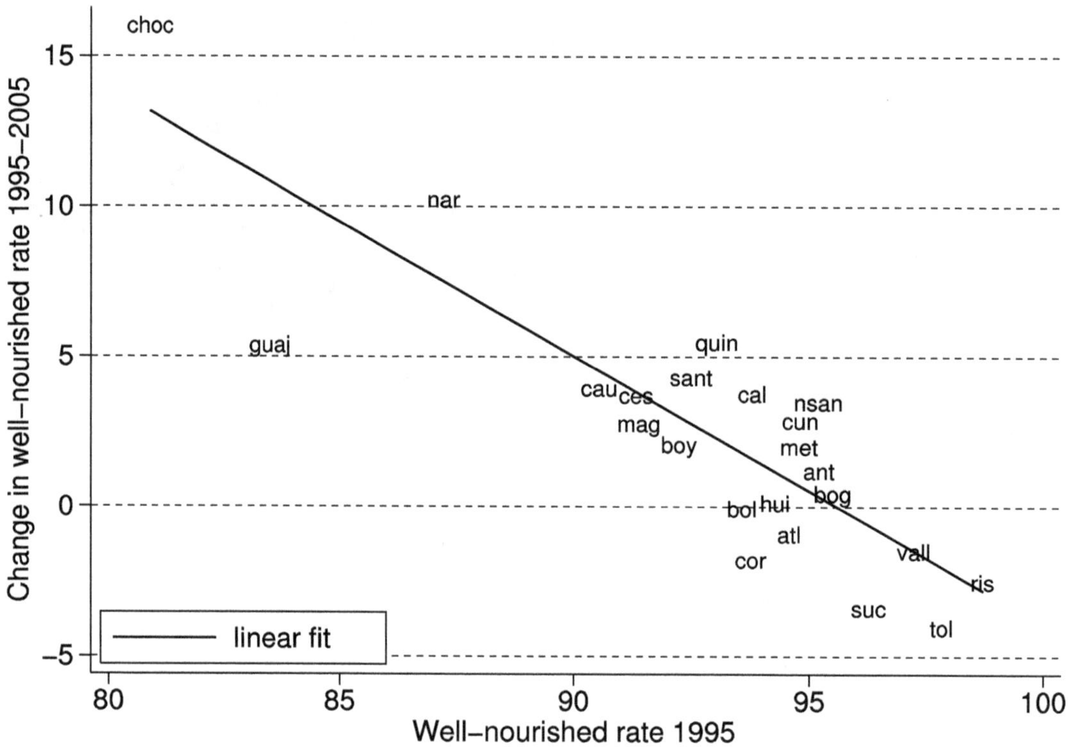

Source: Own calculations based on data from DHS

Figure 4.14: Univariate Kernel Density Estimators of Relative Well-nourished Rate. 1995 and 2005.

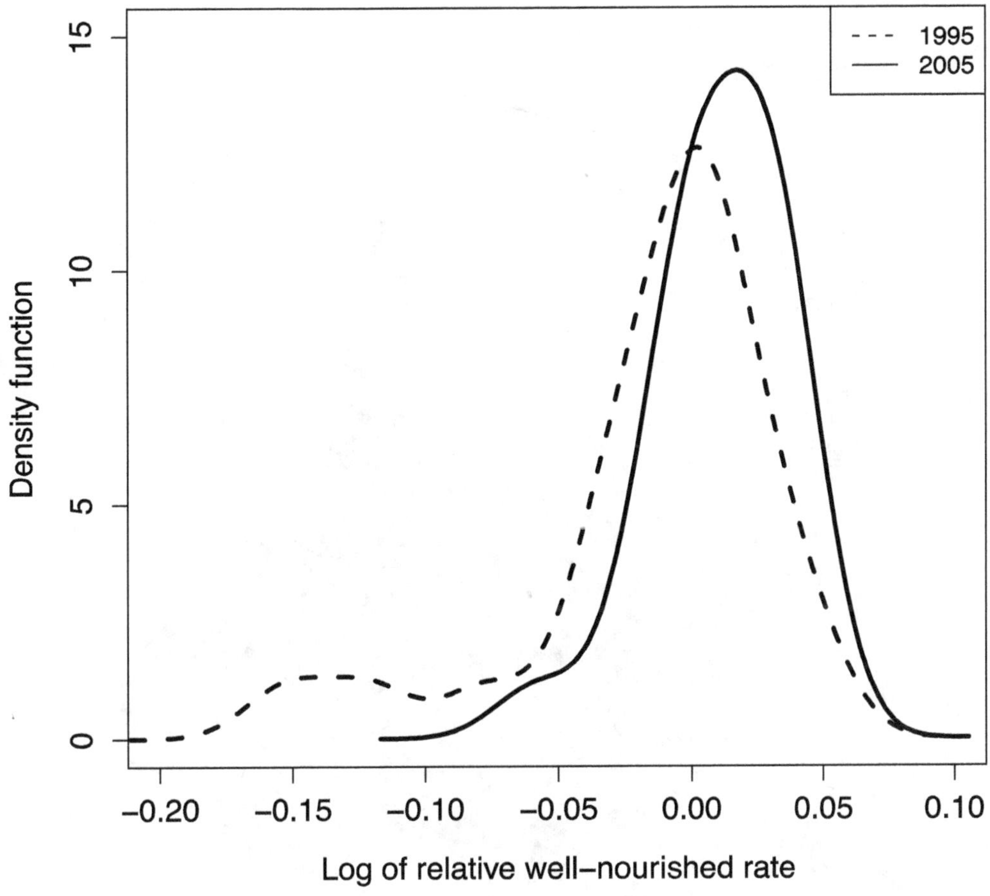

Source: Own calculations based on data from DHS. Variables relative to the national average and in logs.

Figure 4.15: Bivariate Kernel Density Estimators of Relative Well-nourished Rate. 3D Representation. 1995 and 2005.

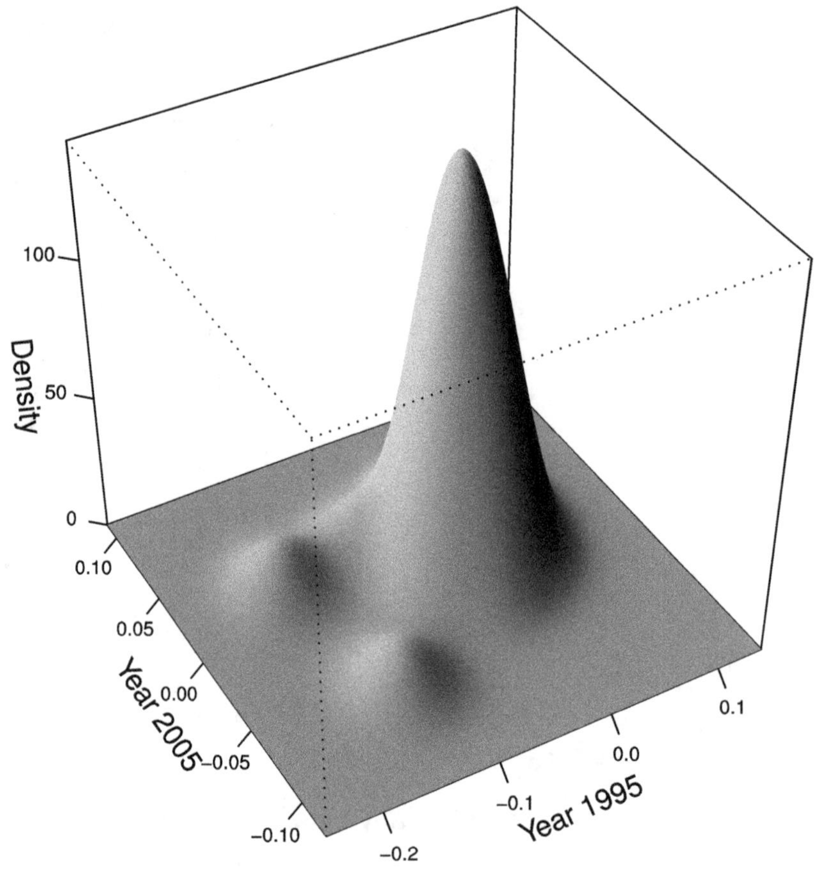

Source: Own calculations based on data from DHS. Variables relative to the national average and in logs.

Figure 4.16: Bivariate Kernel Density Estimators of Relative Well-nourished Rate. Contour Plot. 1973 and 2005.

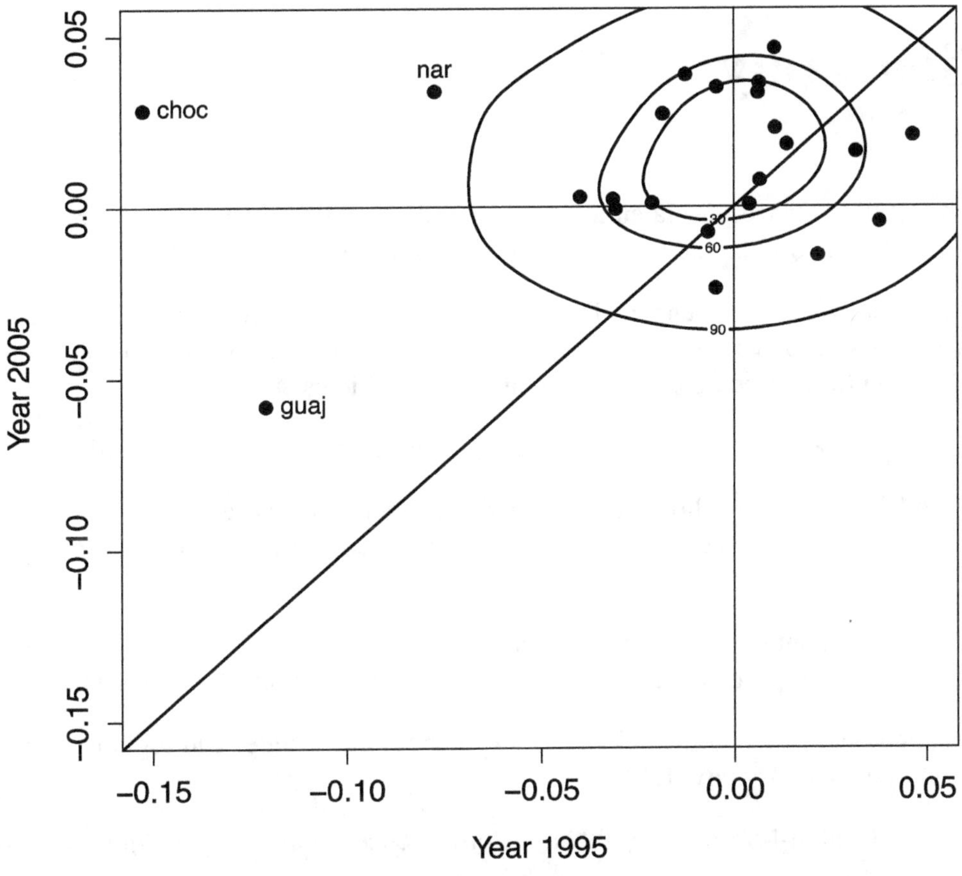

Source: Own calculations based on data from DHS. Contours at drawn at the 30%, 60%, and 90% which are upper percentages of highest density regions. The points represent the 25 observations. Points outside the 90% contour are identified. A 45 degree line is added to the plot.

Bibliography

Aguirre, K. (2005). Convergencia en indicadores sociales en Colombia: Una aproximación desde los enfoques tradicional y no paramétrico. *Desarrollo y Sociedad*, (56):147–176.

Aguirre, K. (2008). Convergencia: Del análisis del nivel de actividad económica a las variables sociales. Una revisión de la literatura del caso colombiano. Documentos de CERAC 8, Centro de Recursos para el Análisis de Conflictos.

Ardila Rueda, L. (2004). Gasto público y convergencia regional en Colombia. (45).

Barón, J. (2003). ¿Qué sucedió con las disparidades económicas regionales en Colombia entre 1980 y el 2000? Documentos de Trabajo sobre Economía Regional 38, Banco de la República.

Barrera, F. and Domínguez, C. (2006). Educación básica en Colombia: Opciones futuras de política. Technical report, Departamento Nacional de Planeación, DNP-MERDP.

Barro, R. J. and Sala-i-Martin, X. (1991). Convergence across states and regions. *Brooking Papers on Economic Activity*, 1:107–182.

Barro, R. J. and Sala-i-Martin, X. (1992a). Convergence. *Journal of Political Economy*, 100:223–251.

Barro, R. J. and Sala-i-Martin, X. (1992b). Regional growth and migration: A Japan-United States comparison. *Journal of Japanese and International Economies*, 6:312–346.

Barro, R. J. and Sala-i-Martin, X. (2004). *Economic Growth*. MIT Press, Cambridge, MA, second edition.

Beck, N. (2001). Time-series-cross-section data: What have we learned in the past few years? *Annual Review of Political Science*, 4:271–293.

Beck, N. and Katz, J. N. (2007). Random coefficient models for time-series-cross-section data: Monte Carlo experiments. *Political Analysis*, 15:185–195.

Bès, M., Hernández, R., and Oliva, C. (1998). Descentralización en Colombia: Nuevos desafíos. Estudios Económicos y Sectoriales RE3-98-002, Banco Interamericano de Desarrollo. Departamento Regional de Operaciones 3, División de Países 5.

Bettencourt, L. M. A. M., Lobo, J., Helbing, D., Kühnert, C., and West, G. B. B. (2007). Growth, innovation, scaling, and the pace of life in cities. *PNAS*, 104(17):7301–7306.

Birchenall, J. and Murcia, G. (1997). Convergencia regional: una revisión del caso colombiano. *Desarrollo y Sociedad*, (40):273–308.

Birdsall, N. and Szekely, M. (2003). Bootstraps not band-aids: Poverty, equity and social policy in Latin America. Working Papers 24, Center for Global Development.

Bloom, D. E. and Canning, D. (2007). Mortality traps and the dynamics of health transitions. *PNAS*, 104(41):16044–16049.

Bonet, J. (1999). El crecimiento regional en Colombia, 1980-1996: Una aproximación con el método shift-share. Documentos de Trabajo sobre Economía Regional 10, Banco de la República.

Bonet, J. (2007). ¿Porqué es pobre el Chocó? Documentos de Trabajo sobre Economía Regional 90, Banco de la República.

Bonet, J. and Meisel, A. (2006a). El legado colonial como determinante del ingreso per cápita departamental en Colombia. Documentos de Trabajo sobre Economía Regional 75, Banco de la República.

Bonet, J. and Meisel, A. (2006b). Polarización del ingreso per cápita departamental en Colombia, 1975 - 2000. Documentos de Trabajo sobre Economía Regional 76, Banco de la República.

Booysen, F., van der Berg, S., Burger, R., Maltitz, M. v., and Rand, G. d. (2008). Using an asset index to assess trends in poverty in seven Sub-Saharan African countries. *World Development*, 36(6):1113–1130.

Bourguignon, F. (2004). The poverty-growth-inequality triangle. Working Papers 28102, The World Bank.

Branisa, B. and Cardozo, A. (2009a). Regional growth convergence in Colombia using social indicators. Ibero America Institute for Econ. Research (IAI) Discussion Papers 195, Ibero-America Institute for Economic Research. URL http://www2.vwl.wiso.uni-goettingen.de/ibero/papers/DB195.pdf.

Branisa, B. and Cardozo, A. (2009b). Revisiting the regional growth convergence debate in Colombia using income indicators. Ibero America Institute for Econ. Research (IAI) Discussion Papers 194, Ibero-America Institute for Economic Research. URL http://www2.vwl.wiso.uni-goettingen.de/ibero/papers/DB194.pdf.

Brock, W. and Durlauf, S. N. (2001). Growth economics and reality. Mimeo, Department of Economics, University of Wisconsin.

Canova, F. and Marcet, A. (1995). The poor stay poor: Non-convergence across countries and regions. CEPR Working Paper.

Cárdenas, M. (2007). Economic growth in Colombia: A reversal of fortune? Departamento Nacional de Planeación - Archivos de Economía No. 2402.

Cárdenas, M. and Pontón, A. (1995). Growth and convergence in Colombia: 1950-1990. *Journal of Development Economics*, 47:5–37.

Cardozo-Silva, A. R. (2008). Pro-poor growth in Colombia from 1996 to 2005. In Klasen, S. and Nowak-Lehmann D., F., editors, *Poverty Inequality and Migration in Latin America*, volume 20 of *Goettingen Studies in Development Economics*, pages 87–107. Peter Lang Verlagsgruppe.

Cass, D. (1965). Optimum growth in an aggregation model of capital accumulation. *Review of Economic Studies*, 32:233–240.

CEGA (2006a). *Ingreso, Consumo y Ahorro en los Departamentos de Colombia: 1975-2000*, volume 2. Universidad de Los Andes/Centro de Estudios Ganaderos y Agrícolas, Bogotá.

CEGA (2006b). *Sistema Simplificado de Cuentas Departamentales de Colombia: 1975-2000*, volume 1. Universidad de Los Andes/Centro de Estudios Ganaderos y Agrícolas, Bogotá.

Clark, D. (2005). Sen's capability approach and the many spaces of human well-being. *The Journal of Development Studies*, 41(8):1339–1368.

DANE (1990). *La Población de Colombia en 1985: Estudios de Evaluación de la Calidad y Cobertura del XV Censo Nacional de Población y IV de Vivienda*. Bogotá.

DANE (2007). *Colombia. Proceso de Conciliación Censal 1985-2005*. Bogotá.

DANE (2008). Metodología de cuentas departamentales. Technical report, Departamento Administrativo Nacional de Estadística.

Datt, G. and Ravallion, M. (1992). Growth and redistribution components of changes in poverty measures : A decomposition with applications to Brazil and India in the 1980s. *Journal of Development Economics*, 38(2):275–295.

Davidson, R. and MacKinnon, J. G. (1993). *Estimation and Inference in Econometrics*. Oxford Univ. Press, New York.

Davison, A. and Hinkley, D. (1997). *Bootstrap Methods and Their Application*. Cambridge Series on Statistical and Probabilistic Mathematics. Cambridge University Press, Cambridge.

Departamento Administrativo Nacional de Estadística, (DANE) (2008). Cuentas nacionales anuales base 1994. Electronic publication. www.dane.gov.co.

Departamento Nacional de Planeación DNP (2002). Evaluación de la descentralización municipal en Colombia: Balance de una década. Technical report, Departamento Nacional de Planeación DNP, Dirección de Planeación Nacional, Bogotá.

Díaz, A. M. and Sánchez, F. (2004). A geography of illicit crops (coca leaf) and armed conflict in Colombia. Documentos Cede 001917, Universidad de los Andes-CEDE.

Díaz, A. M. and Sánchez, F. (2004). A geography of illicit crops (coca leaf) and armed conflict in Colombia. Documentos CEDE 2004-19, Universidad de los Andes-CEDE.

Díaz, Y. (2003). ¿Es necesario sacrificar equidad para alcanzar desarrollo? El caso de las inequidades en mortalidad infantil en Colombia. Documentos CEDE 2003-11, Universidad de los Andes-CEDE.

DNP (2004). Evaluación de dos métodos de imputación de ingresos totales en la población en edad de trabajar con encuestas de hogares. MECOVI: Taller 14, imputación de datos en las encuestas de hogares: los procedimientos metodológicos y sus implicaciones. Resúmen y conclusiones.

DNP (2006). Metodología de medición y magnitud de la pobreza en Colombia. Mimeo, Misión para el Diseño de una Estrategia para la Reducción de la Pobreza y la Desigualdad. Departamento Nacional de Planeación (DNP-MERDP).

DNP (2008). Distribución de los recursos del Sistema General de Participaciones provenientes del crecimiento real de la economía superior al 4% de la vigencia 2006. Documento Conpes Social 115, Departamento Nacional de Planeación (DNP), Consejo Nacional de Política Económica y Social.

Dollar, D. and Kraay, A. (2002). Growth is good for the poor. *Journal of Economic Growth*, 7(3):195–225.

Drèze, J. and Sen, A. (1989). *Hunger and Public Action*. WIDER Studies in Development Economics. Oxford University Press, Oxford.

Duclos, J.-Y. and Wodon, Q. (2004). What is "pro-poor"? Cahiers de recherche 0425, CIRPEE.

Duong, T. (2008). *ks: Kernel Smoothing*. R package version 1.5.6.

Duong, T. and Hazelton, M. (2005). Cross-validation bandwidth matrices for multivariate kernel density estimation. *Scandinavian Journal of Statistics*, 32:485–506.

Durlauf, S. and Quah, D. (1999). *The New Empirics of Economic Growth*, volume 1, chapter 4, pages 235–308. North Holland Press.

Durlauf, S. N. (1996). Controversy on the convergence and divergence of growth rates. *The Economic Journal*, 106:1016–1018.

Durlauf, S. N. (2001). Manifesto for a growth econometrics. *Journal of Econometrics*, 100:65–69.

Durlauf, S. N., Johnson, Paul, A., and Temple, Jonathan, R. W. (2005). Growth econometrics. In Aghion, P. and Durlauf, S. N., editors, *Handbook of Economic Growth*, volume 1A, pages 555–677. Elsevier.

European Commission (1996). *First Report on Economic and Social Cohesion*. Office for Official Publications of the European Communities, Luxembourg.

Feres, J. C. and Mancero, X. (2001). El método de las necesidades básicas insatisfechas (NBI) y sus aplicaciones en América Latina. Estudios Estadísticos y Prospectivos 7, Economic Comission for Latin America and the Caribbean, CEPAL. United Nations.

Ferreira, F. H. and Ravallion, M. (2008). Global poverty and inequality : a review of the evidence. Policy Research Working Paper Series 4623, The World Bank.

Filmer, D. and Pritchett, L. (2001). Estimating wealth effects without expenditure data – or tears: An application to educational enrollments in states of India. *Demography*, 38(1):115–132.

Foster, J., Greer, J., and Thorbecke, E. (1984). A class of decomposable poverty measures. *Econometrica*, 52(3):761–766.

Fuentes, J. A. (2005). Violent conflict and human development in Latin America:The cases of Colombia, El Salvador and Guatemala. Ocassional Paper 10, United Nations Development Programme, Human Development Report 2005.

Gaviria, A., Medina, C., and Mejia, C. (2006). Assessing health reform in Colombia: From theory to practice. *Economía*, 7(1):29–72.

González, J. I. (2001). Imparcialidad financiera y equidad. Otra lectura del informe de la Organización Mundial de la Salud. Año 2000. *Revista de Gerencia y Políticas de la Salud*, 1(1):39–47.

Gores, C. (2007). Which growth theory is good for the poor? *European Journal of Development Research*, 19(1):30–48.

Granados, C. M. (2008). ¿Contribuyen las reformas al progreso social?, El caso de los servicios de acueducto y alcantarillado y la mortalidad infantil en Colombia 1990-2004. Documentos CEDE 2008-07, Universidad de los Andes-CEDE.

Grimm, M. (2007). Removing the anonymity axiom in assessing pro-poor growth. *Journal of Economic Inequality*, 5(2):179–197.

Grimm, M., Harttgen, K., Klasen, S., and Misselhorn, M. (2008). A human development index by income groups. *World Development Volume*, 36(11):2527–2546.

Grosse, M., Harttgen, K., and Klasen, S. (2008a). Measuring pro-poor growth in non-income dimensions. *World Development*, 36(6):1021–1047.

Grosse, M., Harttgen, K., and Klasen, S. (2008b). Measuring pro-poor progress towards the non-income millennium development goals. In McGillivray, M., editor, *Achieving the Millennium Development Goals*, pages 123–150. Palgrave Macmillan, Studies in Development Economics and Policy edition.

Grün, B. and Leisch, F. (2008). FlexMix Version 2: Finite mixtures with concomitant variables and varying and constant parameters. *Journal of Statistical Software*, 28(4):1–35.

Günther, I. and Grimm, M. (2007). Measuring pro-poor growth when relative prices shift. *Journal of Development Economics*, 82(1):245–256.

Günther, I. and Klasen, S. (2009). Measuring chronic non-income poverty. In Addison, T., Hulme, D., and Kanbur, R., editors, *Poverty Dynamics*, chapter 4. Oxford University Press.

Haddad, E. A., Perobelli, F. S., Bonet, J., and Hewings, G. J. D. (2008). Structural interdependence among Colombian departments. Borradores de Economía 517, Banco de la República.

Härdle, W., Müller, M., Sperlich, S., and Werwaltz, A. (2004). *Nonparametric and Semiparametric Methods*. Springer Series in Statistics. Springer, Berlin.

Hernández, G. H. (2004). Impacto de las regalías petroleras en el departamento del Meta. Ensayos sobre economía regional, Banco de la República, Centro Regional de Estudios Económicos Villavicencio.

Hernández, M. and Obregón, D. (2002). *La Organización Panamericana de la Salud y el Estado Colombiano: Cien Años de Historia, 1902-2002*. Organización Panamericana de la Salud, Bogotá.

Hernández Flórez, M. (2007). La pobreza en Colombia: Un fenómeno multidimensional. Tésis maestría en economía, Universidad de los Andes, Bogotá, Colombia.

Homedes, N. and Ugalde, A. (2005). Las reformas de salud neoliberales en América Latina: Una revisión crítica a través de dos estudios de caso. *Pan American Journal of Public Health*, 17(3):210–220.

Jazmín, C., Rivera, M., and Castañeda, M. Y. (2004). El malestar de la salud en Colombia. Informe Especial 303, Contraloría General de la República.

Jones, M., Marron, J., and Park, B. (1991). A simple root n bandwidth selector. *Annals of Statistics*, 19:1919–1932.

Kakwani, N., Khandker, S., and Son, H. H. (2004). Pro-poor growth: concepts and measurement with country case studies. Working papers 1, International Poverty Centre, United Nations Development Programme.

Kakwani, N. and Pernia, E. M. (2000). What is pro-poor growth? *Assian Development Review*, 18(1).

Kakwani, N. and Son, H. H. (2008). Poverty equivalent growth rate. *Review of Income and Wealth*, 54(4):643–655.

Kanbur, R. (2002). Conceptual challenges in poverty and inequality: One development economist's perspective. Working Papers 7242, Cornell University, Department of Applied Economics and Management.

Kenny, C. (2004). Why are we worried about income? Nearly everything that matters is converging. *World Development*, 33(1):1–19.

Kenny, C. (2005). Why are we worried about income? Nearly everything that matters is converging. *World Development*, 33(1):1–19.

Klasen, S. (2000). Measuring poverty and deprivation in South Africa. *Review of Income and Wealth*, 46(1):33–58.

Klasen, S. (2008). Economic growth and poverty reduction: Measurement issues using income and non-income indicators. *World Development*, 36(3):420–445.

Kolenikov, S. and Angeles, G. (2009). Socioeconomic status measurement with discrete proxy variables: Is principal component analysis a reliable answer? *Review of Income and Wealth*, 55(1):128–165.

Lal, K. (1999). Implementation of the 1993 SNA in Canada - backcasting issues. Technical report, System of National Accounts Branch. Statistics Canada.

Lasso Valderrama, F. J. (2002). Nueva metodología de encuesta de hogares. ¿Más o menos desempleados? Archivos de Economía 003282, Departamento Nacional de Planeación (DNP-MERDP).

Lee, K., Pesaran, M. H., and Smith, R. (1997). Growth and convergence in a multi-country empirical stochastic Solow model. *Journal of Applied Econometrics*, 12:357–392.

Leisch, F. (2004). FlexMix: A general framework for finite mixture models and latent class regression in R. *Journal of Statistical Software*, 11(8).

Leisch, F. and Grün, B. (2008). *flexmix: Flexible Mixture Modeling*. R package version 2.2-3.

Libhaber, M. and Foster, V. (2003). Health. In Giugale, M. M., Lafourcade, O., and Luff, C., editors, *Colombia: The Economic Foundation of Peace*, chapter 15, pages 433–462. World Bank, Washington D.C.

Londoño, J. L. and Szekely, M. (2000). Persistent poverty and excess inequality: Latin America, 1970-1995. *Journal of Applied Economics*, III(1):93–134.

Long, J. S. and Ervin, L. H. (2000). Using heteroscedasticity consistent standard errors in the linear regression model. *The American Statistician*, 54(3):217–224.

Maddala, G. S., Trost, R. P., Li, H., and Joutz, F. (1997). Estimation of short-run and long-run elasticities of energy demand from panel data using shrinkage estimators. *Journal of Business and Economic Statistics*, 15:90–100.

Maddala, G. S. and Wu, S. (2000). Cross-country growth regressions: Problems of heterogeneity, stability and interpretation. *Applied Economics*, 32:635–642.

Magrini, S. (2004). Regional (di)convergence. In Henderson, J. V. and Thisse, J. F., editors, *Handbook of Regional and Urban Economics*, volume 4, chapter 62, pages 2741–2796. Elsevier.

Masanjala, W. H. and Papageorgiou, C. (2004). The Solow model with CES technology: Nonlinearities and parameter heterogeneity. *Journal of Applied Econometrics*, 19:171–200.

Mazumdar, K. (2003). Do standards of living converge? A cross-country study. *Social Indicators Research*, 64:29–50.

McCulloch, C. E. and Searle, S. R. (2001). *Generalized, Linear, and Mixed Models*. Wiley Series in Probability and Statistics. John Wiley and Sons, New York, NY.

Meisel, A. (2007a). La Guajira y el mito de las regalías redentoras. Documentos de Trabajo sobre Economía Regional 86, Banco de la República.

Meisel, A. (2007b). ¿Por qué se necesita una política económica regional en Colombia? Documentos de Trabajo sobre Economía Regional 100, Banco de la República.

Meisel, A. and Vega, M. (2007). The biological standard of living (and its convergence) in Colombia, 1870-2003 - A tropical success story. *Economics and Human Biology*, 5(1):100–122.

Micklewright, J. and Stewart, K. (1999). Is the well-being of children converging in the European Union? *The Economic Journal*, 109(459):692–714.

Moser, C. and Felton, A. (2009). The construction of an asset index measuring asset accumulation in Ecuador. In Addison, T., Hulme, D., and Kanbur, R., editors, *Poverty Dynamics*, chapter 5. Oxford University Press.

Murad R., R. (2003). Estudio sobre la distribución espacial de la población en Colombia. Technical Report 48, CELADE/CEPAL.

Neumayer, E. (2003). Beyond income: convergence in living standards, big time. *Structural Change and Economic Dynamics*, 14(3):275–296.

Nuñez, J. and Espinosa, S. (2005). Pro-poor growth and pro-poor programs in Colombia. Documentos Cede 003379, Universidad de los Andes-CEDE.

Observatorio de Derechos Humanos (2003). Informe anual de derechos humanos y DIH. Technical report, Vicepresidencia de la República, Colombia. Observatorio del Programa Presidencial de Derechos Humanos y DIH, Editorial ABC.

Ocampo, J. A., Pérez, M. J., Tovar, C., and Lasso Valderrama, Francisco Javier, F. J. (1998). Macroeconomía, ajuste estructural y equidad en Colombia: 1978-1996. Archivos de Economía 00079, Departamento Nacional de Planeación (DNP).

Oeppen, J. and Vaupel, J. W. (2002). Broken limits to life expectancy. *Science*, 296(5570):1029–1031.

Olshansky, S. J., Carnes, B. A., and Cassel, C. (1990). In search of Methuselah: Estimating the upper limits to human longevity. *Science*, 250(4981):634–640.

Parra, C. E. and Salazar, N. (2000). La crísis financiera y la experiencia internacional. Boletines de Divulgación Económica 1, Departamento Nacional de Planeación, (DNP).

Pinheiro, J. C. and Bates, D. M. (2000). *Mixed-Effects Models in S and S-Plus*. Statistics and Computing. Springer, New York, NY.

Pinto Borrego, M. E., Vergara Ballen, A., and Percipiano Lahuerta, Y. (2005). Costos generados por la violencia en Colombia: 1999-2003. Archivos de Economía 00277, Departamento Nacional de Planeación (DNP).

Posada, C. E. (2004). Un choque al activo externo neto y el ciclo económico Colombiano. Borradores de Economía 001606, Banco de la República.

Pritchett, L. (2000). Patterns of economic growth: Hills, plateaus, mountains, and plains. *World Bank Economic Review*, 14:221–250.

Profamilia (2005). Salud social y reproductiva en Colombia, encuesta nacional de demografía y salud. Technical report, Profamilia.

Quah, D. (1993a). Empirical cross-section dynamics in economic growth. *European Economic Review*, 37(2-3):426–434.

Quah, D. (1993b). Galton's fallacy and tests of the convergence hypothesis. *Scandinavian Journal of Economics*, 95(4):427–443.

Quah, D. (1996). Empirics for economic growth and convergence. *European Economic Review*, 40(6):1353–1375.

Quah, D. (1997). Empirics for growth and distribution: Stratification, polarization and convergence clubs. *Journal of Economic Growth*, 2(1):27–59.

R Development Core Team (2008). *R: A Language and Environment for Statistical Computing*. R Foundation for Statistical Computing, Vienna, Austria.

Ram, R. (1982). Composite indices of physical quality of life, basic needs fulfillment, and income: a 'principle component' representation. *Journal of Development Economics*, 11(2):227–247.

Ramsey, F. P. (1928). A mathematical theory of saving. *Economic Journal*, 38:543–559.

Ravallion, M. (2009). Why don't we see poverty convergence? Policy Research Working Paper Series 4974, The World Bank.

Ravallion, M. and Chen, S. (1997). What can new survey data tell us about recent changes in distribution and poverty? *World Bank Economic Review*, 11(2):357–82.

Ravallion, M. and Chen, S. (2001). Measuring pro-poor growth. Policy Research Working Paper Series 2666, The World Bank.

Ravallion, M. and Chen, S. (2003). Measuring pro-poor growth. *Economic Letters*, 78(1):93–99.

Ravallion, M. and Chen, S. (2004). Pro-poor growth : A primer. Policy Research Working Paper Series 3242, The World Bank.

Rojas, F. (2003). At the crossroads of decentralization: Recentralization, federalization. In Giugale, M. M., Lafourcade, O., and Luff, C., editors, *Colombia: The Economic Foundation of Peace*, chapter 31, pages 871–896. World Bank, Washington D.C.

Sahn, D. E. and Stifel, D. (2000). Poverty comparisons over time and across countries in Africa. *World Development*, 28(12):2123–2155.

Sahn, D. E. and Stifel, D. (2003). Exploring alternative measures of welfare in the absence of expenditure data. *Review of Income and Wealth*, 49(4):463–489.

Sala-i-Martin, X. (1996). The classical aproach to convergence analysis. *The Economic Journal*, 106:1019–1036.

Sánchez, F. (2006). Descentralización y progreso en el acceso a los servicios sociales de educación, salud y agua y alcantarillado. Technical report, Departamento Nacional de Planeación, (DNP-MERDP).

Sánchez, F. and Palau, M. D. M. (2006). Conflict, decentralisation and local governance in Colombia, 1974-2004. Documentos CEDE 2006-20, Universidad de los Andes-CEDE.

Sarmiento, A., Angulo, R. C., and Espinoza, F. A. (2005a). Informe Bogotá cómo vamos.

Sarmiento, A., González, J. I., Alonso, C. E., Angulo, R., and Espinosa, F. (2005b). Crecimiento pro-poor en Colombia: 1996-2004. Archivos de Economía 283, Departamento Nacional de Planeación, (DNP).

Sen, A. (1985). *Commodities and capabilities*. North Holland, Amsterdam.

Sen, A. (1998). Mortality as an indicator of economic success and failure. *Economic Journal*, 108(446):1–25.

Sen, A. (1999). *Development as freedom*. Knopf, New York :, 1st. ed. edition.

Sen, A. (2002). *El Derecho a No Tener Hambre*. Universidad Externado de Colombia, Bogotá.

Sen, A. K. and Foster, J. E. (1997). *On economic inequality*. Clarendon Press; Oxford University Press.

Serra, M. I., Pazmino, M. F., Lindow, G., Sutton, B., and Ramirez, G. (2006). Regional convergence in Latin America. IMF Working Paper 125, International Monetary Fund.

Sheather, S. J. and Jones, M. C. (1991). A reliable data-based bandwidth selection method for kernel density estimation. *Journal of the Royal Statistical Society*, 53:683–690.

Shioji, E. (1997). It's still 2 percent: Evidence on convergence from 116 years of the US states panel data. Economics Working Papers 236, Department of Economics and Business, Universitat Pompeu Fabra.

Solow, R. M. (1956). A contribution to the theory of economic growth. *Quarterly Journal of Economics*, 70:65–94.

Son, H. H. (2003). Approaches to defining and measuring pro-poor growth.

Temple, J. (1999). The new growth evidence. *Journal of Economic Literature*, 37:112–156.

Tenjo Galarza, F. and López Enciso, E. (2003). Creidit buble and stagnation in Colombia, 1990-2001. *Colombian Economic Journal*, 1(1):151–191.

UNICEF (1998). *The State of World's Children: Focus on Nutrition*. UNICEF, New York.

United Nations (2004). *World Population to 2300*. United Nations Population Studies No. 236. United Nations, New York.

UNODC (2006a). Coca cultivation in the Andean region for 2005. Technical report, United Nations Office on Drugs and Crime.

UNODC (2006b). World drug report 2006. Technical report, United Nations Office on Drugs and Crime.

Vélez, C. E., de la Brière, B., and Millán, N. (2001). Poverty and welfare in rural Colombia during the last two decades. Mimeo. The World Bank, Washington, DC.

Vélez, C. E. and Robles, M. (2008). Determining the paramenters of axiomatically derived multidimensional poverty indices: An application based on reported well being in Colombia. In Kakwani, N. and Silber, J., editors, *Quantitative approaches to multidimensional poverty measurement*, chapter 12, pages 210–225. Palgrave Macmillan, Houndmills, Basingstoke, Hampshire.

Velez, E., Harding, D., and Sarmiento, A. (2003). Education. In Giugale, M. M., Lafourcade, O., and Luff, C., editors, *Colombia: The Economic Foundation of Peace*, chapter 21, pages 611–651. World Bank, Washington D.C.

von Maltzahn, R. and Durrheim, K. (2007). Is poverty multidimensional? A comparison of income and asset based measures in five Southern African countries. *Social Indicators Research*, 86(1):149–162.

Wand, M. P. and Jones, M. C. (1995). *Kernel Smoothing*. Monographs on Statistics and Applied Probability 60. Chapman and Hall, London.

Wasserman, L. (2006). *All of nonparametric statistics*. Springer Texts in Statistics. Springer, New York.

World Bank (2003). *Tertiary Education in Colombia. Paving the way for reform.* World Bank.

World Bank (2008). World development indicators 2008. Technical report, World Bank, Washington, DC.

World Bank (2009). *World Development Report 2009: Reshaping Economic Geography*. The World Bank, Washington, DC.

Permissions

All chapters in this book were first published by Peter Lang International Academic Publishing Group by Adriana Rocío Cardozo Silva; hereby published with permission under the Creative Commons Attribution License or equivalent. Every chapter published in this book has been scrutinized by our experts. Their significance has been extensively debated. The topics covered herein carry significant information for a comprehensive understanding. They may even be implemented as practical applications or may be referred to as a beginning point for further studies.

We would like to thank the editorial team for lending their expertise to make the book truly unique. They have played a crucial role in the development of this book. Without their invaluable contributions this book wouldn't have been possible. They have made vital efforts to compile up to date information on the varied aspects of this subject to make this book a valuable addition to the collection of many professionals and students.

This book was conceptualized with the vision of imparting up-to-date and integrated information in this field. To ensure the same, a matchless editorial board was set up. Every individual on the board went through rigorous rounds of assessment to prove their worth. After which they invested a large part of their time researching and compiling the most relevant data for our readers.

The editorial board has been involved in producing this book since its inception. They have spent rigorous hours researching and exploring the diverse topics which have resulted in the successful publishing of this book. They have passed on their knowledge of decades through this book. To expedite this challenging task, the publisher supported the team at every step. A small team of assistant editors was also appointed to further simplify the editing procedure and attain best results for the readers.

Apart from the editorial board, the designing team has also invested a significant amount of their time in understanding the subject and creating the most relevant covers. They scrutinized every image to scout for the most suitable representation of the subject and create an appropriate cover for the book.

The publishing team has been an ardent support to the editorial, designing and production team. Their endless efforts to recruit the best for this project, has resulted in the accomplishment of this book. They are a veteran in the field of academics and their pool of knowledge is as vast as their experience in printing. Their expertise and guidance has proved useful at every step. Their uncompromising quality standards have made this book an exceptional effort. Their encouragement from time to time has been an inspiration for everyone.

The publisher and the editorial board hope that this book will prove to be a valuable piece of knowledge for students, practitioners and scholars across the globe.

Index

M

N

P

R

S

U

W

www.ingramcontent.com/pod-product-compliance
Lightning Source LLC
LaVergne TN
LVHW080602210926
848485LV00003B/92
* 9 7 8 1 6 4 7 2 5 4 1 8 6 *